Common Sense

Art Robinson reminds us of America's special journey down a freedom road of liberty, justice, prosperity, charity, and American exceptionalism – a road paved with common sense. A road that led our nation away from the tyrannies that have ruled the world for thousands of years.

This is a road of individual liberty. People are the ultimate resource – human dynamos that can climb any mountain, bridge any river, and overcome any challenge to make our world better, if they are free to do so.

We must continue down this road of liberty – for ourselves, our children, and our country, and as an example to people in other nations who are struggling to lift themselves from poverty and tyranny.

Our country has stumbled over those in Washington who want power and money. They seek to turn us back upon the older road of history – a road of subservience to the state and those who rule it – a road of slavery.

We must not turn back. Ours is the great experiment in freedom. We must not give up our liberty to politicians, to corporatists, to bureaucrats, to socialists, or to other power seekers.

We must rid our government of the career politicians who now control it and return to a smaller, benign Constitutional government, watched over by citizen volunteers in Congress who make sure that our liberty is protected from all challenges – from abroad, from within, and from government itself.

Published by
Art Robinson
P.O. Box 1250
Cave Junction, Oregon 97523

COMMON SENSE IN 2012

LIBERTY, JUSTICE, PROSPERITY, AND CHARITY FOR AMERICA

ART ROBINSON

I dedicate this book to my family and to the many Americans whose foresight and courage have given us liberty. I trust in God to give our generations the wisdom to preserve that liberty.

TABLE OF CONTENTS

Contents

PREFACE

This book is for the voters of Congressional District 4 in Oregon. It explains, to the best of my ability, the issues facing us all in the 2012 elections.

Throughout our District and our nation, tens of millions of citizen volunteers have risen up in an effort to return our country to the path of Liberty and Justice.

We are Republicans, Democrats, Constitutionalists, Libertarians, Independents, and many other groups concerned about our country's future.

And, we are all Americans. We are all different, but we share a common love for our country and for fundamental human rights and principles.

In times past, national elections have been about our differences. There are many varied ideas among us about the directions our country should go and the goals it should reach.

Our Constitutional Republic is uniquely designed to permit us to resolve those differences within a framework that simultaneously preserves the individual rights to Life, Liberty, and the Pursuit of Happiness for every one of us.

This election is different. Today, the framework of Liberty itself is in great danger. This danger is political, economic, social, and ethical. The problem is so serious that Americans of all political persuasions are banding together to solve it. After our country is back on track, we can again debate our lesser differences.

We have elected to public office and entrusted with legislative and economic power too many individuals who place their personal ambitions above the best interests of our country. These people have strayed so far from our national principles that their actions now endanger us all.

To be sure, the corruption that threatens us is not just political. Throughout our country there are people in industry, business, banking, finance, education, medical care, science, and other pursuits who also act in unprincipled ways. There have always been such people, and there always will be. The frailties of human nature afflict us all – some more than others.

Our problem is that too many of the career politicians who now control our national Congress have formed improper self-serving alliances. They have used the money and power we have entrusted to them in ways prohibited by our national Constitution. They have shared our trust, our resources, and our national strength with too many corrupt special interests.

Congress has created debts so large that they endanger our economy; created a bureaucracy that over-regulates every aspect of our lives; over-taxed our people and our businesses; given huge amounts of our national treasure to special interests that have no right to our money; and embroiled us in a seemingly endless series of conflicts with other nations.

These and other congressional actions have had tragic effects on our prosperity.

Tens of millions of us can no longer find real work to

support ourselves and our families, and tens of millions more live in anxiety that their jobs may soon be lost.

Those of us who are older find that our private savings for retirement are imperiled and the public savings for retirement we entrusted to Congress in Social Security, Medicare, and other programs are threatened.

Those of us who are younger find that our educational system no longer adequately prepares us to compete effectively and that opportunities to work are diminishing.

Those of us in the most productive years of middle age find that, no matter how hard we work, we cannot save the resources necessary to care properly for our families and plan adequately for our futures.

Our country has not fallen, but it has stumbled. It has stumbled over the actions of unprincipled career politicians, primarily those in the U. S. Congress.

When our country was founded, there were no "political careers." Our Congress was intended to be comprised of citizen volunteers, who served briefly as a public service and then returned home to resume their ordinary lives. By electing people of integrity and ability who had no self-interest in building "careers" in government, we were largely protected from systemic corruption in Congress.

Our Founders established a nation where the rights of the individual stood above the state. They created a Constitution that protected each person from the state. And, they created a Congress where every member is sworn to uphold that Constitution. Finally, they arranged that Congress would be elected frequently, so that the people could make sure that it protected their freedoms.

There are many ways to view our current problems. It is obvious, however, that something is badly amiss in

Washington. It is quite clear that we need new management of our national affairs.

In 2010, I volunteered to provide that new management for the citizens of Oregon Congressional District 4.

I would serve as a citizen volunteer. I have absolutely no interest in becoming a career politician.

In 2010, 44% of the voters chose me and a greater number voted for the 24-year incumbent.

Had that election campaign been fought with integrity, including real debates on the issues between the contenders and honest representations of their differences, I could have concluded that the majority of the voters preferred that our country continue down the road of over-taxation, over-regulation, over-spending, and over-indebtedness that my opponent represents and has voted for in Congress for 25 years.

Instead, however, it was clear that the 130,000 people who voted for me do not want to continue on the present course and that a great many of those who did not vote for me were misled as to my accomplishments and goals. The last section of this book entitled "Correction of DeFazio Misrepresentations" replies to the many misleading and false claims that have been made by my opponent.

Moreover, individual voters have made more than 13,000 personal financial contributions to our campaign. In 2010, those voters put up 42,000 campaign signs on their own initiative. Our campaign purchased the signs, but all were put up by volunteers. We have received tens of thousands of expressions of support from the public. I owe these people the best effort I can possibly make toward the national goal that they represent.

So, I decided to run again in 2012 and to write this

book. During the 2012 campaign, I will use all of my resources to make sure that the voters know the truth about the dangers that face our country and the skills, experience, and good judgement with which I will handle them.

Readers will notice repetition in this book. Some ideas are so important that they bear repeating. Also, I expect that many people will not read the whole book, but will turn to the chapters about the issues that most interest them. Each chapter must stand alone. The organization of this book moves from politics to principles to issues. An idea that applies to more than one chapter is necessarily repeated.

I do not ask that you agree with everything in this book. I only ask that you read what I have written, and draw your own conclusions.

It is my hope that, if you do so, you will grow to like the author, you will trust the author, and you will conclude that the policies he will follow, if elected, will be good for the people of our District, good for Oregon, and good for our nation.

Respectfully yours,

Art Robinson
March, 2012

INTRODUCTION

"The cause of America is, in a great measure, the cause of all mankind. Many circumstances have, and will arise, which are not local, but universal, and through which the principles of all lovers of mankind are affected, and in the event of which, their affections are interested."
Thomas Paine, *Common Sense* (1776)

The stakes were high in February 1776. Paine, a recent immigrant, saw how high they were. Delegates of the colonial governments were considering secession from the British Empire. The Empire was increasingly seen as a threat to liberty. Less than a year later, on December 23, 1776, Thomas Paine introduced his pamphlet *The American Crisis* with the words,

"These are the times that try men's souls. The summer soldier and the sunshine patriot will, in this crisis, shrink from the service of their country; but he that stands by it *now*, deserves the love and thanks of man and woman."
Thomas Paine, *The American Crisis* (1776)

Six nights later, George Washington and the Continental Army – including the men who would become the first and fifth Presidents of the United States – crossed the Delaware in their famous attack on the British, which re-energized the American cause.

For five more terrible and grueling years, Americans fought against Big Government tyranny. They fought for Liberty and Justice. And, finally: On October 17, 1781, British General Cornwallis surrendered to George Washington at Yorktown.

The Great Experiment Begins

The War for Independence over, Americans lived under a confederation until, on September 17, 1787, the Constitutional Convention completed its work in Philadelphia and presented it for ratification by the citizens of each state. After ratification in 1788, it went into effect.

With this, America became a Constitutional Republic.

The Bill of Rights, the first ten Amendments to the Constitution, was ratified effective December 15, 1791.

This Constitutional Republic unleashed in North America the greatest experiment in liberty in all of human history. Even though it was the work of men and therefore subject, in its construction and its implementation, to the imperfections of men, the new Republic permitted the citizens of the United States to accomplish great things.

As a result, many hundreds of millions of Americans have lived with the great blessings of freedom and liberty and billions of the world's people have been inspired by America in their efforts to lift themselves from poverty and tyranny through the example of the United States.

America Is Exceptional

As American economist Julian Simon demonstrated,[1] people are the ultimate resource. Human beings always produce more than they consume and thereby increase in prosperity, if they are free to do so. Our Constitutional Republic guaranteed individual liberty and protected it with justice. The result was "American Exceptionalism" – a two-century demonstration of the wonderful things a free people can accomplish.

As Thomas Paine wrote, it was "common sense" that a continent would not be ruled by an island and that a free people would not be ruled by a King. Therefore, he advised that it was best that separation from England take place sooner rather than later because the necessary suffering and difficulties would only become greater with time.

As the Founding Fathers knew, it was also common sense to acknowledge that some individuals are always present who seek to gain power over others through misuse of political processes. So, they formed a government, but also bound that government down by the chains of a Constitution that would protect the citizens of the United States from such people.

It was also common sense that the American nation would thrive so long as American Liberty survived, as we have been reminded by many great Americans from Benjamin Franklin to Booker T. Washington to Ronald Reagan.

In recent decades, however, America has stumbled. We still retain our custom and culture; we still recall our heritage of American exceptionalism; we still proclaim our allegiance to our Constitutional Republic; and we still enjoy much of the prosperity made possible by the momentum of past accomplishments.

Yet, we also share an uneasy realization that something is amiss – that our heretofore shining future is dimming and our vision and opportunities are clouding in an unfavorable way.

We have allowed our country to drift away from the legal protections specified in our Constitution. We have permitted our prosperity to be diminished by means of a continually increasing burden of over-taxation, over-regulation, and over-indebtedness that has been placed on the backs of American workers and entrepreneurs by government. This burden has become so great that many Americans are no longer able to maintain their prosperity and are no longer able to compete successfully.

These circumstances have diminished our personal well-being and our national well-being. Virtually everyone in our body politic is adversely affected. This includes not only those in private enterprise, but also those whose lives depend upon governmental programs, since those programs are funded by resources created by private enterprise.

America is Still Exceptional

We live in the greatest country on earth. While our country has serious problems in Washington, we are heirs to the wealth, traditions, customs, and culture bequeathed to us by two centuries of the most free people who have ever walked the earth. It is our responsibility to pass this freedom on to those who will come after us.

A Return to Liberty

A growing uprising is spreading throughout the United States. This is and will continue to be peaceful, because our Founding Fathers wisely gave us a government that can be controlled by peaceful means.

This movement has been joined by citizens within the Republican, Constitution, Libertarian, and Independent Parties and many other informal parties. It also involves people within the Democrat Party. Even many of those who advocate big government now realize that a bankrupt and over-reaching government cannot survive and that liberty is threatened by such a government.

Most Americans, even those actively involved in this movement, would prefer to be doing other things. They just want to be left alone to enjoy their freedoms.

The outcome of these events is as certain today as was the outcome of the original American conflict in Thomas Paine's day. There was no doubt that America would ultimately be freed from England. Only the timing and the extent of suffering during the events were unknown. Thomas Paine argued correctly that common sense dictated that the separation be made sooner rather than later.

Now, throughout the United States, tens of millions of Americans – more with each passing month – are demanding a return to more freedom and less government. They are demanding an end to runaway taxation, regulation, and debt. They are demanding a return to the principles of our original Constitutional Republic.

The United States will return to a government of liberty and justice. Common Sense predicts nothing less.

It is not common sense that a people who have been free for more than 200 years will give up their freedom to a gaggle of career politicians and their retainers in Washington.

We hope that Thomas Paine will forgive us from borrowing upon his title, but there really is none better. As he warned our ancestors two centuries ago, we must assure that our country is guided by Common Sense.

A Special World

I am going to give you some of my background, mainly as a way for you to become better acquainted with me. I also want to remind you of a special world, a world that some of us have been forgetting. Most of us remember. Younger people may not.

As a boy growing up in Houston and Victoria on the Gulf Coast of Texas, I was educated as all children are educated, by example. With luck, most of our examples are positive. Sometimes, we also learn by counter examples and by painful experience.

Work was the dominant activity in our home. My father, a mechanical engineer educated at Iowa State University, and the team of engineers and construction workers he directed ultimately carried out the design and construction of 10 large petrochemical plants.

Though most of this work was done at his office and in the plants, our kitchen table was covered with engineering drawings almost as frequently as it was covered with food.

Ted Robinson was literally in love with chemical plants – a love that has enhanced the lives of many Americans with the products of those plants, such as the plant at Sea Drift, Texas, which was built to make polyethylene for everything from pipes to grocery bags.

Ted Robinson

Ted Robinson, whose life's work with his wife Zelma beside him and thousands of coworkers whom he led, provided – and still provides – polyethylene for Americans

Scheduled "work" occupies the life of a typical American about 8 hours per day, 5 days per week, 50 weeks per year, or about 2,000 hours each year. We sleep, on average, about 2,500 hours. The remaining 4,000 hours (the total, on average, is 8,766) is used in various other ways. For most of us, however, work is more than a 2,000 hour activity. During the other hours, we think about our work; sometimes we dream about our work; and often we carry out work-related activities in various unscheduled ways.

Homemakers with children, like my mother, typically work most of the time they are awake, as do people like my dad, for whom work was recreation as well as employment.

He rarely stopped thinking about his chemical plants. The lives of those who are blessed by work they greatly love are constantly enriched by this activity, which is more a way of life than it is a means of earning a living.

As a boy, I saw the work of my parents, but I had no experience that caused me to reflect upon the circumstances that made it possible. My dad just kept building chemical plants. I never heard him mention government.

One thing was entirely evident. Work was – as they wanted it to be – the central activity of my parents' lives. Had their work been taken away, they both would have suffered greatly – and not just from the loss of income.

When my Dad lost his life in an Air India Boeing 707 crash on the top of Mont Blanc on January 24, 1966, at the age of 55, my mother lost the love of her life, and she lost her career. Without him and without her reason for being and her life's work, she lived just one more year.

The Importance of Meaningful Work

Work – a "job" in our current parlance – is far more than a means of earning money. It is integral to our lives. This is why I have placed job creation at the heart of my campaign for Congress. The terrible loss of American jobs is a crisis for our country and for tens of millions of people.

After college at Caltech and graduate school at the University of California at San Diego, I was immediately given a job on the faculty at UCSD. My thoughts then were, "This is great. I am going to get to play all of my life, and people are going to pay me besides." Research work and teaching were so much fun for me that, having no family, I worked almost every waking hour in these activities.

When I see today so many members of academia using the freedom they enjoy within the universities to work minimally, teach minimally, run constantly to out-of-town meetings, and generally avoid hard work, I feel sorry for them. Perhaps this is the reason that they have so many personal problems. They are unhappy in their work.

> "The secret of success is to make your vocation your vacation."
>
> *Mark Twain*

Work – "jobs" – however, does not just automatically happen. The activities with which we earn the resources required to live and which give meaning to our lives depend on many things. Primarily they depend upon liberty. We must have the freedom to work, to use the resources that we need, and to employ others to work with us.

The desire to work is built into us. It is a part of our nature. That we desire to work – both for subsistence and for enjoyment – is self evident. It is simply "common sense."

Not so obvious, however, are the conditions that lead to our having fulfilling jobs and work – conditions that automatically arise in a free society and just as automatically depart as freedom diminishes.

To be sure, a slave "works," but a slave does not have a "job" in the sense that an American means a job. A slave labors in tyranny. A free man works.

Yet a meaningful job requires many things. It requires the capital to pay for machinery and raw materials. It requires a market for the items produced. It requires a market in which the money earned can be traded for the products of the work of others. And, more than anything else, it requires circumstances that assure freedom and continuity of the environment needed for work and sufficient liberty to excel in competition with others who are doing similar work.

People automatically work when they have liberty. People are the ultimate resource. People always work and produce more than they consume – and thereby become increasingly prosperous – providing they are free to do so.

The United States contains, within its borders, a vast wealth of natural resources. The American people could not exhaust those resources in thousands of years. All that is required for the continued advance of this great country is sufficient freedom for Americans to do that which comes naturally to them – to work.

Yet, this work is being taken away from tens of millions of Americans. Jobs – fulfilling or otherwise – are now in short supply, and an estimated 30 million Americans are unwillingly out of work.

Employment Opportunities Lost by Congress

Our economy is healthy when about 30% of our workers are employed in manufacturing and the remaining 70% are employed in services to the manufacturing workers and to those who provide services to the manufacturing workers. Services include barbers, auto mechanics, retailers, grocers, truckers, teachers, bankers, and others in thousands of different professions who use the wealth created by manufacturing and profit from personal savings to enrich our lives.

Graphs A and B show data from the U.S. Bureau of Labor Statistics. In the 1950s, about 30% of all Americans

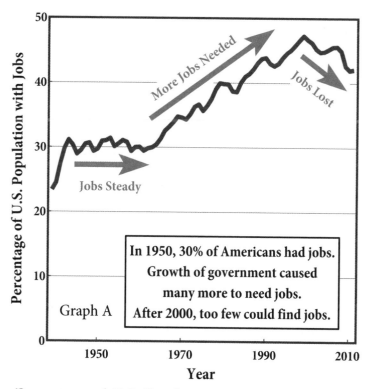

Percentage of U.S. Population With Non-Farm Jobs

Initially at 30%, employment rose from the 1970s to 2000. By then 50 million more people needed work to maintain their living standards. Congress made prosperity harder to maintain. After 2000, needing even more work, fewer people could find it.

held "jobs." About 10% of the total population or one-third of the workers were in manufacturing. There was typically one "breadwinner" per family.

As the economic conditions of many families gradually deteriorated from the 1970s onward, more and more people entered the work force. Increasingly, both parents needed to work. They worked in efforts to maintain family standards of living in an economy that was gradually being strangled by congressional over-regulation, over-taxation, over-spending, and over-indebtedness.

In about the year 2000, however, the situation finally became so unfavorable that the American economy began a sharp turn downward. More and more people could not find jobs at all, so overall employment dropped.

The percentage of Americans with non-farm jobs rose from 30% in 1965 to 47% in 2000 and then fell to 42% in 2010. That 5% fall is the approximately **15 million jobs lost** during the current ongoing economic crisis. The trend upward that was interrupted in 2000 would probably have reached about 52% by 2010, so the real deficit of jobs for people who want and need employment is actually about 10% or about **30 million jobs**.

Meanwhile, manufacturing, mining, and logging jobs fell from 10% of the total population in the 1950s to 6%. in 2000, with a sharper drop from 6% to 4% after the year 2000 – much lower than the percentage required for good economic health.

The U.S. stock market reflects the simultaneous decline in the value of American industry. Graphing the Dow Average in dollars is not useful because the government has printed so many dollars that the dollar no longer serves as a reliable long-term measure of value. This dollar printing also makes real returns on savings negative, with disastrous effects on seniors and others on fixed income.

Look at Graph C, however, of the Dow Average as priced in gallons of gasoline – a measure of value we all face every day. Priced in gasoline, the Dow has fallen 6-fold since 2000, and there has been no post-2009 rally. In the chapter of this book entitled *Sound Money*, there is a graph

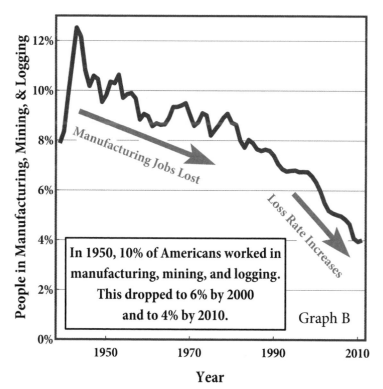

Percentage of Population Employed in Manufacturing, Mining, & Logging

The percentage of Americans working in manufacturing, mining, and logging fell steadily until 2000, when the drop worsened. Congress caused these job losses. From 2000 to 2010, an average of 10 factories and 2,000 manufacturing jobs were lost every day.

showing a similar drop in the Dow vs. other commodities.

These three graphs show the economic price the American people have paid for the loss of liberty caused by career politicians in Washington. This is the cost of the over-taxation, over-regulation, over-spending, and over-indebtedness that our nation has endured – as I will show in this book – at the hands of the U.S. Congress.

Presidents, bureaucratic agencies, local and state governments empowered or mandated by Congress, and others contribute to these things, but all federal actions are funded, allowed, or made possible by Congress.

This economic problem can only be corrected by getting rid of the members of Congress and their retainers whose mismanagement has caused it and replacing them with people of common sense.

Manufacturing

Americans have lost their jobs largely because our country has lost much of its manufacturing industry. Since the 1950s, the percentage of American workers employed in manufacturing has dropped from 10% to 4%.

The loss of manufacturing jobs shown in graph B above can be summarized another way. **The United States has lost, on average, 10 factories and 2,000 manufacturing jobs per day – every day – for the past 10 years.**

It is our manufacturing industries – from steel in the Northeast to lumber in the Northwest – that form the foundation of our economy. We have plenty of natural resources for our industries. The natural resources of the United States are so vast in every category that we could not even begin to exhaust them in a thousand years.

For example, American coal, oil, natural gas, and methane clathrate resources are vast. These four forms of hydrocarbon energy are industrially inter-convertible, so we can use the least expensive to produce the more expensive. There are today industrial plants converting coal to oil as the Germans did during World War II, and plants

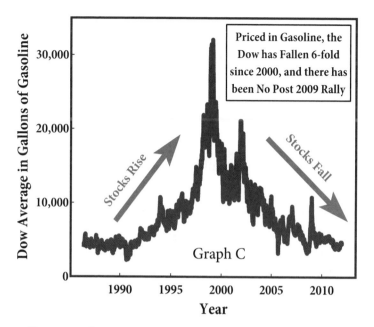

Dow stock average priced in gallons of gasoline.

Measured vs. real value (the price of gasoline) rather than dollars, the Dow peaked in 2000, and has declined dramatically since. There has been no real stock rally from the lows of 2009.

converting natural gas into oil.

Methane clathrates (natural gas in special forms of ice in the ocean) are so abundant that they exceed all oil, coal, and natural gas combined. Methods of recovering methane from clathrates are just being developed. Our hydrocarbon natural resources are essentially inexhaustible.

Likewise, our uranium and thorium reserves can fuel our nuclear power industry for thousands of years. Wind, sun, and hydroelectric resources are also extensive. We only need to use those technologies that are most practical and economical – a choice that can best and most wisely be made by free people competing and using their talents and abilities, and certainly not by Washington politicians.

Yet our energy industry, hobbled by the tentacles of big government, cannot now even supply our own needs. We have been importing 30% of our energy. With our economy in a slump, it is now 20%.

A Stumbling Economy

When an American buys a spoon, or a dish, or some other widget made in China, somewhere else in America an American must manufacture something of equivalent value that is purchased by a resident of China. We must trade things of real value.

The actual situation is, of course, more involved. People trade all sorts of widgets and natural resources, between many countries. But the principle is the same. Real products and resources must be exchanged, not pretend products and resources, such as the government "printed money" that is now being created under congressional authorization.

If pretend resources worked, we could simplify things greatly. We could just outsource the printing of money to the Chinese, too. Then the Chinese could manufacture the goods *and* the money; pay themselves; and then ship the goods to us. We could merely stop by the Walmart warehouse and pick up the things we want, without paying at all!

Our politicians have printed up trillions of dollars in recent years and distributed these dollars to their political cronies and campaign donors to "jump start" the economy. This has not improved the economy.

> *"In the Carboniferous Epoch we were promised abundance for all,*
>   *By robbing selected Peter to pay for collective Paul;*
>   *But, though we had plenty of money, there was nothing our money could buy,*
>   *And the Gods of the Copybook Headings said: 'If you don't work you die.'"*
>   **Rudyard Kipling**

Congress has also borrowed trillions of dollars, using us as the collateral for their debts. Those debts must be serviced, which is one reason my opponent in the 2012 campaign, Peter DeFazio, advocates raising taxes. He wants to service the debts he and those like him have run up in the past and also tax away capital to buy more votes – even though that capital is badly needed elsewhere to create jobs in our stumbling economy.

Without liberty, we cannot manufacture the things we need for our own use and for trade. When government taxation, regulation, and spending become too high, our businesses, industries, and workers cannot function competitively. Without liberty, we cannot work effectively.

We must get the dead hand of government off the backs of the American people, so that our jobs will return, and our people can prosper.

Each real dollar spent in our economy must be earned by someone's useful productive work. Either the worker or business – or another person or business to whom their savings and profits are entrusted – spends that dollar.

New inflated paper dollars, whether printed up under

Congressional authorization or printed by counterfeiters in a hidden basement, only harm our economy. (More on this in the chapter *Sound Money.*)

People are the ultimate resource. They turn the natural resources of our nation and resources that we buy from other nations into goods and services. People always produce more than they consume – if they are free to do so.[1] Therefore, prosperity tends to steadily increase.

Why then is our prosperity decreasing? Why are so many Americans without jobs? The reason is that Big Government has taken away too much of our freedom. We are no longer able – under the conditions set by our government – to produce as much as we consume.

In times past, **America was known for producing the highest quality and lowest priced products in the world, and we had the highest wages in the world.**

Now, with government confiscating our wealth and liberty at every turn, we have reduced our quality, raised our prices, and lowered our wages in attempts to compensate. The result? People the world over, including Americans, are buying elsewhere, and our prosperity is falling.

The American economy – the combined work and expenditures of the people of the United States – is consuming more that it produces. Therefore, in order to maintain prosperity, our governments (federal, state, and local) and people have borrowed tens of trillions of dollars – more debt than can ever be repaid.

This situation can no longer be covered up by more borrowing, so our nation is sliding toward bankruptcy. Lost jobs and diminished prosperity are the result.

Why are we producing too little and accumulating vast amounts of debt? There is just one reason: big government, especially that controlled by Congress, has taken away so much of our liberty that we can no longer produce enough goods and services to maintain our way of life.

1. *Federal Regulations* levied and overseen by regulatory agencies, such as the Environmental Protection Agency, Department of Energy, and others, have become so extensive that American workers and businesses spend a large part of their time and resources complying with them. While most of these agencies were started with good intentions, they have grown to include millions of bureaucrats who demand that Americans spend too much of their time and money satisfying regulations, rather than doing productive work.

These regulatory agencies did not exist during most of our history. They are recent creations of Congress. Most of these agencies should be closed, and their legitimate activities delegated to the states and the people, where they constitutionally belong – and to small federal offices reporting directly to Congress.

Reduction of federal regulations to a level that conforms to common sense would cause the largest economic boom in American history – and it would not cost the American people one cent. In fact, it would reduce federal expenditures now required to pay millions of government bureaucrats and their non-governmental counterparts who spend their time shuffling regulatory paper.

Regulatory agencies also stand between American workers and the natural resources they need to produce useful products. In Oregon, they stand between Oregonians and their mineral and forest resources. Federal regulations have placed a very large part of our country's abundant mineral, energy, timber, and agricultural resources beyond the reach of our industries and workers.

Congress has empowered a freedom-destroying bureaucracy. We need a new Congress and fewer bureaucrats.

2. Federal Taxes take money away from the wages of workers and profits of businesses and reduce the capital available for business, industry, and jobs. To be sure, part of these dollars are spent for services that are constitutionally required, but a large part of these tax dollars are wasted and spent imprudently.

Moreover, Congress has created many "unfunded mandates" – things that the federal government demands that state and local governments do, but for which federal resources are not provided. This raises our state and local taxes to pay for federal programs.

These taxes are paid by everyone, not just those who are directly taxed. On average, half of every dollar earned by an American is taken in taxes – even from workers who pay no income taxes.

When we buy automobile fuel, for example, we pay state and federal fuel taxes. We also pay the taxes of the fuel company, taxes of the worker who dispenses the fuel, taxes of the farmer who produces the food consumed by that worker, taxes of the teacher who teaches the farmer's children, and so on. It is estimated that, on average, 22% of the cost of all our purchases is this additional hidden tax.

Almost every time dollars are exchanged, the government takes some of those dollars by taxing the people engaged in that activity. All of these taxes accumulate in the cost of everything we buy.

Politicians want us to believe that taxes fall largely on "profits," "gains," and the "rich." In fact, all taxation is inherently regressive. It falls most heavily on the middle class and the poor. Taxation works its way into the price of everything. A poor man's dollars are few and therefore much more precious, so he suffers the most from taxation.

3. Federal Debt has grown so large that service of this debt is draining away huge amounts of resources that are needed for the production of goods and services by American industry and workers.

Debt also requires collateral. The lender must have confidence that the borrower will repay, either with earnings or with some other asset that he holds. What have our career politicians in Congress pledged in collateral for the tens of trillions of dollars in debt, both actual and obligated, that they have accumulated?

Congress has pledged in collateral for its debt one primary asset: **the future labor of the American people.** This means we have all been pledged as involuntary servants for this debt – we and our children and our grandchildren. Slavery, of course, has been illegal in the United States since the end of the Civil War. Nevertheless, this is our situation.

Debt – accumulated by political overspending by the U.S. Congress – is an additional crushing burden that has been placed on the backs of American workers.

During his over-long tenure in Congress, my career politician opponent and his big-spending colleagues have spent about $50 trillion. Yet, federal income was only about $40 trillion. So, the debt has risen by about $10 trillion.

This spending has purchased lots of re-election campaign support for these career politicians, but it has been impoverishing us and our country.

The result of runaway over-regulation, over-taxation, and over-indebtedness – all caused by the U.S. Congress, which controls these activities – is that much of American industry has been forced, in order to remain competitive, to move abroad where economic freedom is greater.

We now import, for example, $300 billion in energy each year. This energy could be produced in the United States, but lack of economic freedom makes it impractical to do so. This costs us $300 billion each year – on average, $3,000 from each American family.

And, we lose more than $3,000 per family. High imported energy costs cause our energy intensive industries to move abroad, so we lose jobs and pay more for imported products, too.

> We are apt to shut our eyes against a painful truth . . . For my part, whatever anguish of the spirit it may cost, I am willing to know the whole truth; to know the worst; and to provide for it. *Patrick Henry*

As American industry has moved abroad and businesses within the United States have contracted under the burden of federal over-regulation, over-taxation, and over-spending, the American economy has contracted. Thus we have lost tens of millions of American jobs.

To be sure, the government issues statistics monthly that purport to show that our GDP (gross domestic product) is slowly rising. These statistics are, however, bogus. They measure the money that changes hands, without regard to whether the exchange involves useful work. Moreover, the GDP estimates are also artificially high because they are corrected by artificially low estimates of price increases.

As most Americans realize in their daily lives, their economic circumstances are worsening and becoming more precarious. This is because real GDP is actually falling, contrary to government claims.

Abundant meaningful employment opportunities and American prosperity will not return until the reasons for their loss are eliminated. We must get rid of the career politicians in Congress who have done this to our country, replace them with citizens with common sense, and then make sure Congress gets the government off our backs.

As recently as 40 years ago, with American products the highest quality and least expensive in the world and American wages the highest, other developed countries constantly complained of the "brain drain." Their most productive people came to the United States, where there was more economic liberty. This is no longer our situation. We must rid ourselves of the policies that have harmed our country and get our economy moving again.

During the 2012 election, Washington politicians will pretend that the election contest is between those who receive money or other benefits from the government vs. those who are taxed by government to obtain that money. They hope that those who receive "benefits" from government will re-elect them.

The truth is quite different.

In fact, it is those dependent on government programs who are in the greatest danger from the politicians who are ruining our economy.

At greatest risk are those who receive Social Security, Medicare, and veterans benefits; those who receive food stamps and other welfare payments; those who work at all levels of public education; those who maintain American roads and bridges; those who work to defend America from foreign threats; those who deliver our mail; and those who work in other aspects of our public sector.

As over-regulation, over-taxation, and over-spending impoverishes our country, it also impoverishes our government. An over-burdened private sector cannot produce the wealth required to pay for these governmental programs. As these programs diminish or close for lack of funds, those dependent upon them will suffer the most.

In the 2012 election, we are all in this together. We must return common sense to the U.S. Congress.

Congressional Mismanagement

A successful business executive once told me that the mark of good management in his company was when he could leave for vacation and things went along just as smoothly without him. If instead there were constant crises requiring his attention, something was wrong.

An American Secretary of State of long ago once said that the job of the Department of State is to create boredom. If everything was going so well for the United States around the world that there was little interest in foreign affairs, then he was doing his job well.

In 2010, however, I listened to a woman describing a recent opportunity to visit her congressman (not DeFazio). She said the visit was very exciting.

There he was, floating through the capitol; surrounded by retainers; constantly making important decisions; responding to emergencies – large and small; bending briefly toward a nearby aide to ask how to vote on a new law; conferring with lobbyists; entertaining dignitaries; speaking sagely to the media; and yet finding time for a nod and smile to her and other admirers. Wow! How fortunate that our country has such supermen!

And yet, how wrong is this picture!

Our Constitution did not establish a big government where the individual is subservient to the state and officers of the state, as had ordinarily been the case in previous world history. The Constitution instead established a small government where the liberty and rights of the individual are ascendant. From this difference has flowed the success of our nation.

The Constitution actually gives Congress the authority to do things that should require very little time. To be sure, the Congress is authorized to pass laws, but, after 200 plus years, we surely by now must have most of the laws we need. We should be getting rid of unnecessary and wasteful laws, rather than piling on more.

Congress should collect modest taxes for the country's needs; make certain the Department of Defense has the resources to secure our freedom; pay the country's debts and pay for the operations of the other branches of government; carry out its few other functions as efficiently and quietly as possible; and then *keep out of our way*.

In 2013-2014, Congress needs to do lots of work to get rid of unnecessary laws and bureaucracies that our country can no longer afford; repeal laws that have diminished our liberty; and revise our taxation and federal spending so that they enhance our liberty rather than diminish it.

Congress needs to make sure that obligations are met to our seniors, veterans, and other groups by arranging more money to flow directly to those people, rather than flowing through a myriad of bureaucrats and special interests who deplete the funds.

Congress needs to work toward the ultimate objective – a Congress that also creates boredom. We will know that Congress has succeeded when Americans can listen to the evening news for weeks without hearing much of anything about what the government is doing.

Congress also needs to reduce the perks of congressional office so that self-serving career politicians find little incentive to occupy these positions. Lavish retirements, big expense accounts, special opportunities that make congressmen wealthy (as is my millionaire opponent Mr. DeFazio), and other perks available to those who improperly use the power of congressional office should end.

Congress needs to return to the intentions and wisdom of our Founding Fathers. This requires that we get rid of the career politicians and return to a Congress where capable citizen volunteers are trusted to fill congressional positions for short terms in order to make sure our country's business is carried out properly.

Congress must lift the burdens of over-regulation, over-taxation, and over-indebtedness off of the backs of the American people.

This burden is not going to be lifted by the same career politicians who put it there. These politicians must be replaced by Americans with common sense.

Part I

POLITICS

1

WHO IS ART ROBINSON?

"There is no distinctly Native American criminal class . . . save Congress."

Mark Twain

The Candidate

> Art Robinson is a successful scientist, businessman, and father. He lives with his family on their family farm in Josephine County and works at the Oregon Institute of Science and Medicine.
>
> Art is asking voters to elect him as a citizen volunteer in Congress. We must clean up the mess in Washington, especially in the Congress.
>
> Art's opponent is a 13-term, 25-year career politician. We can't rely on the career politicians who have created the problems in Washington to fix them.

Who is Art Robinson, and why vote for him?

After all, Congress has bankrupted our government, broken virtually all of its key promises, ignored the Constitution, behaved in uncountable dishonest ways, badly damaged our economy, destroyed tens of millions of

American jobs, and created innumerable regulations and agencies that constantly interfere in our lives.

Anyone who seems to want to join this disreputable group should be automatically suspect.

That's what this book is about. Congress is making life miserable for the Robinsons, too. I have volunteered to serve a term in Congress and perhaps more if necessary to help solve Oregon District 4's part of this problem. It's time to rid ourselves of the career politicians in Congress who are doing so much damage to our country and our way of life.

This book explains why retiring our current 13-term, 25-year congressman and electing me will be good for everyone in Oregon Congressional District 4, for Oregon, and for our nation. Part of this book is about the overall way our country should be governed, but most of it is about specific issues of special concern to all of us now.

The Founding Fathers intended that the elective positions in our federal government be filled by citizen volunteers. Citizens, whose lives and accomplishments indicated that they could be trusted with the public business for one or two terms of office, were to be selected by popular vote.

Usually these people would serve as caretakers to keep government on track and doing the few things specified for it in the Constitution, but sometimes they would be elected to solve a special problem that had arisen.

Well, we sure have a special problem in Washington today! The problem is that our elective offices are not filled by citizen volunteers at all, but instead by self-interested career politicians who have taken our country down a road that threatens our way of life.

Career politicians stay too long. Citizen volunteers

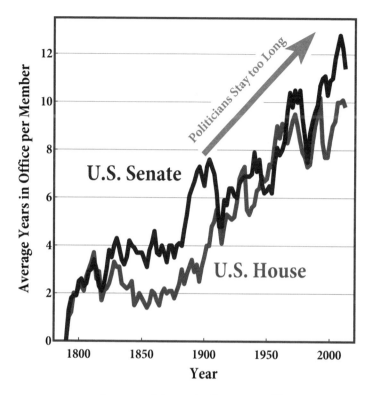

Average Years in Congress[74]

During the first century, the average tenure of members of the House and Senate was 2 and 4 years, respectively. (These are averages for sitting members at intervals, so average total tenure per member is a little longer.) Those members were citizen volunteers. Today, the averages are 10 and 12. These members are career politicians. Their careers create a conflict of interest between their self-interests and the best interests of our nation.

serve and then return to their life's work. After 10-plus years in Washington, career politicians have little to which to return. Getting re-elected becomes more important to them than the best interests of our nation.

You will not find ordinary politics in this book because I am not a politician. I am a father, scientist, and businessman. When a problem arises, I seek a solution to the problem and then solve it.

Fathers usually, but not always, successfully solve problems. Scientists solve some problems, but not others. It is the nature of science to chip away at the mysteries of the physical world and unravel problems a few at a time. Businessmen successfully solve most of the problems in their businesses. They must do so to stay in business.

Politicians, by contrast, seldom solve problems and usually don't propose solutions, except at election time. Politicians are "very concerned" about the problems. They will "bring all necessary resources to bear" on the problems. They will "not allow" the problems to continue. America "will be secure." Everyone "will" be prosperous. And, of course, their opponents "will not" solve problems, but will make matters worse. If one listens carefully, however, the specifics are usually left out or are contrived and bogus.

> **"I don't make jokes . . . I just watch the government and report the facts."**
> **Will Rogers**

My opponent, for example, is now claiming that raising taxes on the fuel markets would lower gasoline prices.[77] This is obviously not common sense. He hopes to gain votes by playing to public dissatisfaction with higher prices.

We have a few people in government who are not really politicians even though they have been in Washington for a long time. Congressman Ron Paul is a physician who has delivered thousands of babies. Imagine how many problems he has successfully solved in his work!

Ron Paul recently proposed that federal expenditures be reduced by $1 trillion per year beginning in 2013 and that five federal agencies, including the department of energy and the department of education be closed. Whether one agrees with the specifics of this proposal or not, it would sure go a long way toward balancing the federal budget and freeing Americans from federal over-regulation. It is considered, however, to be poor politics.

By proposing a specific solution, Ron Paul has made some voters nervous. Many worry that the $1 trillion reduction would take away some perk that they enjoy or that closing an agency would affect their own advantages.

This places him at a disadvantage to the politicians who assure that "the budget must be balanced" and government "must work effectively," but carefully avoid specific actions that would accomplish this.

When pressed, the career politicians in Washington formed a "committee to work on the problem" of saving $1 trillion gradually over a period of *ten* years. Even if reached, this goal would not even stem the increase in government spending, much less lower it.

The deficit is already more than $1 trillion *each and every year and is increasing rapidly,* so the committee goal was to solve less than 10% of the real problem, and it failed to do even that. The important thing was to be seen by voters as "very concerned" and "working hard on" the problem.

During the 2010 campaign, we were honored that our friend Harrison Schmitt came to Oregon and campaigned with us. Dr. Schmitt is a Caltech-educated scientist; he is the last man who piloted a spacecraft onto the surface of the Moon; and he served one 6-year term as Senator from New Mexico.

He told me that, when he was in the U.S. Senate, he was an oddity because he was a problem solver. The other 99 senators, politicians all, became nervous with a problem solver in their midst. *Problems* are a career politician's political capital - not the *solutions*. Solutions make some voters nervous, and can be inconvenient at election time.

When Harrison Schmitt was landing on the Moon, had he radioed back that he was "very concerned" and "ready to give assurances" of success, it would have been cold comfort to his colleagues. He needed to solve multiple problems in real time without equivocation and without error.

He did.

In deciding to campaign for us, Dr. Schmitt knew that my view of America's Constitutional Republic, the way it should function, and the policies it should follow are very similar to his own.

He also knew that both our campaign chairman Dr. Noah Robinson and our candidate Dr. Art Robinson are, like him, professionally successful, Caltech-educated scientists. We all three have offered ourselves as problem solving citizen volunteers. At this point in its history, this is what our nation and our people need.

Who Is Art?

So, who exactly is Art Robinson? What follows is a brief biography, combined with some relevant national history.

Freedom in the 1950s

In Victoria, Texas, young Art Robinson reads with pride in his grade school *Weekly Reader,* that Americans produce most of the world's steel, concrete, aluminum, machine tools, automobiles, chemicals, food, and many other products. The United States is the powerhouse of the world. America is filled to the brim with citizens who are the hope and example of freedom to people everywhere – many of whom still languish in war, poverty, and tyranny.

American products are the best quality and the lowest priced. And, American wages are the highest in the world. The "brain drain" is a constant concern in other countries as productive people throughout the world flood into America to work and live as free men should – unfettered by government tyranny.

Ted Robinson, Art's father, is completing the design and construction of the Union Carbide polyethylene plant at Sea Drift, Texas – his love of engineering driving him to produce the finest machinery possible and his work unimpeded by the tentacles of government. Multitudes of such men are at work throughout the land.

Freedom in the 1960s

Nuclear power – the greatest technological advance in human history – is being installed throughout America, providing low cost, safe, clean electrical energy for the next leap forward in world freedom and prosperity. Americans are going to the Moon, and plan to go to Mars. The computer revolution has begun, and the world watches in awe. Is there nothing that free Americans cannot accomplish?

Ted Robinson has built chemical plants in the U.S., Puerto Rico, Brazil, Scotland, England, Belgium, India, and Japan. American know-how in thousands of industries spreads hope and freedom everywhere. Homi Bhabha fathers nuclear energy in India – the first step in lifting a billion people from the bondage of poverty.

High over the French Alps on January 24, 1966, two explosions are heard, a Boeing 707 is gone, Homi Bhabha and Ted Robinson are dead – buried in the snow at the top of Mont Blanc.

America doesn't miss a beat. She has tens of thousands of engineers and scientists. They are leading hundreds of thousands of their younger peers and tens of millions of productive people who are working to turn their dreams and knowledge into reality.

Art has graduated from Caltech. Awarded his PhD at the University of California at San Diego, he is appointed to the faculty there. He is just one more man with the freedom to live and work within the great American experiment in liberty.

Art and his students and colleagues discover molecular clocks that time the aging of protein molecules and also make discoveries in nutrition and preventive medicine.

Art and Laurelee - September 1988

Freedom Falters in the 1970s

America is in trouble. Washington is flooded by career politicians, pursuing personal goals rather than the best interests of our country. They trade their votes for power and money to those who bid the highest.

These politicians begin crippling American industry with taxation and regulation. They stop the building of nuclear power. They are uninterested in the manned exploration of Mars and beyond.

America is adrift, and her people are turning inward. Envy and fear of technology begin to be taught in American public schools – replacing reverence for the American Constitutional Republic, individual human liberty, and the values that built our nation.

Art Robinson and his scientist wife Laurelee have left UCSD and founded an Institute with Art's long-time friend and colleague Linus Pauling. They have originated a new discipline – now known as "metabolic profiling" – a revolutionary medical advance.

As president and research professor of their institute, Art assumes that their medical discoveries will soon be available to the American people. He is naive. The tentacles of Washington politicians have already reached American medicine – choking off innovation.

American medicine – with a legacy that freedom made possible – is still the finest in the world, but costs far too much as a result of politicians whose expansion of taxation, regulation, and litigation is gradually strangling free enterprise in all American industries.

Steel, aluminum, machine tools, automobiles, chemicals, and the multitudes of other American products that Art admired in his *Weekly Reader* are still being made – but the industries making them are moving abroad, unable to thrive in the American political climate. Medical care cannot easily move abroad – it just costs more and stagnates under the assault from Washington.

Freedom's Hope in the 1980s

Ronald Reagan is elected, the Soviet Union nears defeat, and President Reagan begins to cut away the political cancer that has been consuming the American dream. He proclaims that it is "Morning in America," and real hope returns.

Reagan moves to free American workers and industries. He reduces taxation and regulation and an economic resurgence results, but Reagan is soon gone – and career politicians regain control.

Art and Laurelee move to Oregon in 1980, and with

colleagues establish the Oregon Institute of Science and Medicine. They also work with the Reagan Administration on civil defense, and Art writes a platform plank on civil defense at the 1988 Republican Convention.

By November 1988, they have 12-year-old Zachary, Noah 10, Arynne 8, twins Joshua and Bethany 6, and Matthew 18 months.

It is Armistice Day, November 11. President Reagan presents a wonderful speech. All of the Robinsons seem to have a stomach flu, but by morning, they are much better – except for Laurelee.

Laurelee is dead.

The report states that she died from acute idiopathic hemorrhagic pancreatitis – her pancreas released enzymes that punctured an artery. She was ill for just 24 hours.

She was 43 years old.

The Robinsons Growing Up Together - 1995

A silent, almost eerie calm settles upon the Robinson children. Their grief is deep, but it does not harm them. The loving hand of God quiets, it comforts, it gently leads. It is a thing unseen.

A Scientist and Six Children

Art entered a very different life. The Lord raised the children, Art ran errands, and the seven Robinsons grew up on the farm together.

They continued the civil defense work – traveling cross country many times together, publishing tens of thousands of copies of instructions and books that the Federal Emergency Management Agency, FEMA, distributed to emergency responders throughout the United States, and building civil defense displays purchased by the federal government and displayed to millions of Americans.

Without Laurelee, their home school became an exercise in self-learning, and Art and the children, with help from friends and colleagues, gradually developed a self-teaching curriculum and an array of children's books that they now publish.

In 2011, more than 60,000 American children used their award-winning curriculum for grades 1 through 12. The six children put each other through college and graduate school with this family business.

Zachary, Noah, Arynne, Bethany, and Matthew earned BS degrees in chemistry – Zachary, Noah, and Matthew completed those degrees in two years at college. Joshua earned a BS in mathematics.

Zachary and Arynne then earned doctorates in veterinary medicine from Iowa State University. Noah earned a

Matthew Robinson - 1999

Matthew earned a BS in chemistry from Southern Oregon University in just two years. He entered Oregon State University to earn a PhD in nuclear engineering. He is pictured here with the excellent historical novels of G.A. Henty that he and his family publish. These books have been widely used in American education for more than a century.

PhD in chemistry from Caltech – finishing in three years and publishing four research papers in the *Proceedings of the National Academy of Sciences*. In 2011, Joshua, Bethany, and Matthew were graduate students at Oregon State University – all working to earn PhD degrees in nuclear engineering.

The seven Robinsons divided the work as needed, with some adjustments. After five years of one-course meals – twice a day, Art is permanently replaced in the kitchen by his hungry peers. Today, the children still do their farm work on weekends home from school.

The whole family and their colleagues gradually built the Oregon Institute of Science and Medicine into a world-class laboratory for the study of molecular clocks and biomedical research.

Their recent publications involve studies of a protein involved in Alzheimer's and Parkinson's diseases, research on human aging, and improvements in diagnostic medicine. Robinson publications are highly respected and widely read by scientists throughout the world. One research publication – Art's favorite – is authored by all seven Robinsons. They all participated in the work.

The Robinsons love music and resurrect church pipe organs as a hobby. They have also republished most of the

Assembling a Pipe Organ in 2007

Noah, Matthew, and Joshua Robinson assembling a pipe organ. As a hobby, they rescue and restore classic pipe organs.

recorded works of the great gospel singer George Beverly Shea – a project in which they have produced 27 CDs with more than 400 songs.

By 2011, Art has written the pro-science, pro-technology, pro-free enterprise newsletter *Access to Energy* for 18 years, inheriting this work from scientist and refugee from Communism, Petr Beckmann. *Access to Energy* is science for laymen in areas of interest in human affairs. One-third of the subscribers are scientists and engineers.

As a result, Art was asked by *The Wall Street Journal* to write the lead editorial in their edition published during the Kyoto global warming meeting in Japan, where Vice-President Al Gore attempted to impose energy rationing on the American people. Art and Zachary wrote this editorial, and Art and Noah wrote another on this subject for the *The Wall Street Journal* a few years later.

Based on a scientific review article they authored entitled "Environmental Effects of Increased Atmospheric Carbon Dioxide," the Robinsons and their colleagues circulated a petition by mail that has been signed by more than 31,000 Americans with university degrees in physical science – urging the government not to ration and tax energy supplies on the basis of the scientifically invalid claims of human-caused global warming.

These signatures demonstrate that Al Gore's claim of a scientific consensus favoring his opinions is entirely untrue. This petition has helped to delay crushing new energy taxes on American families.

The hard work, principles, academic excellence, personal accomplishments, and productive enterprises of the Robinson family have, by example, inspired and helped many other American families.

Art Robinson in 2010

Nation in Crisis

It is 2012. The dead hand of government has crippled the American juggernaut. Suffering under crushing over-taxation, over-regulation, and over-indebtedness, Americans are not even self-sufficient in energy, buying energy from unstable nations abroad.

Lost jobs, lost homes, lost savings and retirement plans, and lost hope for a future as prosperous as their parents and grandparents: Americans are watching as their way of life, prosperity, and hopes for the future slip away.

That way of life was built on American freedom – freedom that permitted each American to produce more than he consumed and to prosper. Their liberty has been taken away by career politicians – including the 13-term congressman from Oregon District 4.

Influenced by demagoguery, the American people have made a terrible mistake. They have elected too many self-interested politicians to Congress, who hold the American Constitution, the American Republic, and the American people to be less important than themselves.

Trillions of dollars have been misspent by Congress – money taxed, printed, or borrowed from China and other competitors. There is little indication that the profligate spending in Congress will end.

Many think the American people will soon be forced to declare national bankruptcy. Do these politicians care at all about the people, except at election time?

Empathy

There is a story about a man who comes home from work to find his wife very upset. She has been treated in an insulting way during the day. "He was just awful," she sobs. "I felt so embarrassed."

"This is entirely unacceptable and will never ever happen again," her husband storms. He immediately telephones the offending party, demands and obtains an apology, and makes certain it will never happen again. He then hangs up the phone, comments that the problem has been solved, and then asks his wife, "What's for dinner?"

To his astonishment, his wife bursts into tears.

He solved the problem, but he did not take time to sympathize with her. She wanted to talk with him about the incident. She wanted him to feel her pain and commiserate with her. This was a major part of her day. She wanted him to share it with her.

His wife was right, and her example is not restricted to women. Both men and women want their problems solved, and they want them solved by people who understand the pain that these problems have caused for them.

President Clinton understood this. He told voters, "I feel your pain." This was important to his being elected.

As a result of their mother's death, my six children were raised entirely by their father. Mothers are usually more skilled at empathy. Without a mother, we needed to adapt.

Together we became a great seven-person phenomenon, a wonderful experience for all of us.

It is painful to see my fellow citizens and my country harmed. When nations or people are charmed onto a wrong path through emotional manipulation, the results can be disastrous.

Some of the worst tyrants in history have been very talented orators, who have led tens of millions of people onto paths of misery and death.

The husband in the story who failed to empathize with his wife was probably not quite what he seemed. He loved his wife and may well have suffered more than she when he learned of her mistreatment. Yet, she did not understand.

As you read this book, you will constantly meet, in the writer, a problem solver – a problem solver who feels deeply the suffering of each of you and of our nation.

Consider the existence of the book itself. Consider that in 2010 and now again in 2012, the writer turned aside from almost all that he ordinarily enjoys in life to try to help his country and its people. Consider that, if he wins in 2012, he must spend more years away from the pursuits and people he really loves.

Art Robinson definitely feels our mutual pain.

Can Robinson Win?

It has been said that Robinson can't lose. If he wins, he gets to go to Washington and help to solve our country's problems. If he loses, he also wins because he doesn't have to go to Washington.

Robinson also can't win. If he loses the election, he loses. If he wins, he has to go to Washington.

The truth is that I truly can only win. In 2010, we had the wonderful experience of meeting and campaigning with thousands of Oregonians just like us, and of talking with the voters of District 4 about the necessity of common sense in government. We received the votes of 130,000 of our fellow citizens (44% of those who voted) and hope to receive the votes of many more in 2012. This, for us, has been a great honor.

I did lose a little of my good name and reputation. In the final months of the 2010 election, my opponent launched a million dollar media blitz with a series of outright falsehoods about me. This is documented in the section entitled *Correction of DeFazio Misrepresentations* later in this book.

If I believed even 10% of what my opponent said about me then, I would be unwilling to have dinner with myself. And, I know some of my fellow citizens believed him. This time, I hope that everyone will know the truth.

When you have read this book, you will know the answer to the question "Who is Art Robinson." As a friend of mine has said, you will have received your "2012 election flu shot" – immunization against the false statements about Robinson that may be offered during the campaign.

Please give me your vote. Don't vote for me or against me on the basis of my opponent's radio and TV ads and propaganda fliers during the campaign.

If you read this book, or even skim over the chapter summaries, DeFazio's TV ads in the final 30 days will give you a laugh. "Does this guy really think we are *that* ill-informed?" Yes, he does. But he will be wrong.

Making Things

There is an old adage that there are two sorts of people in the world – those who do the work and those who take the credit. The adage advises that it is best to be among those who do the work – because there is less competition.

America is now torn by a conflict between those who do productive work and those in politics who, in their rush to take credit, impede the workers by over-taxation, over-regulation, and other impediments to liberty.

This conflict was the subject of the famous 1957 novel *Atlas Shrugged*, which is now being released in movie form.

In *Atlas Shrugged*, the producers – "men of the mind" – withdraw. Led by John Galt, the producers go on strike. Atlas (after the mythical Greek god, who carried the world on his shoulders) shrugs, and the world feels the effects.

Now, the conflict envisioned in *Atlas Shrugged* has arrived in America, but the producers are *not* going on strike. Many of them are simply leaving the United States and taking their productive enterprises abroad. This has cost our nation tens of millions of productive jobs.

Many others – myself, my family, and our friends included – have chosen instead to resist. We, along with tens of millions of productive people still in America, are the "men and women of the mind" – those who will never leave their country and will also not give up their efforts to produce.

I am a producer, as are all members of my family – as are our friends and associates in Oregon and across America who have provided the more than 13,000 individual campaign contributions to support my candidacy for Congress. Those in Oregon voluntarily put up more than 42,000 Robinson for Congress signs during the 2010 election. The back cover of this book quotes several such people – and one other.

By contrast, our opponent has spent most of his life as a career politician.

There is much worry in America today – worry of not finding a job, worry of losing a job, worry of not receiving Social Security or Medicare, worry of not receiving a good education, and worry about many other things.

I am worried, too. I represent productive Americans who are worried that the government policies that are inhibiting our work will continue and will increase until our work is largely stopped. Worried that our country will continue its descent toward poverty and tyranny, wherein those who need the products of our work are left destitute, and we ourselves lose our freedom to work.

While there are John Galts among us, the men and women of the mind are not following them. We will not withdraw, and we will not willingly be ruled by self-serving career politicians and their bureaucrat retainers.

In my case, I have set aside time from my work in order to serve my country. I hope that Oregon voters will understand – and that they will grant me the office to do so.

The Right Answers

When my daughter Arynne was growing up, she greatly admired the gospel music of George Beverly Shea. Arynne's mother had also loved Mr. Shea's music.

Arynne collected, as completely as possible, every performance that George Beverly Shea recorded, including 45s, 78s, and long playing records, tapes, and CDs.

Mr. Shea has received many awards. One unusual one is the *Guinness Book of World Record* for singing in person to more people than any other man in history. In his work with Billy Graham, he has sung in person to more than 200 million people. Even now, at the age of 103, Mr. Shea is still singing and lifting the spirits of many people.

Arynne digitized all of Mr. Shea's songs. She made a complete set on CDs, and our family attended a Billy Graham Crusade in St. Louis, in hopes that Arynne would have an opportunity to meet Mr. Shea and give the CDs to him. Ultimately, we were privileged to become friends with this wonderful man and his charming wife.

As a family project, we brought back into print a collection of 425 of Mr. Shea's performances on 27 CDs, which we distribute on the Internet. We play these beautiful gospel songs as we work in our laboratory.

Arynne worked as a volunteer for the Billy Graham organization before she graduated from Bethel College in chemistry and from Iowa State University with a doctorate in veterinary medicine. Attendance at the Crusades, however, gave all of us a greater familiarity with his ministry.

Mr. Graham was a friend, confidant, and spiritual inspiration to eleven American Presidents, including Presidents Truman, Eisenhower, Kennedy, Johnson, Nixon, Ford, Carter, Reagan, Bush, Clinton, and Bush. He

Arynne Robinson & George Beverly Shea

Arynne and Mr. Shea selected his favorite recordings for each of the 425 of his gospel songs that the Robinsons then republished.

brought many millions of people to the Christian faith. If any preacher ever had reason for egotism, he surely does. Yet, he is characterized by great humility.

There are two events that I recall most from his Crusades. The first is standing in a choir of 5,000 people singing *a cappella* the hymn *Just As I Am*. With 5,000 in the choir, one has the sensation that even he is on tune, too. This was a wonderful and moving experience.

The second was a part of Mr. Graham's message. In his sermon, Billy Graham posed a question to his audience. In the familiar style of a minister, this question set the stage for his Biblical answer, which would be expected to follow.

Instead, Billy Graham followed the question with the words: "I don't know."

The use of these words, even when one is a very great authority on a subject, is a mark of true wisdom. I do not pretend to know the answers to all of our nation's problems. My opponent, however, says that he does have the answers.

During his 13-term, 25-year career: Oregon District 4 has lost 90% of its timber industry, including 25,000 timber jobs and tens of thousands of other jobs; the federal debt has risen 700%; federal regulations have risen 50%; America's manufacturing jobs have fallen by 50%; medical costs have risen 100%; our energy industries have fallen far behind; and our nation's future has seriously clouded.

During his tenure, Congress spent $50 trillion, but had only $40 trillion in revenue, creating $100,000 in debt for every American family. Moreover, unfunded promises of Congress now total more than $500,000 per family.

Yet, Peter DeFazio says that he has the answers. If we re-elect him, he will continue his support of: federal EPA actions to increase taxes until fuel use falls by 80%[76] (in a bill DeFazio co-sponsored); impediments to oil drilling; Obamacare, which took $500 billion out of Medicare; more "stimulus" spending; "no" votes on improvements in education; higher taxes; increased regulations; and all sorts of over-spending that will further raise the national debt. And, he will continue to work to put more and more Oregon District 4 land and natural resources off limits to use by the public.

I may not have all the answers, but one thing is very clear. Congressman DeFazio's answers have definitely not worked for District 4, for Oregon, or for our nation.

By reading this book, you will know my thoughts about national issues. My work, if elected, will lead to a brighter future for us all.

2

WINNING

As a non-politician (well, perhaps an anti-politician), I'm running on two principal ideas.

1. The affairs of our Congress are not being conducted with ordinary common sense. This has gotten entirely out of hand and is getting us all into a lot of trouble.

2. The best way to correct this problem is to send new people to Congress, preferably ordinary citizen volunteers who will obey the rules of our Constitutional Republic and act with common sense.

We cannot always expect to have the best people represent us if they must all be volunteers. It's expensive to live, and most people need to earn their livings.

Our family would be willing to send me to Congress as an unpaid volunteer for a few years to help our nation, if

> **Americans are winning. People throughout our nation, Oregon, and Oregon District 4 have risen up by the tens of millions to insist that our government get back on track. They are fed up with their poor representation in Congress.**

that were necessary. The young people in our family would just work harder to make our way.

All across our nation, tens of millions of ordinary Americans like us are rising up in alarm over the craziness in Washington and volunteering to help in all sorts of ways. This is the reason that I am certain that our country, regardless of the darkness on our horizon now, will have a very bright future.

This is also the reason that the citizens of District 4 saw more than 42,000 "Art Robinson for Congress" signs all over their district in 2010. Every one of those signs was put up by a citizen volunteer, eager to end our district's contribution to the problems in Washington. This is the reason 6,000 people sent contributions of their own money to our campaign and 130,000 people voted for me, even though I was almost completely unknown to these voters before the campaign and had never been in politics.

I have no fear of my opponent and his political machine, but I sure would not want to go up against those 130,000 people, whose ranks are growing every day.

If elected, I will do exactly what these voters need by acting upon the principles summarized in this book. And I will make certain that they know exactly what I'm doing.

I am sure that, if the voters of District 4 know the policies that I represent and know the many ways those policies will be good for them personally, for Oregon, and for our nation, we will win the election.

We may, in fact, already be winning. The election in 2010 was close, and many more voters have become dissatisfied with their congressional representation since then. Perhaps writing this book is not necessary.

After all, most Americans have little or no interest in politics. They quite rightly want to go about their lives and exercise their freedom with as little interference from

Campaigning in 2010

government as possible. When they see that Congress is not doing its job, they have a common sense reaction:

"Throw the bums out, and get someone else."

As things are now, that sentence alone should win the election for us. Many voters may not be interested in reading a whole book about this.

This reminds me of an experience I had once in a courtroom in California. It is a good idea to stay out of courtrooms, except as a juror. When I was a young man, I was embroiled in several civil court cases – not by choice, but by circumstance. I won them all, but would have preferred not to participate.

In this case, my opponent was a lawyer and was represented by another, younger lawyer. I had learned from sworn testimony in another case that my lawyer opponent was a user of cocaine. So, I quite naturally started raising questions in court about the possible influence of cocaine on his behavior. Stung by this, he urged his lawyer to get the court to stop my asking these questions.

His lawyer therefore filed a motion, but made the mistake of swearing under penalty of perjury to an affidavit that I could prove was false. The result was a court hearing before a judge on my First Amendment right to ask the cocaine questions and on the lawyer's lawyer's guilt of perjury – an offense endangering his license to practice law.

First, the lawyer defending the lawyer defending the lawyer (you see, by then the opposing lawyer's lawyer needed a lawyer, too, so they were three deep) spoke – reading me out of the human race and urging the court to deny the perjury claim.

Next was my turn. I rose to speak, but after only a few words, the judge said, "Dr. Robinson, you are winning. It is always a good idea, when you are winning, not to say much, and you are winning." So, of course, I sat down.

Now, it was time to hear the First Amendment motion. This time the lawyer of the lawyer rose, and he too read me out of the human race and asked that I not be allowed to take evidence about the cocaine.

(This sort of situation poses serious rhetorical problems. It is a wondrous thing indeed to see how many false and pejorative statements an unprincipled but skilled lawyer who is not under oath can pack into a few paragraphs. An ordinary person could not answer them all in ten times the time allotted, but you surely want to try.)

So again, armed with the notes I had taken during his elocution, I rose to defend myself. And, once again after just a few words, the judge interrupted.

"Dr. Robinson," the judge said, "you are still winning. It is always a good idea, when you are winning, to not say much, and you are winning." So, again, I sat down. The hearings were over.

The court went on to other things, the courtroom being filled with attorneys on other business.

Later, the judge ruled. He ruled in my favor on my First Amendment right to ask about the cocaine. Therefore, my lawyer opponent gave up and settled the case in my favor.

The judge didn't rule on the perjury motion against the lawyer's lawyer. The evidence was overwhelming, so the ruling would have had to go against him. There was a rule, however, that I did not know. If I didn't make the charge in open court, the judge didn't have to rule. By getting me to sit down, he saved the lawyer's license.

Who will win this election? The answer is that almost any Oregonian with ordinary honesty, integrity, and common sense should be preferred by voters over the representation that we have now. The Congress is failing.

The winners of this election must be the people of our district, of Oregon, and of our nation. Since these same people are the voters, the future should be very bright.

This Book

I've been writing all my life, primarily scientific articles filled with the jargon and esoterica of science. I also write a newsletter read by scientists and laymen who are interested in science and human affairs.

Readers will recognize that the writer of this book is not a politician. No politician would risk telling this much of the truth. Yet, this is what our country needs. Citizen volunteers who have the experience to know the truth; the honesty to tell it; and the common sense to apply it to the problems in Washington.

It is very unlikely that a reader of this book will agree with everything I have written. This is why most candidates do not write books like this. They do not want to offend anyone or give their opponent ammunition.

I am not a politician. I believe that I have a responsibility to tell voters everything about my views that may be relevant to their votes. A citizen volunteer has no "political career" to protect. This makes him a far better choice.

Please consider the totality of my views and abilities when you consider whether or not you like me, trust me, and think my policies will be good for you.

Please give me the privilege to serve you in Congress.

3

AMERICA'S PROVEN FORMULA
FOR SUCCESS

Yes, this is a campaign book. But it is not like any campaign book you have ever seen. First of all, much of this book is about what I call **America's proven formula for success**. This formula has provided success for millions of individuals, their families, their churches, their businesses, their schools, and for the nation as a whole.

The America that we have partially lost in my lifetime can be restored. More than that, this nation can become far better than it was when I was growing up in the 1950s.

It can do this if voters decide to elect individuals

> American Liberty and Justice for all people has led to American Prosperity and Charity. These are the ingredients of American Exceptionalism.
>
> When Big Government improperly reduces individual liberty, our people and institutions – both public and private – suffer.
>
> We have allowed big government to intrude too far into the American formula for success. We must rein in that government.

at every level of political office who are committed to implementing the formula that made the United States of America the "shining city on a hill" that all the world admired – and this doesn't mean Capitol Hill!

America has stumbled, but she has not fallen. America is in trouble, but she can get out of trouble. Some Americans in recent years have been forgetting the American formula for success.

Older Americans remember a nation that was built by implementing the formula. But, over time, if people fail to remind themselves of the principles that made them successful and made the nation successful, their children and grandchildren may not know these principles. If we return to the formula that many of us have partially abandoned, we can recover and build something even better.

The World in 1800

In 1800, give or take 20 years, the Western world began the most momentous technological change it has ever seen. The economic world of 1800 in the United States, the year that Thomas Jefferson was elected President, was not fundamentally different from the economic world in 1750, 1700, 1600, or even 1500. It was an agrarian world. In the newly formed United States, anyone who went inland 100 miles or more entered a wilderness that had not changed much in 1000 years.

In terms of technology, the world of 1800 was primitive. Think about this. The following inventions had never been heard of: the automobile, airplane, farm tractor, commercial electricity, radio, television, antibiotics, microcomputer, and a vast number of other inventions.

If we could go back to 1800, we would probably not recognize some of the tools, and we would not know how to use many of them. We could easily recognize the social institutions and political institutions of America in 1800, but we would not be skilled in the use of 1800 tools.

What is my point? This: people do not change, but their tools change. The fundamental principles of ethics do not change, but the means of production change. What parents teach their children about right and wrong does not change, but the courses in the schools change.

If we spend time teaching our children the principles of ethics, plus skills that go back to ancient Egypt, such as reading, writing, and mathematics, our children will be better prepared for the world they will face than if we send them into schools that focus on teaching "real world" subjects, but not ethics and the "three Rs."

Why is this? Because students with a positive work ethic, a positive personal ethic, and a positive social ethic can gain the basics of any field that they have the ability and perseverance to master. They can do this rapidly if they have been taught the fundamentals and if they know right from wrong and are willing to use right principles.

The technical skills of classroom education can be picked up rapidly, but ethical skills – especially if not learned early in life – can take a long time to master.

Our family developed a home school curriculum. It is on 22 CD-ROM disks and covers kindergarten through the second year of college. It is designed so that the students can teach themselves. More than 60,000 children now use this curriculum.

My children have all been very academically successful using this curriculum. They developed a lot of it themselves. The secret of their success is only partly due to their innate intelligence. They are bright young people, but that isn't the main source of their success.

They learned how to work; they learned how to think; they learned how to discipline themselves; and they learned how to budget their time. These are the basics of academic success. Most parents know this. Parents have been teaching this to children for a very long time.

The Key Is Ethics

And ye shall know the truth, and the truth shall make you free.   John 8:30

The key to success is ethics. This applies to individuals, and it applies to every institution that people are associated with. The principles of ethics are easy to state but difficult to practice. One list is called the Ten Commandments.

> **"There is but one straight course, and that is to seek truth and pursue it steadily."**
> **George Washington**

There are other similar lists, and, because our civilization was constructed in terms of these ethical principles, our people grow up thinking in terms of these principles as if they were common knowledge. These principles were once a part of every American's concept of common sense.

Common sense still prevails in America. Some Americans have departed from what the founders of this country regarded as common sense, but it is still part of the inheritance of most Americans. It is a very important legacy from the past.

Americans generally are practical people. They are down to earth people. They are hands-on people. They are "show me" people. They share a common formula.

The Formula for Success

There are a lot of aspects of America that have led to its enormous success over the last 200 years. Key aspects can be boiled down into a formula. This formula is easy to remember. It is this:

Liberty plus Justice produces Prosperity and Charity. In the language of science:

$$L + J \to P + C$$

Charity here means far more than gifts and welfare. If one ignores this formula, his success will be limited. No matter what field you are in, if this is missing, you will find it much harder to be successful.

In this book, I'm going to cover several important areas of modern life. I'm going to focus a lot on economics, but we all know that economics is only part of life. A person who is economically poor can live a very good life. A person who is rich can fail. We teach our children this from a very early age.

We do not teach our children that getting rich is the essence of a good life. But Americans do respect wealth because they understand that prosperity often comes as a result of liberty, justice, and charity.

Charity

And now abideth faith, hope, charity, these three:
but the greatest of these is charity.
First Corinthians 13:13

What we ordinarily think of as charity is inescapably voluntary. It is counterproductive to take by force from the rich and give to the poor. This is not justice, and it is not charity. Charity is a willing act.

We know where government "charity" always leads: "Take from the rich and give to the poor" involves deducting 50% for handling. Then it goes up to 60%, and government takes more and more from the middle class as well – and even from the poor. Eventually the poor just serve as an excuse for those in power to give to themselves.

Moreover, the "charity" in *First Corinthians* does not concern just gifts to the poor. It is a state of mind and system of actions that lead to an admirable life.

Charity suffereth long, and is kind; charity
envieth not; charity vaunteth not itself, is not puffed
up,
Doth not behave itself unseemly, seeketh not her
own, is not easily provoked, thinketh no evil;
Rejoiceth not in iniquity, but rejoiceth in the
truth;
Beareth all things, believeth all things, hopeth all
things, endureth all things.
First Corinthians 13:4-7

I am especially fond of this section of First Corinthians because it describes the Robinson childrens' mother perfectly. Laurelee's every word and action was a human embodiment of this definition. Laurelee Robinson was a living example of this entire passage.

In the 23 years since she died, we have often been guided by this passage. The message of Laurelee's life is in the entire passage, not just in a part.

When Laurelee died on November 11, 1988, there was a short Biblical quotation on the chalk board that she used for the childrens' home school. The last thing Laurelee wrote for them on their chalkboard was:

> *Trust in the Lord with all thine heart; and lean not unto thine own understanding.*
> *Proverbs 3:5.*

Proverbs goes on to say:

> *In all thy ways acknowledge Him, and He shall direct thy paths.*
> *Proverbs 3:6*

As is implicit in the Bible and in similar wisdom found elsewhere, our actions are voluntary and flow from human liberty. Without liberty, we are not free to choose.

Even He who speaks to us through the Bible does not force us to live in a sensible way. He instead tells us how to live, gives us examples to illustrate His message, and leaves us free to choose our own path. If we choose an unwise path, we suffer the consequences.

God, Himself, does not force us to live as He knows is best, but politicians and their bureaucratic retainers in Washington try to force us to live as they think best. They seem to place themselves even higher than God.

Which kinds of ordinary charity are most valuable to people who are truly poor, disadvantaged, and in need of a helping hand? This depends upon the recipients.

Some people are afflicted in ways that will require help all of their lives. Others are able-bodied people who fall on hard times through no fault of their own. These will be restored to productivity and self-esteem if they receive a temporary hand up.

So long as a society has liberty and justice, it will have the prosperity to provide this kind of charity. Without liberty and justice, it will not have these resources.

Actually, all people need charity from all other people.

Read First Corinthians 13:4-7 carefully. It warns against envy, pride, unseemliness, selfishness, rashness, evil thoughts, iniquity, untruthfulness, closed mindedness, lack of hope, and lack of forbearance.

The underlying assumption of the biblical message is the right of each person to life, liberty, and the pursuit of happiness. Life is given by our Creator along with individual liberty and advice about the best ways to pursue happiness.

Charity is a high aspiration for any individual, any society, and any nation.

The System of Liberty

America today is threatened by a system of compulsory political "charity," which is undermining the system of liberty. What system of liberty? The system of liberty that was understood by the Founding Fathers of our country.

Economist Adam Smith called this the natural system of liberty. It is the liberty that the men who wrote the Constitution hoped would be preserved by the restraints they placed on the central government.

They planned that Americans would be free to follow their dreams under a legal order that protected life, protected liberty, protected property, protected freedom of speech, protected freedom of religion, and gave hope to millions of people.

The immigrants who came to the United States by the millions did not come here to get on the welfare rolls. There were no welfare rolls. They came here because they recognized that the United States offered a system of liberty, which did not exist in any other part of the world.

America had lots of land, lots of resources, lots of opportunity, but above all, there was a system of liberty and justice that encouraged people to become creative and hard working. It enabled them to gain access to capital (real savings and accumulated profits, not printed money), and this capital enabled them to build successful enterprises.

American productivity became the wonder of the world and was known as "American Exceptionalism." As the economist Julian Simon proved,[1] people are the ultimate resource. People always produce more than they consume if they are free to do so. Americans were free and they had, as they still do today, essentially unlimited natural resources, so they built the most prosperous and productive nation the world has ever known.

The nation they built was an inspiration to the whole world. Billions of people have worked to lift themselves from poverty and tyranny by following the example of the United States – until recently. What has happened?

Why has our great nation stumbled? Why is it losing its prosperity and charity? It is losing these things because an out-of-control government is taking away the people's liberty and their access to natural resources, and is beginning to withdraw their access to a system of justice.

> We are not born as slaves. Slavery, to a slave master or slavery to a government are the same. Both violate our fundamental right to liberty.

Over-taxation, over-regulation, over-indebtedness, and bureaucratic big government domination is taking away liberty and justice from the American people. These things are under control of the U.S. Congress. It is Congress that has authorized runaway big government, and only Congress can bring it back under control.

Congress has forgotten the formula that made America successful. Once again, the formula is this:

Liberty + Justice → Prosperity + Charity

Where people have liberty protected by justice, they become more prosperous and act with true charity.

When governments reduce people's liberty, they reduce productivity, which leads to reduced charity.

Politicians promise to pass laws that will protect the poor, but after the laws are passed, there are more poor people, more bureaucrats administering the programs, and less liberty. Because there is less liberty, there is soon less productivity, and when there is less productivity, there will soon be reduced charity and even more poor people.

Rival Formulas

There are two alternative formulas at war with the American formula of success. The first rival formula is this: **Governmental Confiscation of Property produces Charity**. This formula violates common sense. It assumes that the government will reliably provide charity with money taken from the people. This formula is wrong.

$$GCP \neq C.$$

There are also some misguided people who believe a second formula. They have been misled into believing that: **Property Confiscated by Government Creates Jobs, so Seizure then produces Prosperity.** This makes no sense either.

$$PCG \neq J \text{ and } S \neq P$$

When the taxman comes to take his pound of flesh, throughout the history of man, taxpayers have reacted negatively. If the taxman takes too much, they work less. They don't see any point in working in order to pay the taxman. *People do not want to work for the taxman.*

This formula says taxation creates capital. This violates common sense. Savings and profits are capital. Unearned capital is rarely used wisely by the taker, so it's partially lost, along with the jobs it would have made possible. Government confiscation doesn't produce prosperity.

$$GC \neq P.$$

This is common sense. Unfortunately, common sense has become increasingly scarce over the last 40 years in Congress. As common sense has become more scarce, formulas that don't work have become more popular.

What I am saying is that *politicians in the United States have steadily abandoned the formula that made this country the most free, most just, most prosperous, and most charitable country on earth.*

Liberty + Justice → Prosperity + Charity

This formula made America great, and this is what will reverse America's current decline from greatness.

We must vote to abandon rival formulas that have proven destructive, decade after decade, and which have led to the crises – more than one – that face us today.

There is a way out. It looks as though we have reached a dead end, but there is a detour sign. The detour sign will take us back on the highway of success that has made the United States the greatest country in history.

4

HONESTY IN POLITICS

In science, honesty is not just the "best policy," it is the only successful policy. A scientist cannot change the physical world, so, if he is not honest in his work, the truth eventually invalidates his work and wastes his time and that of his coworkers.

When my coworkers and I write a scientific research paper, we read it over dozens of times. It is not style or manner of presentation that causes us to do so. We are re-reading primarily to make certain that nowhere in the paper is there a single sentence or figure that gives the slightest false impression of our research results.

> **We should insist on integrity in the people that we elect to Congress. Our country is in too much trouble now to risk anything less.**
>
> **A citizen volunteer who has a distinguished career in science, a profession requiring complete and rigorous honesty, is especially well suited for Congress.**

We are also rereading to make sure that there are no "errors of omission," where we have failed to mention anything that we know of that could change the interpretation of our work.

Although I have been privileged to participate in quite a lot of excellent research work published in many major scientific journals (see pages 370-371), my reputation for integrity is my most important professional possession.

We have found politics to be a lot different regarding honesty, although my opponent appears to be somewhat extreme, even for politics.

What some would rather politely call "errors of omission" and "incorrect statements" are his stock in trade. I discuss many of these in the section on "Correction of DeFazio Misrepresentations" at the end of this book.

Typically an individual afflicted with these faults finds a sentence, phrase, or other item in the writing or speeches of his opponent which, if quoted by itself, twisted in meaning, and out of context, misrepresents the truth. Sometimes, he even invents a statement that was not said.

For example, my opponent's large billboard on Highway 5 in 2010 showed me saying, "Energy company CEO's shouldn't pay taxes." This statement is entirely fabricated.

In publishing this sentence that he falsely attributed to me on the billboard, he fabricated a statement that I did not make and would never make. This is an outright lie.

See the chapter *Corrections of DeFazio Misrepresentations* below for more on this.

By FEC rules, DeFazio's billboard was also supposed to contain a disclaimer saying it was put up by his campaign. It does. Can you read it? It is the almost invisible text at the bottom, just under his misleading web site address, where he publicizes his campaign falsehoods.

When a gaggle of these false statements are strung together it looks like the radio ad on the next page. (Accompanied by music similar to that of the Twilight Zone).

DeFazio supplemented this advertisement with an appearance on national network television where he falsely claimed that I live in a "survivalist compound" and that my campaign is supported by secret donors.

And, no doubt we will hear again in 2012 his claim that I am a tool of Wall Street. Nothing could be further from the truth.

There are special interests that will pay for ads like these to elect a politician whom they know is dishonest because they think he will use his dishonesty to get favors for them. Voters should not let this happen.

If we re-elect to Congress career politicians who lie like this, we deserve the mess in Washington.

After two and a half decades of active participation in the taxation, regulation, overspending, and deficits that have entrapped our nation in a seeming inescapable

Fraudulent DeFazio Billboard on Highway 5.
Art Robinson has never made this statement.

False DeFazio 2010 Campaign Radio Ad

"Picture a world where everything has gone terribly wrong.

"There's nuclear waste in our drinking water. Big oil and its executives run everything and the special interests pay no taxes at all, so we pay their share.

"Social security's privatized and millions of seniors will go broke if the stock market crashes again. Kids roam the streets because public schools have been abolished.

"It's a nightmare and its Art Robinson's vision for America . . . . Don't let this happen. If this horrifying world isn't where you want to live, vote against Art Robinson's wrong priorities and extreme values.

"I'm Peter DeFazio, candidate for Congress, and I approve this message. Paid for by DeFazio for Congress."

The claims in this ad are false. Do we want representatives in Congress who tell such falsehoods? What would he be willing to say about any other citizen who displeases him?

mire of unbalanced budgets and debt, Mr. DeFazio is now representing himself as opposed to these things that he supported. His earlier record is conveniently omitted.

I have done my best to truthfully represent my opponent's policies in this book. I even sent two draft copies to him, one to each of his two addresses, asking that he suggest revisions of any aspect that he thought in error. He made no suggestions. Later, I sent him two copies of the first edition of this book, asking that he suggest changes in any errors that he thinks it contains. Again, he made no suggestions. I did this a third time. There has, so far, been no response.

The 2012 campaign should consist of a public debate of the relative merits of my policies on the issues vs. my opponent's. That is why I have repeatedly challenged him to debate – in public and without the protection of moderators. He refuses to do so.

In an unguarded moment off microphone during the campaign, DeFazio was heard to say, "I can't afford to debate." With this sort of claims to defend, he sure can't!

While proof reading this book, Noah and I noticed that I had written a sentence favorable to the financial services industry. The next sentence, however, said that I oppose companies that make corrupt deals with Congress to get unfair advantages and public money. We decided to combine the two sentences into one because our opponent was sure to quote the first without the second.

We did, but I don't expect that to deter him.

The very extreme false and negative campaigning that voters have seen from my opponent in 2010 and now in 2012 was not so prominent in his previous campaigns. Then, he felt confident that he would win. Under pressure now from a real threat to his seat in Congress, he is frightened. A career politician who has done little else in life and has come to love greatly the perks of his career becomes very fearful if it looks like he may lose his position.

Too long tenure in Congress creates a conflict of interest for every member of Congress. With Congress as a career, each action he takes is weighed against his self-interests as compared with the interests of the nation. Many choose their interests first. My opponent is not unique. With billions of dollars to spend – dollars that can be spent to ensure their re-elections, temptation is just too great.

We need to return to the intent of our Founders – that Congress should be made up of citizen volunteers.

Will Rogers was a great and perceptive comedian, who turned many hilarious phrases on the antics of politicians. If we just had Will Rogers and Mark Twain with us today, the two could help us all to laugh these career politicians out of office – and our problems would be solved.

They lived, however, at a time when human nature and politics were clearly on view, but when our country was not faced with problems as dangerous as those of today.

Our problems today are not humorous. If they were, I would not be offering precious years of my life and work to help in solving them.

Today, it is more important than at any previous time in our nation's history that we confine public discourse and debate as closely as possible to the truth.

To that end, a citizen volunteer with a lifetime of experience in a profession requiring strict adherence to the truth can make a unique contribution.

5

NAMING THE BILLS

Congress's career politicians and their staffers (many congressional offices are mostly run by their chiefs of staff, while the congressmen enjoy the perks of office) have a wonderful time dreaming up names for the bills – an activity that is in the dubious tradition of American stings and hustles.

It works like this:

First, they give the bill or amendment a name that even old Scrooge couldn't vote against. Two recent examples:

Patient Protection and Affordable Care Act
Saving American Democracy Amendment

> The bills that Congress passes should be honestly named; should contain only provisions relevant to that name; and should be short and well-enough written that any citizen or member of Congress can conveniently read and understand them.
>
> When a congressman votes for a bill, he should be held responsible for all of its content and effects.

Second, they lard up the bill or amendment with all sorts of deals and provisions that please the Washington establishment and help assure their re-election support. These additions often bear no relation to the bill's name.

Third, the bill is cast into almost unreadable language and so many words and pages as to obscure its real purposes. The bill is passed, and often its provisions become known to the voters later, who predictably react in opposition to many of them.

Fourth, based on polls of voters, the congressman comes out against those provisions that the voters most oppose.

So, the congressman gets to first bask in the glory of the wonderful goals reflected in the bill's name. Then, he gets to appear rugged and tough as he later rails against offending provisions in the bill he voted to pass.

Voting on the bill is often rigged. Voting along party lines is expected of congressmen who want to have their party's support for re-election. So, the votes are carefully counted before the actual vote.

Then the party bosses award "passes" to those congressmen who face close election contests or whose district voters are especially likely to be offended by the bill. Passage is left to other congressmen.

This was the case in Oregon District 4 with the 906-page *Patient Protection and Affordable Care Act*, which is now better known as *Obamacare*. This was a close vote, and Oregon voters were split about evenly on the issue as reflected in the *name* of the bill and *claimed* benefits.

The long bill itself was not understandable without reading thousands of pages of other documents it referenced that were not submitted with the bill. It is unlikely that anyone who voted for this bill actually read the bill and its essential references.

Yet, my opponent cast one of the deciding votes for the bill. Many Oregon voters had already expressed anger about it, but it was apparently decided that there were other Democrats in the House who would be damaged more by a "yes" vote.

When voters learned the contents of the bill, very strong opposition to its many repressive provisions was widespread among voters in District 4.

So, DeFazio has now come out against numerous provisions in the bill he voted for. As they say in political sound bites, "He was for it before he was against it."

But, while he was for it, he voted it into law.

There is no danger the "Saving American Democracy Amendment" that DeFazio is co-sponsoring with his fellow socialist Bernie Sanders will ever be passed. Its provisions are so radical that he wouldn't even get the votes from most Democrats if they actually read the Amendment. [2,3]

In this case, he hopes that the name alone along with his false and misleading claim that the bill will rein in "corporate greed" and "election corruption" will garner votes.

I think that every bill passed in Congress should be printed on only a few pages and in clear enough language that any person with ordinary reading skills can understand it in less than an hour of study.

A Congressman should not vote for any bill unless he is willing to stand behind all of its provisions if it passes.

6

CAMPAIGN FINANCE

The House of Representatives shall be composed of Members chosen every second Year by the People of the several States, and the Electors in each State shall have the Qualifications requisite for Electors of the most numerous Branch of the State Legislature.

No Person shall be a Representative who shall not have attained to the Age of twenty five Years, and been seven Years a Citizen of the United States, and who shall not, when elected, be an Inhabitant of that State in which he shall be chosen.

Article 1, Section 2

It was understood from the beginning of our nation that elections with more than one candidate would

> **Congress has arranged the campaign finance laws to favor re-election of incumbents. Thus has arisen a class of long-term career politicians, who have replaced the citizen volunteers who filled the Congress during our nation's first hundred years.**
>
> **We should change these laws. Our country's interests must not fall victim to personal ambition.**

take place. It isn't possible to wax nostalgic for the past when discussing media fairness to candidates. As soon as George Washington retired, even in presidential elections, newspapers of that day published scurrilous and untruthful attacks on candidates they opposed.

Our campaign goal is to make sure that all of the voters in Oregon District 4 understand the ways in which my election will be beneficial for them, for Oregon, and for our nation.

Our opponent's goal, illustrated by his campaign in 2010, will be to keep the voters from hearing our message and to replace that message with a false one.

We must, of course, raise the money needed to deliver our message. The Founding Fathers are silent about this in the Constitution. But Congress has not been silent. Career politicians have voted themselves many tax financed and regulatory advantages that give them special advantages over challengers during elections.

As a consequence, even though Congress has a failed approval rating of only 10% with voters, most incumbents are re-elected. Some incumbent advantages include:

1. Large tax-financed subsidies for mail and other campaigning are given to incumbents. These are excused as resources for "communication" with their constituents.

District 4 voters frequently receive such fliers and phone calls from my opponent at taxpayer expense.

2. There are no enforced restrictions on the receipt of campaign funds from corporations and other special interests whom the congressmen have favored in their congressional actions.

3. Funding restrictions permit larger contributions from special interests than from private individuals.

4. Election rules require names, addresses, and, when available, occupations of all contributors of more than $200 be sent to the Federal Election Commission and publicly displayed. There is no privacy protection for these donors.

In the 2010 campaign, DeFazio actually demeaned and ridiculed specific individuals in public speeches who, he had learned from FEC reports, had contributed to our campaign. In 2012, he is at it again, with campaign literature that maligns individual supporters of our candidacy.

The Oregon 2010 Senate candidate, Jim Huffman, wrote an account in *The Wall Street Journal*[4] about his difficulty in raising campaign funds because potential supporters were afraid to offend the current Senator, possibly resulting in retribution. The Senator would see a record of their contribution.

5. FEC rules allow the filing of entirely bogus FEC complaints, without penalty for false and specious claims.

During 2010, the DeFazio machine filed several bogus FEC claims against our campaign that were demonstrably false, and then sought publicity for those claims before they were inevitably dismissed by the FEC. This cost our campaign tens of thousands of dollars in legal fees, with no method available to recover these costs after the claims proved fraudulent.

6. There are no practical restrictions on misuse of congressional power against challengers. The first letter I received from DeFazio in response to our debate challenge after winning the Republican nomination contained a veiled warning directed against my employer.[63]

Bogus DeFazio FEC claims were later filed against my employer, my family, and even against a retailer, whose only crime was that he sells our home school curriculum.

Funding Sources[5,6]

Career politician Peter DeFazio remains in office with campaign financing from special interests, mostly outside Oregon, that he does favors for in Washington.

Peter DeFazio - 2008
$729,421

Art Robinson - 2010
$1,314,672

Peter DeFazio - 2010
$1,315,473

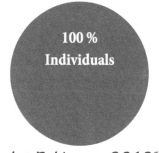

Art Robinson - 2012*
$221,496

Peter DeFazio - 2012*
$449,686

*The data is through December 31, 2011.[5,6] Reports are quarterly.

These FEC complaints included many false statements for which there is no FEC remedy.

7. Prejudicial congressional actions against those who dare to support those who run against incumbents are not regulated. Many national organizations have "incumbent policies" wherein they avoid association with challengers, specifically to insulate themselves against incumbent retribution.

So, what will the sources of funds be in the 2012 congressional campaign in District 4? Contributions in 2010 are the best indication.

DeFazio spent $1,484,241 in 2010.[5,6] Some of this money was raised in 2007-2008 but not spent because he had little competition then. In 2007-2008, he received $729,421,[5,6] 66% from special interests and only 34% from private individuals. In 2009-2010, he received $1,315,473,[5,6] 49% from special interests.[5,6]

His larger percentage from individuals in 2009-2010 was partly due to an emergency effort on his behalf late in the campaign by leftist organizations, including MoveOn.org, which has a very large individual donor base.

We expect DeFazio to raise and spend at least $2 million in 2011-2012. He is very worried about defeat.

Robinson spent $1.28 million in 2010.[5,6] In 2010 he received $1,314,672,[5,6] more than 99% from individuals.

Individuals can contribute a maximum of $5,000, providing $2,500 (this was $2,400 in 2010) is given before the primary election. There were two primary elections in 2010 because of the Independent Party primary (in which Robinson received 56% of the vote, and DeFazio received 39%), so an extra $2,400 was possible.

Special interests are allowed to give twice as much to a

candidate than are individuals, so DeFazio also had larger single contributions than did Robinson.

Moreover, DeFazio's lavish contributions from corporate special interests are understated. In a recent DeFazio FEC report of $10,400 in contributions (all reported received on a single day, May 2, 2012) from "individuals", $7,400 of DeFazio's "individual" contributions actually came from executives; $2,000 came from an executive's wife; and $1,000 from a "retired" executive.

These corporations receive special treatment from DeFazio at public expense. In two of these cases, high executives in the corporations were disguised in the FEC report as mere workers, when they are actually CEOs of the corporations. This sort of shenanigan is hidden corporatism or crony capitalism.

In 2010, about 20% of Robinson's support came from private individual maximum contributions of $2,400. More than 80% was from people who contributed $5, $25, $50, $100, or more (but not $2,400), many contributing more than once. There were about 6,000 such Robinson contributors.

Both candidates were also supported by "independent expenditures." These are groups that advertise for the candidate but are not permitted, under FEC rules, to have contact with the candidate or his campaign.

While DeFazio gets plenty of help from his own "independent expenditures," he became very upset when similar help was provided to Robinson, too.

Campaigns, by independent groups and by the candidates, are required to report their sources of funds to the FEC quarterly, with shorter intervals as the election nears. In late September 2010, TV ads from an independent source in favor of Robinson began to appear. The independent expenditure donors paying for this would not be revealed until the next reporting date of October 15.

Contributors to the DeFazio and Robinson campaigns would also not be reported until October 15. All contributions to the campaigns, independent or otherwise between July 1 and October 1, were, at that time, unknown to the public and the campaigns, except for their own.

With the date for reports a couple of weeks away and counting on fooling the public who did not know the procedures, DeFazio and Rachel Maddow attacked Robinson on national television with the false claim that Robinson had "secret" contributors, who might even be criminals.

Moreover, they claimed Robinson did not even to care to know who his advocates were. (I did not know, and could not until October 15.) They called Robinson and his supporters "money launderers."[42,43] This false claim could equally well have been made against DeFazio, since his campaign had not yet reported its fund sources either.

DeFazio launched this "exposé" on Maddow's MSNBC show with his ridiculous and false claim that Robinson lives in "a survivalist compound on Social Security," and the show went on down hill from there.

On October 15, the campaigns, including the independent expenditures, reported their donors, and the DeFazio-Maddow road show quietly faded away.

So it goes with campaign finance.

Political professionals, in all parties and with few exceptions, view elections almost entirely in monetary terms. Candidates are expected to raise lots of money.

It is expected that Congressmen, once elected, will grant "access" and favors to those who contribute. They reward their friends and punish their opponents.

I would never do this, nor would I use my congressional office to treat any citizen better or worse than any other, regardless of his contributions, politics, or opinions.

The over-dependence on campaign money needs to stop. Yet, we cannot cast a vote to stop it unless – you guessed it – we raise enough money to win the election. When television smear season begins, we must neutralize the smears, and television time is very expensive.

Perhaps this book will help. Those who read it are not going to be influenced by television propaganda.

When voters learn the many ways in which our representation of District 4 in Congress will be good for them, for Oregon, and for our nation, they will want to help us be elected. Many readers will be inclined to contribute to the Robinson campaign – and we very much hope that you will do so, too. You can contribute at www.ArtForCongress.com, or by mail at: Art Robinson for Congress, P.O. Box 1250, Cave Junction, OR 97523.

Money should not be a factor in selecting our Congress. An ability to raise money is not a skill required to do a good job in Washington.

Moreover, the monetary and regulatory rules should be level – favoring neither incumbents nor challengers.

In 2012, DeFazio is loudly complaining about Robinson's financial support (from 6,000 contributors). Challengers are supposed to lose from lack of funds.

Still, DeFazio has a lot more campaign funds than Robinson because he has spent 25 years pleasing corporate and other special interests. The financial playing field is not level, but it is far too level for DeFazio's comfort.

7

NUTRITIONAL THERAPY FOR CONGRESS

Many nutritional remedies have been proposed for the prevention and treatment of human diseases, especially for cancer. One of these involves a diet that consists entirely of raw fruits and vegetables. There are many anecdotal accounts of people who stopped or reversed the growth of malignancies by means of this diet.

Much more research needs to be done before the usefulness of this technique for reducing the growth rate of human cancer is accurately evaluated.

Anecdotal accounts are not considered very scientific. Individual observations upon one's self are subject to indi-

---

We need to put big government on a diet. And the money that we do give to it should go directly to fund obligatory programs – national defense, our seniors, our veterans, and other necessary activities.

Buying votes by shoveling our money to special interests and other forms of wastefulness should stop, even if it deprives our career politicians of the campaign cash for re-election.

vidual error and lack statistical validity.

One day long ago, two proponents of this diet, Arnold and Edie Mae Hunsberger visited me in my office at the Institute for Orthomolecular Medicine, which Linus Pauling and I founded in Menlo Park, California in 1973. (We later renamed it the Linus Pauling Institute of Science and Medicine.)

Mr. Hunsberger was an industrialist. He founded U.S. Elevator Corporation, then the third largest elevator company in the United States. Arn was like my father in that he was completely in love with his work and with his wife, Edie Mae. When he was president of U.S. Elevator, his colleagues continually found him inside elevators and covered with grease because he just loved to work on these machines. They tried futilely to convince him that, as president of a large corporation, he needed to be well-dressed and in his office.

Arn's "executive" behavior was much more common among American industrialists and entrepreneurs during the early development of our country. We would be better off if this were still the case today.

One of Arn Hunsberger's innovations was the glass elevator. He built the first one on a building in San Diego. Today, transparent elevators are widely used.

There came a day when Arn had to choose between his two loves – the elevators and Edie Mae – because Edie Mae became a victim of cancer.

Choosing Edie Mae, he quit his work and the two of them traveled around the world searching for a cure for her. Ultimately, the cancer regressed under the dietary regime of a lady in Boston, Ann Wigmore, then the foremost proponent of raw fruit and vegetable diets for cancer.

Nutrition and Cancer

Dick Willoughby and Ruth Reynolds showing one of their hairless mice to Martin Kamen, who was the discoverer of Carbon 14. Underfeeding the mice improved their health and reduced the growth rate of cancer by 10-fold. Underfeeding Congress's appetite for money would improve the health of our nation, too.

The Hunsbergers wanted this therapy to be more widely accepted and urged me to carry out experiments to test its validity in a scientific manner.

It happened that technician Dick Willougby and I had built a facility for studying the growth rate of cancer in hairless mice as a function of diet. With the help of another technician, Ruth Reynolds, Dick and I were carrying out experiments with this equipment.

So, I decided to test the Hunsbergers' hypothesis. We fed 50 mice on the Wigmore raw fruit and vegetable diet and measured the growth rate of the cancer squamous cell carcinoma. The results were spectacular. The growth of cancer was suppressed more by this than by anything else that had ever been tested in this experimental system.

So, I devoted much of our mouse facility for the next two years to studying this. We later expanded the work to the lab of my former graduate student and colleague Dr. Fred Westall who was then in charge of Jonas Salk's laboratory at the Salk Institute. We carried out 59 experiments with approximately 2,000 mice.

The result was that we could vary the growth rate of squamous cell carcinoma over a ***20-fold range*** by means of diet alone, suppressing the growth rate of cancer relative to control by a factor of ***10-fold***. See "Suppression of Squamous Cell Carcinoma in Hairless Mice by Dietary Variation" by Arthur B. Robinson, Arnold Hunsberger, and Fred C. Westall, *Mechanisms of Ageing and Development* **76** (1994) 201-214.

While there are many details, the results of this work are easy to summarize. The better the nutrition, the faster the cancer grew. For example, at the optimum percentage of protein, the cancer grew vigorously, but, at percentages of protein in the diet above or below the optimum percentage of protein, it grew more slowly.

Raw fruits and vegetables turned out to be simply a pleasant way to eat less. While vegetables, such as spinach, have a rich mix of nutrients, they are low in calories. Spinach has an excellent nutritional balance, but one would need to eat 20 pounds of spinach per day to satisfy a normal human caloric requirement.

The people restricting their diets to only raw fruits and vegetables were starving their cancerous tissues. They were also starving their healthy tissues, but cancers need more nutrients, and so are preferentially hurt.

Many people have reported starving their cancers into remission by means of raw fruit and vegetable diet restriction, but this has never become a medically approved procedure. There is ongoing research on special chemical agents that restrict nutrient delivery to individual tumors.

There is also a very large amount of research showing that essentially all animals, from fruit flies to rabbits, live longer and healthier lives if their diets are restricted below the amounts of nutrients that they would normally eat.

Our bodily tissues efficiently and effectively perform the functions required to keep us alive. Cancer tissues are different. They use more than their share of nutrients; grow wildly and uncontrollably; interfere with the work of our normal tissues; do not do their own work properly; and eventually wreak so much havoc in our bodies that our normal tissues are no longer able to do their work, which leads to death.

The cancerous tissues are more dependent upon large amounts of nutrients than normal tissues. So, when we put the mice on a restricted diet, the normal tissues gained an advantage over the cancerous tissues, and the cancerous tissues grew much more slowly.

Put Congress on a Diet

The analogy between cancer in these mice and the shenanigans of the U.S. Congress is eerily applicable.

Congress has been over-feeding the government. It has been over-feeding it so much – with every dollar that it can beg, borrow, or steal by means of taxes, loans, and money printing – that the malignancy of too much government has run amuck.

The normal economic and social institutions of our country are those that automatically arise in a nation of free people. Those institutions are trying to do their jobs today, but they are being interfered with by a giant malignancy that crowds them out, takes away their resources, and prevents them from functioning properly.

The tendrils of this malignancy are everywhere. At first glance it looks like our other institutions. It says that it is striving to do good things for us that our normal institutions do not do as well.

Yet, before it was here – before it infected our body politic – we were doing very well. Now, because we are surrounded everywhere by the tentacles of big government, the work we need to do is not getting done.

Like a cancer, big government needs a lot more resources to operate than private enterprise. It wastes great amounts of money to do the same jobs, and it does its work more poorly because, like a cancerous tissue, it is no longer under the control of normal common sense.

Congress is responsible for essentially all government activities because it has Constitutional control over their eating habits – it decides how much money they receive. While many missteps are blamed on the president, in fact the president cannot do anything without money given to him by Congress.

It was not necessary to target each malignant cell in the mice or the activities of each tendril of cancerous tissue to control the growth of systemic cancer. We just cut off the general supply of nutrients. The normal cells then gained an advantage, and the system tended toward good health.

Masquerading as Normal

The obvious political response to this analogy is that it seems to equate many essential activities to malignancies.

"Are you equating care for seniors, benefits for veterans, education, medical research, mail delivery, defense of our nation, and all sorts of other government activities with tendrils of malignant cancer?"

Of course not!

Many of these activities are necessary and valuable things that Congress and big government have taken over even though Americans were doing them better and more efficiently before government interfered.

Other things are proper functions of government.

Cancerous tissues are derived from normal tissues. They are tissues that have legitimate and essential roles in our bodies and our health. When they become cancerous, they stop doing their jobs properly and also interfere with other tissues that are still normal and functioning well.

This is a very important distinction, especially at election time.

A candidate who questions any aspect of big government is said to be against the underlying cited *reason* for *every* governmental program.

Proposing ideas to improve Social Security is said to be an effort to end current payments to seniors.

Proposing ways to better defend our country is said to be opposition to national defense.

Proposing to improve the schools is said to be opposition to children and their education.

Proposing a reduction in federal funding to sustainable levels is said to be opposition to all of the wonderful activities that government has now put its nose into.

This political posturing – in which our career politician in District 4 is expert – is like saying a proposal of a cure for brain cancer is really an effort to destroy the brain.

Voters should not be misled by this kind of propaganda. Just because an activity is meritorious does not mean that it should be done by government. Just because an activity is now being done by government does not mean that it should be this way in the future. And, just because an activity should be done by government does not mean that it cannot be done more effectively and efficiently.

Moreover, if the patient is so overfed that he is having difficulty even with ordinary common sense activities, it is a good idea to put him on a diet. His various organs and tissues will sort out how his nutrients are best allocated.

It is time to put Congress and the run-away big government that Congress has created on a diet. Congress has been "pigging out" at the expense of American economic freedom by running out-of-control programs enabled by over-taxation, over-regulation, over-borrowing, and money printing.

It is time to get rid of the long-term members of Congress responsible for this, especially those who have consistently promoted big government programs, like the 25-year career congressman from District 4.

A prominent advocate of better nutrition once published a book entitled *Let's Eat Right to Keep Fit*. Congress should see that our government does this, too.

Part II

PRINCIPLES OF LIBERTY

8

CONGRESS AND OREGON

This is a book about what is wrong with politics in America. It is also about what is wrong with politics in Oregon. Finally, it is about what is wrong with politics in the Fourth Congressional District in Oregon.

The problems can be summarized in two words: **Big Government.**

Let me offer an analogy. Assume that you are in a canoe, floating down a river. You have been told that, at some point, you must head for shore. Why? Because there is a huge waterfall ahead.

You enjoy the canoe ride. You have a great time. The day is warm. Everyone is laughing. You know about the falls, but you don't head for shore.

> The people in District 4 are in economic danger – both those in the rural areas and those in the relatively more prosperous urban areas – those in private businesses and those in public employment.
>
> There are two reasons for this. Congress has acted irresponsibly, and Oregon District 4 has had especially poor congressional representation.

Then you hear a faint sound, like a waterfall. It grows louder. You become concerned. You try to warn your fellow adventurers. But they are drinking and are feeling no pain. "We had better head for the shore," you say. No response.

The noise grows louder. "We really ought to head for the shore," you insist. They laugh at you. "Worrier!" Now you are getting scared. You have a life jacket. You can jump and swim for the shore. But you try to persuade your associates one more time.

That is why I am running for Congress. I can hear the sound of the falls. I hope you can, too. The rapids ahead are labeled "federal deficit" and "federal debt." And we all should be very worried about them.

The Federal Deficit

We all know about the annual federal deficit. It is more than $1 trillion and rising. Congress spends more than $1 trillion per year more than it collects in taxes. It is almost impossible to conceive of $1,000,000,000,000 (trillion). All those digits represent dollars that must be borrowed. These days, much of America's public debt is owed to foreigners. A lot is owned by China. What happens if the Chinese stop buying U.S. debt? What happens to interest rates when the U.S. government can't borrow more money?

The government can also borrow from the Federal Reserve, our nation's central bank. Where does the Fed get the money? It is printed – created out of thin air.

The Fed adds digits to a computer entry and uses the computer entry to loan money to the government. The problem comes when this money gets into the economy. Prices eventually increase – by a lot! When the Federal Reserve prints money, there are ultimately unpleasant results.

Yet, Congress keeps running deficits of more than $1 trillion per year. The official debt is now over $15 trillion. But the actual debt, if we factor in all of the federal government's promises and obligations, is at least $65 trillion, and some economists estimate it at over $100 trillion. None of this has been funded. It is all secured by the property and future labor of the American people.

The lower estimate of $65 trillion is about $650,000 for each American family. How long is your family going to have to work, save, and do without to accumulate $650,000 to pay off its share of this debt?

Congressmen tell us that they are working on this problem. They tell us that they are working to reduce the deficit by 100 billion dollars per year. Their cuts, if they occur, will not even stop the annual rise in the deficit, much less lower it.

Congressmen also tell us that under no circumstances will they ever vote to reduce payments to seniors from Social Security and Medicare. They won't, but they will make those payments with dollars that buy a lot less. They themselves will retire on very generous congressional pensions, and live very well.

Why doesn't Congress balance its budget? You have to balance your budget. I have to balance my budget. Why doesn't Congress do so? I have an answer.

Congress's Credit Card

Imagine 535 people. You hand a credit card to each of them. You let them spend all they want. And the constituents of all the members of Congress will have to pay the bill, no matter how much money each one spends. How much incentive is there to save money by spending as little as possible? If you say the answer is none, go to the head of the class.

The estimated budget for the current fiscal year is $3.6 trillion.[69] Therefore, the average expenditure per member of Congress is about $7 billion per year.

If you were to hand a credit card to these 535 people, I am sure that you would put a spending limit on the card. That is what the debt ceiling is supposed to do. The trouble is, Congress controls the debt ceiling. Congress will not accept any limit on its debt. Every attempt to limit debt has failed in Congress. **My opponent has voted many times to raise the debt ceiling.**[7]

Congress intends to keep spending until it cannot extract enough money from taxpayers, or borrow enough money from China, or get enough printed money from the Federal Reserve.

Congress not only does not pay off the principal, it keeps borrowing more to pay the interest. We all know what's going to happen – the same thing that would happen to a private credit card holder.

Will the professional politicians in Congress pay for their promises? No, they won't. Eventually their credit card will fail. Will they cut spending that affects them personally, such as Congressional pensions? You can be sure that *this* will not happen soon. Congressmen know that they have already spent the trust funds for Social Security. They are not going to depend on it.

There is probably going to be a huge governmental financial failure at some point, and anyone who has extended credit to the United States government will find that the government IOUs are worthless. This means everyone who has paid his Social Security taxes and his Medicare taxes and expects to be paid back in his old age will be disappointed. This is going to happen unless we get rid of the career politicians in Washington who have created and are continuing this problem.

Oregon is at a Turning Point

Oregon's economic problem is easy to state: *lots of resources, lots of poverty – especially in the southern part of District 4.* About 25% of the people in Josephine County receive Food Stamps.

Oregon Congressional District 4 comprises 17,181 square miles and seven counties, including Benton, Coos, Curry, Douglas, Josephine, Lane, and Linn, with parts of Benton and Josephine excluded.

District 4 is larger in area than the nation of Switzerland and has vastly greater natural resources than Switzerland. Yet District 4 households earn less than half as much as households in Switzerland.

Why are the households of District 4 so poor by comparison? Answer: The Swiss are far more free of government meddling, so they can produce more per person.

For example, business taxes in Switzerland average about 14%. Most of these taxes are levied by local government. Oregon corporations labor under a tax burden of 41%, of which 7% is state and 34% is federal for companies earning about $500,000 – and ranging upward to 47% for larger enterprises.

Corporate taxes are, of course, taxes on the people – the workers, stock holders, and customers of the corporations.

Capital (profits and savings) that is taxed away from businesses cannot be used to provide jobs or to provide higher wages to those who are already employed.

District 4 includes about 300,000 households, with a median income in 2010 of about $42,000.[8] The Oregon median is about $49,000. Within the District there is a wide range of median household incomes. By county they are[8]: Curry $37,000, Coos $37,000, Josephine $38,000, Douglas $40,000, Lane $43,000, Linn $46,000 and Benton $48,000.

So, in Switzerland where corporations have such low taxes, what is the fate of the ordinary person? The median household income in Switzerland is about $120,000.

One big reason for its especially low household income is that District 4 has very poor political representation in the U.S. Congress.

In Benton County, hundreds of millions of dollars flow into Oregon State University each year from political sources. So, it has been more difficult to convince voters in Benton County that there is danger ahead. Yet, they are in the most danger.

I think the political situation in Benton County is going to change. I think the voters there are ready for a change. Why? I'll tell you:

Because the economy keeps getting worse. Even many voters whose wealth depends on government are now in danger of losing their entire incomes.

Congress, including our own career politician, just became so greedy that they are killing the golden goose of freedom. If economic liberty is not restored, rural Oregon citizens will continue to have hard times, but many will find ways to get by. This is easier in rural areas. The urban citizens who depend, directly or indirectly on Washington money, however, are in danger of losing everything.

The sugar daddy in Washington is now essentially broke. Daddy is hanging on with loans, deals, and various short term fixes, but he is almost out of options.

It is still not too late to save both those who do and do not depend on Washington, but this will not be done by the same congressmen who created this problem. If it is done at all, it will require new congressmen who work to restore the liberty that America has lost.

Voters with low incomes (or, without jobs, no incomes) are ready for a change in congressional representation. *Now voters who still have jobs and good incomes are figuring out that they, too, are going to be losers if Washington's economic policies are not reversed.* We should win in 2012. It will be the year of recognition that things are getting worse for urban residents, too, and not just for people in the rural areas of Oregon.

This situation today is very different from 2010. Political and financial trends are rapidly accelerating. Oregonians will, if these trends are not reversed, suffer sharply lower real incomes, especially those in the more affluent areas. Even the level of prosperity that we have today, may well become a wistfully remembered rarity in the near future.

Common Sense

It isn't necessary for everyone to be alike in order to work together with common sense.

We raise sheep on our farm. If a ewe is unable to raise her lamb, we raise the lamb. On one occasion, when Arynne was raising a lamb, a duck and a goose the children had raised from chicks were also living in the yard.

The lamb, goose, and duck grew up together in the yard and the fields near our house. They became inseparable. Regardless of their very different personalities, they were the best of friends. One never saw the ewe and the goose alone. They were always together. Sometimes the duck would briefly be seen alone because her legs were shorter and she was a little absent minded, so she was occasionally temporarily left behind.

When a person walked near to the three, the goose made a great show of protecting them, arching and hissing, and, when they appeared to be safe, preening and squawking in braggadocio for her defensive triumph.

When the lamb grew into a ewe and had lambs of her own, the goose and duck were a little confused. At first there was suspicion. The goose tried to protect the ewe

Three Friends

Checking on the Lambs

from her lambs. When the ewe was sheared, there were also some tense moments. She looked a lot different. Who was this interloper, and where was their friend? Nevertheless, the friendship endured. They were devoted to one another.

Consider the many differences between these three. In goals and life styles, sheep, geese, and ducks are a lot more different than people. Yet, they solved their mutually different problems with equanimity and good sense. In the years they lived together, I never witnessed an argument.

Ultimately, the friendship ended because they under-estimated their preparations for a common defense. The goose's efforts were sufficient with respect to the Robin-sons and their visitors (who actually posed no threat at all), but they forgot that their safety also depended upon an Akbash sheep guard dog, who lived near the house, too.

One winter, the three increased their daily circuit to include a field too far from the house for the dog to provide protection, and something ate the goose and the duck. The predator was probably a coyote, bobcat, or cougar, since all three come into our fields.

The defensive advantages of one's homeland compared with adventures abroad are too easily forgotten.

Without her friends, the ewe just sat down in the yard and mourned. She no longer even walked around, and she gained lots of weight. She did continue her friendships with the FedEx lady and UPS man who gave her treats, but, distraught, she lived only a few months longer.

If these three could live together with peace and common sense with respect to their various interests, one would think that congressmen could, too. Unfortunately, it is not this way. Those we have today are more interested in careers, perks, and winning elections.

They are unwilling to consider their own careers as less important than the interests of our nation. This is the reason that the Congress should be filled by citizen volunteers with common sense, instead of career politicians. Is it too much to expect members of Congress to have at least as much common sense as sheep, geese, and ducks?

Our current batch of politicians also have too little real concern for the predators in the world – except when posturing at election time. A strong military defense is essential, but it is also a good idea not to over-reach into places that are not our concern.

Had the ewe, goose, and duck discussed their trips to the upper field and one of them suggested that perhaps they were straying too far from home, I doubt that the others would have accused the third of unpatriotic behavior.

9

LIBERTY AND RESPONSIBILITY

We the People of the United States, in Order to form a more perfect Union, establish Justice, insure domestic Tranquility, provide for the common defence, promote the general Welfare, and secure the Blessings of Liberty to ourselves and our Posterity, do ordain and establish this Constitution for the United States of America.   Preamble

Liberty and responsibility are always linked. *Liberty enables individuals to become more responsible. If you do not have liberty, you cannot have responsibility.*

> **Our obligations as free citizens are to do all that we have agreed to do and to not encroach on other people or their property.**
>
> **We are not intended to become involuntary servants. Yet, Congress has borrowed and obligated more than $600,000 per American household and used each one of us as the collateral for these loans.**
>
> **This is an entirely unacceptable encroachment upon our Liberty. The congressmen who have done this should be removed from office.**

When an individual is held legally liable for the outcome of his actions, he must be given freedom to make the decisions about what he ought to do. If someone is holding him liable, it would be unjust if the person imposing the sanctions did not grant him liberty of action.

At the same time, anyone who attempts to escape responsibility for his actions in a free society has a moral problem. He is trying to say that he is not responsible for his actions. He prefers not to be held accountable for what he does, despite the fact that he has liberty of action to do as he pleases.

> **"This will be the best security for maintaining our liberties. A nation of well-informed men who have been taught to know and prize the rights which God has given them cannot be enslaved. It is in the religion of ignorance that tyranny begins."**
> *Benjamin Franklin*

These days, he could probably become a multimillionaire in one of the large New York City banks. He would not be held responsible by the government. (Congress has actually encouraged irresponsible bank actions, for self-serving political gain.) American taxpayers would be held responsible. In 2009, the largest banks in the United States made handsome profits and handed out huge bonuses to senior executives.

They were able to do this only because Congress authorized the bailout of these banks. The American public was held responsible for the banks' financial obligations. Congress used public money to save the careers and fortunes of irresponsible bankers, with whom Congress had made deals.

The Federal Reserve even bailed out a lot of European banks. Yet, the Federal Reserve is a creation of Congress and is entirely under its jurisdiction.

When President Obama took office another big bailout was passed. My opponent voted for the Obama bailout when it was first proposed as an $825 billion bailout.[9] He then voted against the final bill[10] after it was reduced to $789 billion. He stated that he opposed the later version because it contained too many tax cuts and not enough spending on infrastructure companies (many of which give him campaign contributions).[11]

He wrote on his official web page, "I am pushing for an economic stimulus package . . ." and went on to advocate "infrastructure" spending. He has supported many other bailouts including the $192 Billion additional stimulus, the $15 Billion GM and Chrysler bailout, and the $60 Billion "Cash for Clunkers."

Involuntary Servitude

Americans oppose slavery because it is morally wrong. So, they should defend liberty because it is morally right.

What we find, however, is that people have been elected to Congress who are making slaves of the American people. The burden of public debt placed on us by Congress is so great that only the economic enslavement of the American people is likely to repay it.

When the United States Congress runs up an on-budget debt of $15 trillion, plus an off-budget debt of more than $50 trillion, it has placed Americans into involuntary servitude. The Congress uses as collateral its ability to take our earnings to pay the obligations of the loans.

The American people are the only collateral valuable enough to pledge for more than $1 trillion per year in additional loans. Lenders lend, and lend only because they believe that the Congress is going to be in a position to extract enough wealth from Americans to make the loan payments.

My opponent has voted hundreds of times for congressional expenditures and debt limit increases that raised the national debt.[7,12]

When he voted in this way, the people of Oregon and people throughout the U.S. were used as collateral for the obligation. Our congressman has apparently had few qualms about doing this to us.

Even recently, in the depths of the worst economic times since the Great Depression, my opponent has been calling for more "infrastructure" spending and higher taxes. (See references[5,6] for a link to a list of the infrastructure corporations and unions that have contributed to his 2010 and 2012 campaigns.)

Yet, the government already has more financial obligations than it can meet. If it collects more taxes as he also advocates,[12] that money should go to pay for Social Security, Medicare, and other obligations and to pay off government debt. The even greater government spending that DeFazio now calls for will further increase the debt and further endanger Social Security and Medicare.

You may not think of yourself as an involuntary servant, but that is what you are. The debt grows larger and you are on the hook to make the payments. So are your children and their children.

Congress has made involuntary servants out of people not yet born. Talk about taxation without representation!

Taxation without representation was one of the main complaints that the American colonists had against Great Britain. They would be astounded today to find taxation of yet-to-be-born children in their own country.

If you think you're a free person, think again. You are obligated to work for the government to pay off the government's liabilities.

> *The rich ruleth over the poor, and the borrower is servant to the lender.*
>
> *Proverbs 22:7*

Officially, the borrower is the United States government. Legally, you are the borrower's collateral. The government is able to go into debt only because lenders are promised by Congress that you really are the collateral for the government's debt.

Two Responsibilities

"1. Do all that you have agreed to do, and
"2. Do not encroach on other persons or their property"

Richard Maybury

These two principles are the basis of common law for a very good reason – they are common sense. These are responsibilities that go along with liberty. Liberty without responsibility makes no sense.

A fault in some men is that they seek power over other men. These men seek to take away liberty and enslave other men for their own purposes.

The U.S. Constitution was written to assure, as much as possible, that a government would exist in the United States that protected our personal liberty.

Men are imperfect, and so are institutions. The authors of the Constitution understood that their Constitution would not be perfect, nor would we. They relied upon the inherent common sense of the people to make up for imperfections – and, for 200 years, events generally justified their confidence.

Always, however, there are challenges to liberty from outside our country and from within. We have successfully defended our country from foreign threats, but, especially over the past 40 years, we have been less successful in overcoming internal challenges.

We were bequeathed a vast continent – rich with natural resources and overseen by a constrained government that was designed to protect our liberty. The result was the most astonishing material, intellectual, and moral advance in the history of mankind.

In America, the natural resources of the earth were combined with the ultimate resource: free and responsible people. People were drawn here by American liberty. They flooded into the United States from all over the earth. The great result of this combination has been called "American Exceptionalism."

This "exceptionalism" is not in our genes or in our viscera. This exceptionalism will arise wherever men – of any race, color, or origin – have liberty and the freedom to use and enhance the natural resources of the earth.

Taxation, Regulation, and Debt

Departing from our Constitution, politicians have built a gigantic governmental organization in Washington that seeks to closely regulate every aspect of our lives, including our doctors, our educations, our use of natural resources, our conditions of work, our commerce, our money, our communications, our farms, our personal associations and speech, our personal incomes when we are young and when we are old, and essentially every aspect of our lives.

Congress has levied taxes – including federal, state, and local taxes and the hidden tax of money printing – that consume about half of everything we earn in order to enhance their own power. Not satisfied with half of everything we earn, these people have also borrowed vast sums of money– pledging the future labor of us, our children, and our grandchildren.

The American people are the collateral for these loans. We have become involuntary servants in our own land. We have allowed ourselves to be enslaved by *taxation, regulation, debt, and litigation* (misuse of the legal system to enforce imposition of governmental power).

We have succumbed to this loss of liberty because of our own success – the exceptional success of the many generations of Americans who have lived in freedom.

Each new incremental tax, each new incremental regulation, each new governmental agency has been justified as filling some special need – and accepted because we felt rich and secure enough to permit it.

Now, however, the intrusions on our freedom have grown unsustainable. Now, we are learning that our prosperity and wonderful way of life depended upon American exceptionalism, while American exceptionalism depended upon American liberty. As we have given up our freedom, we have relearned the economic truth that free people are the ultimate resource.

We must remove the impediments to our liberty that have caused our plight – by removing from office the politicians in Congress who have overseen our enslavement. This done, the return of liberty and access to our natural resources will automatically resolve our national economic difficulties.

People are imperfect. Examples of misbehavior can always be found. Nevertheless, our civilization cannot survive if the principles upon which it is based do not survive.

Liberty is morally right, and slavery is morally wrong. This is the basis of American civilization and American exceptionalism. We must not abandon this principle.

10

THE STATES AND THE PEOPLE

The powers not delegated to the United States by the Constitution, nor prohibited by it to the States, are reserved to the States respectively, or to the people.
Amendment 10

This amendment appears in what we know as the Bill of Rights. The Bill of Rights lists restraints on the federal government. The Founding Fathers who wrote the Constitution and their colleagues agreed to the acceptance of the Bill of Rights – the first 10 Amendments to the Constitution – as an essential part of the Constitution.

All powers that are not specifically given to the federal government in the Constitution are reserved to the states and the people.

Congress has ignored the 10th Amendment. Through laws and agencies it empowers, Congress has improperly taken control of numerous activities.

Congressional controls have entangled us in seemingly endless regulations and diminished our liberty and prosperity. These encroachments upon our constitutional guarantees of freedom must end.

Nevertheless, our congressional representatives – all of whom swear an oath to uphold the Constitution – flagrantly disregard the 10th Amendment. They do this largely by using public funds to pay for government agencies that constantly violate this Amendment and by the issuance of "mandates" that dictate "required" state and local actions.

What excuse do congressmen give for violating the 10th Amendment? Mostly, they just ignore it, without giving any excuse at all. If pressed, some point to the Constitution.

> *"We the people of the United States, in Order to form a more perfect Union, establish Justice, insure domestic Tranquility, provide for the common defense, promote the general Welfare, and secure the Blessings of Liberty to ourselves and our Posterity, do ordain and establish this Constitution for the United States of America."*　　Preamble

> *The Congress shall have Power To lay and collect Taxes, Duties, Imposts and Excises, to pay the Debts and provide for the common Defence and general Welfare of the United States; but all Duties, Imposts and Excises shall be uniform throughout the United States . . .*　　Article 1, Section 8

Citing the phrase "promote (or provide for) the general Welfare," they claim that this permits Congress to do anything it decides will be good for general welfare – anything at all! This is bogus.

By their reading, Constitutional powers could have

consisted of just one sentence. "The government will promote the general welfare." "Hey, guys, do your best."

The Constitution gives, as one of its *goals*, the promotion of the general welfare, and then goes on to establish – by means of the body of the Constitution and Bill of Rights – the rules of government that will be followed in order to do that. The 10th Amendment is one of those rules.

We are beginning to see a state-level movement to insist that Congress honor and adhere to the 10th Amendment. This movement, being inherently constitutional, will increase in coming years. We are going to see a restoration of the constitutional limits that are placed on the power of the government in Washington. I am in favor of such restrictions, because they are essential to liberty, and because they are a part of the Constitution.

To vote in Congress as if these limitations did not exist is a violation of constitutional principle. It is a violation of the member of Congress's oath of office. It is time for states to reassert their authority, as assured by the 10th Amendment.

The Environmental Protection Agency

Let me give you an example of a fundamental violation of the 10th Amendment. There is no constitutional authority for the federal government to regulate the environment inside state borders.

From the very early years of the Republic, it was recognized that the federal government had legitimate jurisdiction to regulate disputes between states, such as disagreements regarding rivers that flow between the states. This is a matter of federal jurisdiction, because the federal government has jurisdiction when the area of dispute has borders on both sides of state boundaries.

But attempts by the federal government to regulate the environment inside state borders are illegitimate. Regulation of the environment is clearly a power *"reserved to the states respectively, or to the people."* Yet, the congressionally authorized and funded Environmental Protection Agency has produced a vast number of unconstitutional environmental regulations that are enforced by federal power.

Recently, the EPA announced regulations on energy producers that is expected to result in closure of 20% of America's coal-fired electricity-generating plants by 2016. This loss of 10% of our country's electricity production will further drive up the cost of electricity and cause many of our remaining energy-intensive industries to move abroad – taking American jobs with them. A multitude of EPA and other agency regulations have hamstrung our energy industries.

The state and people of Oregon should regulate their own environment, as the 10th Amendment clearly provides. The people of Oregon will not permit pollution of their rivers, destruction of their forests, and other devastation of their environment. But, they would also allow the common sense use of their natural resources.

Oregon is a very beautiful state. The environment in Oregon that overreaching Washington congressional bureaucrats at the EPA claim to want to protect from Oregonians is worth protecting because past generations of Oregonians have taken good care of it.

Once career politicians get to Washington, they tend to forget the rules. My opponent, for example, is not raising so much as a whimper of objection to the so-called

"Siskiyou Monument" project in District 4. This project is setting up a federal land grab of hundreds of thousands of acres, including lots of private property.

And my opponent is actually promoting "expansion of the Rogue Wilderness," which will take tens of thousands of more acres of land out of use. The federal government "owns" 70% of Josephine County. Similar congressional land grabs are under way in other District 4 counties and throughout our nation.

Moreover, by agreement with the federal government, the counties in District 4 are supposed to receive timber revenues from hundreds of thousands of acres of federal forest land in those counties (under the 1937 O&C agreement) for use in sustaining local government and local employment. (O&C stands for Oregon and California Railroad Company, which once held this land.)

The O&C agreement provides a share of timber revenues on designated federally-controlled land to Oregon counties, in lieu of property taxes. This is especially important in counties where the federal government controls a very large percentage of the property that would otherwise be subject to property taxes.

Yet, Congress has completely violated the O&C agreement, and our career congressman, in the more than 20 years of this violation, has done nothing effective to reverse it. Instead, he has promoted welfare payments to the county governments. Welfare enslaves the counties to the welfare source. It does not solve the problem. It is also no substitute for a vibrant timber economy.

DeFazio apparently does these things to appease his supporters in the extreme environmentalist movement, a movement that is largely empowered by violations of the

10th Amendment. His votes have earned him a greater than 90% approval rating[13,14,15] from these "environmentalists." Recently, he has been promoting a plan to take away half of the O&C land (permanently), but permit limited logging of the rest – if the courts allow it. It is election time, and he is worried about his perch in Washington. Where has he been for the last two decades, while this problem worsened and our timber industry died?

While he watched, 90% of District 4's timber industry was destroyed, 25,000 timber jobs were lost, and (including service jobs dependent on timber jobs) more than 25% of the economy of the district was ruined.

He did not force the federal government to honor the O&C contracts that it broke. Instead, by helping arrange welfare payments to the counties, he increased his own chances of re-election. He was needed, you see, to keep the welfare coming. This is a textbook example of a career politician living off a problem rather than solving it.

Forest Fires in Southern Oregon

In the southern counties of Oregon, the logging industry has been largely destroyed by the Departments of the Interior and Agriculture. By violating the 10th Amendment and the O&C agreements and by issuing numerous onerous regulations, these agencies – funded and controlled by Congress – have cost tens of thousands of Oregonians their jobs and their homes.

Oregon's natural beauty has been preserved and greatly enhanced by the people who have lived here during the past two centuries. Federal regulation of Oregon's environment and resources is relatively new. Why is it needed now?

In 2002, one of the hundreds of small fires that occur naturally (mostly set by natural causes, such as lightning) in Oregon each summer burned out of control in Oregon District 4. Ultimately the "Biscuit Fire" consumed 500,000 acres of forests, and cost more than $100 million to suppress. It was the most devastating fire in Oregon history.

Why was the Biscuit Fire allowed to burn out of control? It began at three locations in "wilderness areas" where federal agencies would not allow the fire to be extinguished. When Oregon firefighters were finally permitted to fight this fire, it was too late. The "preserved" areas and hundreds of square miles of other forests were ruined. Now, my opponent wants the federal government to add large new swaths of land as "wilderness" areas.

Another example of the utter incompetence of federal land management[64] happened in 1988, in Yellowstone Park, where almost 800,000 acres were burned as a result of specific federal policies not to allow firefighters to put out fires. The policy was reversed after the fire spread, but by then it was too late.

But the Biscuit Fire story is even more tragic. After the fire, federal agencies – with Congress looking on without apparent interest – and federal courts forbade the logging of the burned trees, which could have been milled into hundreds of millions of dollars worth of valuable lumber. *The timber was left to rot, decay, and provide fuel for future fires, and the forests were not restored.* Logging the dead trees would have paid for replanting, enriched forest health, and thousands of jobs for Oregonians.

This senseless waste and environmental devastation would not have occurred if the "State(s) and the people" had been in control of this resource.

Local Control and Liberty

The 10th Amendment was put into the Constitution to protect American liberty. The originators of the Constitution knew that central government would endanger personal liberty, so they sharply limited its powers.

The 10th Amendment protects and underpins the fact that, by law, we live in a "Republic" – a fact that is memorialized in the Pledge of Allegiance. With 50 separate states under 50 separate groups of citizen legislators, it is far less likely that government will go awry.

Interstate competition keeps states from going too far astray from common sense. By example and by citizen preference for states with greater wisdom, those states that have erred will find their way.

When, however, the entire country is under overbearing central control from Washington, this competitive correction mechanism cannot work. Mistakes become entrenched and damage everyone, with little recourse.

If the 10th Amendment were properly enforced and the dead hand of federal regulatory agencies lifted from the backs of American workers, businesses, and industries, the American economy would take off like a rocket. There would be no shortage of jobs. There would be a shortage of workers at low wages. Wages would rise.

Obeying the 10th Amendment and relieving Americans of these unconstitutional regulatory burdens would repeal much of the "regulatory tax." This "tax cut" would not cost the taxpayers a dime. It would save hundreds of billions of dollars in taxes and greatly help to balance the federal budget. The "States respectively, or . . the people" would perform the "agency" functions as the Constitution intends.

11

FREEDOM OF EXPRESSION

Congress shall make no law respecting an establishment of religion, or prohibiting the free exercise thereof; or abridging the freedom of speech, or of the press; or the right of the people peaceably to assemble, and to petition the government for a redress of grievances.   Amendment 1

Religion

The words could not be more clear. "Congress shall make no law respecting an establishment of religion." So, as a congressman, I will never vote for a law or appropriation of funds to do so.

> American freedom of religion, speech, press, assembly, and petition must be carefully protected.
>
> Freedom of religion and freedom of communication on the internet are today challenged by people with various motives. Some politicians in Congress are pandering to these people.
>
> We must be careful that all of our freedoms protected by the 1st Amendment are not abridged.

Religion is fundamental to human existence. Everyone has a religion – even atheists. Most of the people who founded America were Christians. Some were deists, and there were some from other religions. Those here before the Europeans had many different faiths.

Most tyrannies in history have had a religious component. Some were theocracies – completely controlled by religious authorities; some were ruled by dictators who claimed religious authority; and some were ruled by atheists who opposed competition from other religions.

America's Founding Fathers lived in a society in which the Christian Bible was the most important influence. The principle that Life, Liberty, and the Pursuit of Happiness are God-given gifts to every person comes directly from that Bible.

The Founding Fathers were also remarkable scholars, especially of human history.[16] They studied the histories of many past civilizations.

Knowing the many examples of tyrannies that used religion oppressively and restricted individual religious freedom, our Founders were determined that Congress would never do this. So, they wrote the First Amendment to protect religious freedom.

Regardless of this, there are many groups who want to use government to advance a particular religion.

Prominent today, for example, are some atheists who want our public schools to do this. They want classes taught in certain ways to discredit other religions and advocate rules that restrict student prayer. Also, there are Muslims who want their religious laws to supersede our civil laws.

Wherever people are found, their religion will be found – just as will be their manner of speaking, dress, interests, and all of their personal characteristics. It is a violation of their constitutional rights to demand that they leave a part of themselves – their religion – outside the door. So long as they do not encroach upon the religious freedom of others, they are constitutionally protected in our country in peaceful religious activities.

Today, we have people who claim that they are offended to be in the presence of someone who is praying or speaking about his faith.

The Constitution protects freedom of religion from Congress. It does not assure freedom from exposure to people who are practicing their religion.

The Founding Fathers believed that, since life, liberty, and the pursuit of happiness were gifts from God, our nation would endure so long as our people understood this.

Communication

Our individual capabilities to exercise our freedoms have recently been markedly expanded by spectacular advances in communications technology. Almost every person on earth can now communicate with every other person by means of the Internet.

We are all familiar with the many conveniences and idiosyncrasies that the Internet and broader electronics revolution have introduced into our lives. Commerce has markedly benefited, and all sorts of opportunities have arisen from this ongoing technological advance.

The most important effect has been to increase our liberty by making the truth more accessible.

Previously, most people received their "information" from print, radio, and television. These sources require substantial capital and are easily controlled by an elite few. So, if media preferred to tell a lie, it was able to do so effectively by simply suppressing the truth by not publishing it.

The Internet has solved this problem. With free access to the world wide web available to everyone, the truth cannot be hidden. Lies are ubiquitous on the Internet, too, but the truth is there right beside them.

For example, when propaganda for the hypothesis of human-caused global warming was running high, many scientists wanted to oppose this, but their voices were simply not heard in the establishment media.

In 1998 and then again in 2007, my colleagues at the Oregon Institute of Science and Medicine, Harvard, and Rockefeller University and I wrote two well-researched review papers on this subject and circulated them by mail along with a petition to American scientists. The petition urged the U. S. government to take no action on the basis of this failed idea.

We received by mail more than 31,000 signatures of American physical scientists, including those of more than 9,000 PhDs, on this petition.[17]

Our petition reads:

"We urge the United States government to reject the global warming agreement that was written in Kyoto, Japan in December, 1997, and any other similar proposals. The proposed limits on greenhouse gases would harm the environment, hinder the advance of science and technology, and damage the health and welfare of mankind.

"There is no convincing scientific evidence that the human release of carbon dioxide, methane, or other green house gases is causing or will, in the foreseeable future, cause catastrophic heating of the earth's atmosphere and disruption of the earth's climate. Moreover, there is substantial scientific evidence that increases in atmospheric carbon dioxide produce many beneficial effects upon the natural plant and animal environments of the earth."

Before the days of the Internet, this petition and our research review article with its 132 references to the peer-reviewed scientific literature and other definitive sources would have been yesterday's news the day after it was announced and entirely forgotten soon afterward. Many media outlets would have just ignored it.

Instead, with the Internet, our review article became the most widely read review article on this subject in the world, and the petition project has significantly affected public debate. We published the truth, and the Internet made that truth available to everyone.

When the truth and the lie compete on a level playing field, usually the truth eventually wins. The Internet's level playing field is a wonderful tool for the preservation of human liberty.

It is also a great thorn in the side of those who once had monopoly control of the information received by the American people. So, our freedom of speech on the Internet must be carefully guarded.

Many proposals have been made to restrict freedom of communication on the Internet; to place economic barriers in the form of taxes on it; and to inhibit Internet use in various ways.

It is crucial that we make sure that Congress does not pass disabling restrictions on the Internet.

Communications and commerce on the Internet should not be taxed. The Internet should not be restricted .

To be sure, there are many things on the Internet that

each of us, in different ways, would find offensive. I have read, for example, that there is a great amount of pornography on the Internet. I have not seen this, however, because I have never visited those sites.

A willingness to filter out those things we prefer not to see is part of the price of our freedom. Parents should make sure that their children are able to cope with this free environment before they give them access to it.

In our home, we made a rule that no one could use a computer at all until they were 16 or had completed calculus, even though we use computers extensively in our research work.

Had the Internet existed in colonial days, I expect that it would have been mentioned specifically in the Constitution along side freedom of speech. In any case, there is no doubt that freedom on the Internet is covered by the words written into the Constitution by our Founding Fathers.

Speech and Press Freedom

It is self-evident that, if we cannot speak freely, we cannot have liberty. Again, the Constitution says that Congress shall make no law abridging the freedom of speech. That's easy, but what about the laws Congress has made that fund and empower those who do so? The answer is that Congress should not have its nose into everything and be making those laws.

Today, freedom of speech is under assault from another claimed new freedom or "right" – the "right" not to be offended. By means of this claimed bogus "right" not to be offended, freedom of speech about literally any subject can be suppressed.

There are even those who now want all literature that contains "offensive" words to be suppressed. This includes a large part of our literary heritage. Paradoxically, some of those who advocate that racially offensive words not be published are trying to suppress some of our greatest books that were written to oppose racism.

One thing is very clear. "Congress shall make no law abridging the freedom of speech."

As to freedom of the press, the American press has done a pretty thorough job of protecting itself. As the "press" is extended into the Internet, however, we must be watchful. Some people are working to apply censorship to the Internet. This must not be allowed to happen.

Assembly and Petition

These are largely extensions of freedom of speech. People assemble to talk with one another and to support expressed ideas. Congress is not allowed to make laws abridging the right of the people peacefully to assemble and to petition the government for a redress of grievances.

As recent assemblies of many hundreds of thousands of "Tea Party" people and of thousands of "Occupy" protesters show, freedom of assembly is being more-or-less assured in a responsible way. There have been incidents, but most assemblies currently have little difficulty.

The right to petition government is in a little more trouble.

In the 1980s when we were working on civil defense, we could visit any congressional or senatorial office and leave our literature with the secretaries. We thus easily utilized our right to petition.

In 2009, however, Noah and I were not allowed to leave our petition signed by more than 31,000 American scientists at the offices of senators and congressmen. The leaving of petitions in congressional offices is now no longer permitted. Eventually our petition was entered into the Congressional Record.

The right to petition congressional offices should be reinstated. Congress should be easily accessible to all citizens, not just those who buy access with campaign contributions at election time.

The freedoms of religion, speech, press, assembly, and petition must never be abridged by direct or indirect actions of Congress.

12

SOCIAL ISSUES

"Among the natural rights of the colonists
are these: first a right to life; secondly a right to
liberty; thirdly a right to property; together with
the right to support and defend them in the best
manner." *Samuel Adams*

L et us begin with a principle that I hope we all share.
The federal government was never intended by the
Founding Fathers to make individuals good. They saw
government as a necessary institution for protecting
certain essential human rights, especially life, liberty, and
property (economic liberty). They also knew that central
government is a dangerous institution that needs careful
supervision.

> The rights to Life and Liberty should be rigor-
> ously enforced and never compromised, including
> the rights of children before birth and of senior
> citizens.
>
> We should not use the government as a tool for
> social engineering in attempts to control ordinary
> human behavior. This infringes upon our liberty.

They did not see the federal government as an agency of social redemption. They believed that private efforts and local institutions are the proper agencies for uplifting individuals and communities. They did not believe that the federal government should restrict liberty in order to make people more righteous.

This philosophy was very different from the philosophy of the French Revolution. The French Revolution was based on the idea that the state could intervene and make a better society by means of violence. *At the heart of the French Revolution was the guillotine.* The revolutionaries killed tens of thousands of people for opposing a program of government social redemption. They even had an agency called the "Committee of Public Safety," which decided who would be killed. It could also have been translated accurately as the "Committee of Public Salvation." That was how the French revolutionaries viewed their committee.

Later, the Communists believed that the state is the proper agency for the creation of a new mankind. They believed that even the laws of nature would bend to the communist state if enough repression were applied. Stalin believed the state could repeal the laws of genetic inheritance. Lysenko, who was Stalin's pet "scientist" in this, set back Soviet biology by several generations.

The Soviets expected that, if men and women were forced to obey the communist state and those who did not obey the state were killed, then their descendents would automatically obey the state.

Historically, it has been the position of the majority of Americans that the government is dangerous, in the same way that fire is dangerous, and that it should not be allowed to intrude into the lives of American citizens in an endless quest to make everybody better. Many politicians, however, have become persuaded that, if they try to legislate national goodness, they will get more votes.

> **"Government is merely a temporary servant; it cannot be its prerogative to determine what is right and what is wrong, and decide who is a patriot and who isn't. Its function is to obey orders, not originate them."**
>
> *Mark Twain*

The proper function of civil government is to suppress certain specified forms of misbehavior. Actions that threaten the lives, liberty, and property of the citizens are to be deterred. Congress is authorized to protect the fundamental human liberties that our Constitutional Republic was created to preserve.

Our federal justice system was created largely to protect the people from the government and carry out other related functions. Our state justice systems are charged with protecting people from each other. There is some overlap between the federal and state systems of justice.

It is life, liberty, and property that our government was created to preserve. To the extent that these are "social issues," they are of congressional interest.

Liberty

Throughout most of recorded history, the killing or enslavement of people by other people has been the norm. One empire after another was based on these practices, which threatened everyone. Racism played only a minor role in the thousands of years of world slavery. People enslaved each other in vast numbers, usually with little regard to sex, race, or national origin.

During recent times, people around the world have become increasingly intolerant of the enslavement or killing of other people. The excellent example provided by the United States has played a great role in this change, but this was not easy.

The first major blow against slavery was struck by Great Britain, which abolished slavery throughout the British empire in 1833. Slavery existed in the United States until the end of the Civil War in 1865.

At least slavery was *supposed* to have ended in 1865. But when I find that I am forced, like most Americans, to labor for the government during half of each year, I am not so sure.

"Like most Americans?" He is surely wrong. Almost half of Americans pay no state or federal income tax, and, in Oregon, there is no sales tax.

But what do these apparently tax free people do with their money? They spend it. And the prices they pay include the taxes of everyone who has had a role in providing the items they purchase.

There once was a time when, if we had a leak in our plumbing, we called a plumber. I know my parents did, even though they were exceptionally frugal. Now, mostly wealthy people and congressmen call a plumber. The rest of us are down at Home Depot, Grover, Lowe's, Walmart, or some other store buying cheap Chinese plastic pipe to fix our own plumbing. So, there are fewer jobs as plumbers.

The reason for this is that plumbers charge too much, even though they could surely keep our plumbing in better shape. Why the high charges? Because plumbers pay taxes and the people who supply them with parts pay taxes, and the people from whom the plumber buys food pay taxes, and the doctors who keep the plumber and his family healthy pay taxes, etc, etc, etc. When we pay a plumber, less than half of the money actually goes to the plumber.

Less than half? This is because the plumber, especially if he is a good plumber and has managed to build a small plumbing business, is considered "rich," so he pays at even higher tax rates.

"Plumbers are rich?" That may be new news to the plumbers, but it is old news to DeFazio and his socialist friends. They say plumbers are "rich," and want to tax them even more to pay the big bills they have run up in Washington.

But I digress.

Slavery takes away liberty. So, our government is charged with preventing it. The federal government did relatively well in this, until career politicians took over in Washington and enslaved us all with a mountain of debt.

I oppose slavery in all of its forms. This includes opposition to members of Congress who use the American people as collateral for colossal politically-incurred debts and thereby force Americans into involuntary servitude.

Life

The right to life would seem to be a simple subject, but this appears to be an insoluble problem for us still. People greatly value their own lives, but many of them have different views about other people's lives. They do not seem to realize that their own lives are no safer than those of everyone else.

Who has the wisdom or the right to decide that another human being should be deprived of life? The Founding Fathers knew the answer. No one has that right.

Who has the right to decide that a child or a senior citizen will not have a "good enough" life, will not be "enough" loved, will not be "enough" cared for, will not be of "enough" value? No one has this right.

The right to life and liberty applies to every human being. This is what the Founding Fathers intended, and they structured our government to protect life.

It is, of course, different if a criminal is trying to kill my daughter. I have a right to endanger the criminal's life, if necessary, to save her life. This is a special case. There is little disagreement about this.

Linus Pauling and I worked together over a period of 15 years, often on various projects with potential to improve human life. We published many research papers on subjects as diverse as nuclear physics, general anesthesia, and human nutrition.

Linus stated his goal as to "reduce human suffering." My goal was different. I sought to "increase the quality, quantity, and length of human life." When I wrote the articles of incorporation of the research institute that Linus and I co-founded, I wrote the goals of both of us into its statement of purpose.

I decided that Linus's goal was too limited. Scientists might say his "boundary conditions" were too narrow. Suffering can be minimized or even completely eliminated by killing the person. I don't think Linus intended this. He just had not thought the matter through.

Our government permits the killing of unborn children and is beginning to make similar decisions about senior citizens.

My opponent has voted for tax funding of all forms of abortion, including partial birth abortion, which involves the killing of a child while it is being born. I will never vote to support the killing of any child – born or unborn, through funding the killing or otherwise. DeFazio also voted for Obamacare, which sets up panels of bureaucrats who will decide who will receive medical care and who will not. They will decide who will live and who will die.

Senior citizens should be especially concerned about this because Obamacare takes $500 billion out of Medicare. The intention is to end Medicare and transfer all seniors into Obamacare. Then bureaucratic panels will decide on the phasing out of medical care as seniors get older. Members of the Administration influential in drafting this law make no secret of their desire to phase down and eventually phase out medical care as people age. [18, 19]

When the right to human life is compromised, for unborn children, for senior citizens, or for anyone else – once government decides who will live and who will die, we regress toward the past. In the past, before the American experiment, human life was held very cheap.

Our Constitutional Republic was a great step forward in human history with respect to the right of every human being to life. Unfortunately, our country has tragically stumbled in this regard. A further tragic step is Obamacare, which puts our older citizens' lives at risk. I oppose abortion, and I oppose government rationing of medical care.

A man and woman who act in such a way that they are so fortunate as to conceive a human child should be ready to care for that child. If they do not do so, then the child should be cared for by someone among the millions of Americans who would like to adopt a child. If a woman conceives a child, she should take responsibility for the child, at least until it is born.

Unfortunately, there has arisen a bureaucracy that decides which parents are "suitable" and which are not and sets overly oppressive standards. Adoptive parents are rejected, for example, on the basis of age. This bureaucracy should be revamped.

Every child born in America should have a home immediately, and no child should be killed before birth. There are plenty of Americans ready to accept the great gift of these children into their homes.

Not all of these homes are of the type that you or I might prefer. But any home and a chance at life is far better than no life at all.

But what about the mothers? What about the rare situations in which the pregnancy or birth is a medical threat to the mother's life? These very unusual, rare instances should be handled by the doctor and mother as most have been in the past, with common sense and charity.

What about rape? (There are very few children conceived through rape.) Here liberty and life conflict. The woman did not act voluntarily. I believe that life is more important than liberty in this case.

Yes, the woman has been seriously injured, and carrying a child to term is an additional burden. She should be compensated very generously for this injury and for this burden. The mother and the child are both innocent.

We should never allow the deliberate killing of an innocent human being.

My life's work has been devoted to the advancement of scientific knowledge with the goal of increasing the quality, quantity, and length of human life. I regard the opportunity to live a human life upon the earth as a gift of indescribable and inestimable value – any human life, not just a life that someone else happens to think desirable.

Our country is dedicated to life and liberty. Without life, there is no liberty. When expediency conflicts with these principles, we should stand on principle.

Behavior

I have written above about specific issues that involve life and liberty and the responsibility of government to protect them. Both issues are divisive. I hope that those who disagree with me will consider my views on other issues and will decide to send me to Congress regardless of our differences. There is no point in trying to ignore these things. Voters want to know the candidate's views.

Many conservative voters feel that other social views should be promoted and forced by law upon everyone by government. Many liberal voters think so, too. Numerous other groups with labels other than "conservative" and "liberal" also want this. These groups have different opinions as to which views should be promoted.

Let's look at the Constitution. It is the written rules under which we live in the United States. We require that every person elected to Congress take an oath to uphold the Constitution.

While the Constitution clearly intends for the government to protect life and liberty and assure justice, the Constitution is silent on most other issues.

In fact, the Constitution is more than silent. It specifically delegates to the states and the people jurisdiction in all matters not specifically mentioned in the Constitution. The Congress has no business meddling in things that the Constitution does not authorize.

We are all, as human beings, capable of and prone to all sorts of behavior that is not good for us – at least not good for us in some other person's opinion. Moreover, many of the things we get involved in are so unwise that, even as we do them, we ourselves would be willing to admit that they are unwise.

> **"It is by the goodness of God that in our country we have these unspeakably precious things: freedom of speech, freedom of conscience, and the prudence never to practice either."**
> *Mark Twain*

Still, our lives are our own and our freedom is precious. So long as we do not endanger the life or intrude on the freedom of another person, we should be free to make fools of ourselves in any way we wish.

Of course, not everything is black and white. Some ways in which we might wish to exercise our freedom are harmful to the freedom of others. We must compromise through our laws as best we can with common sense.

States, as authorized by state citizens, have more latitude than the federal government. Moreover, state governments are much closer to the people and much more easily regulated by the voters in each state.

In Congress, I shall strive to conduct the people's business under the Constitution that I have sworn to uphold. I will not try to impress my personal social views or the social views of others on the American people by unconstitutional misuse of congressional power.

Republicans

In 2010, I had the nominations of the Republican, Constitution, and Independent Parties and the endorsement of the Libertarian Party. I won the Independent Party nomination by besting DeFazio in the Independent Party primary election. In the general election against him, we received many contributions and votes from Democrats.

In 2012, political party is largely irrelevant. Tens of millions of people across America – from all political parties and views – have joined a vast coalition to protect American Liberty and to restore common sense to Washington. After this is done, we can all resume the debates about our lesser differences.

I have been a Republican all my life, as were my parents. Our family was probably Republican back as far as the party goes. Several generations of my family were Iowa farmers, until my dad, who was an engineer. They were all Republicans. I grew up in Texas, was educated and worked in California, and moved to Oregon 32 years ago.

The Republican Party started in 1854, about the time that my first relatives arrived in Iowa. My mother's side were "Brouhards." John Brouhard came west from Indiana with his family in a covered wagon in 1851. Most of them, including John Brouhard, are buried in the Colo, Iowa, cemetery. The Robinsons lived in northern Iowa.

A local newspaper of August 1850 describes the event

that caused John Brouhard to leave Indiana. According to a witness, Indiana pioneer Dr. Lewis Kern:

"Jesse Lane approached John Brouhard, who, by the way, was a large, raw-boned man and apparently much stronger than Lane. But the Lanes boasted of being of fighting stock. After applying various vile epithets to Brouhard, Lane dared him to fight, and Brouhard said, 'Jesse, I do not want to fight with you here. I am willing to acknowledge that you are the better man than I am and let us make friends.'

"When Aaron Lane, Jesse's brother, drew a ring on the ground and remarked that 'If he was not a d-d coward he would enter the ring and his brother would whip him!' Brouhard replied, 'To show you I am no coward, I will enter the ring,' which he did in a perfectly cool manner, while Lane had his coat off and belt fastened around his waist, foaming with rage. He sprang at Brouhard. The first lick Brouhard knocked off and dealt Lane a blow in the region of the heart. Lane fell over muttering a curse and died."

John Brouhard was tried by jury in circuit court and was acquitted of manslaughter. He was fined three dollars for the "affray" – as the newspaper referred to it.

Lane had a lot of relatives in Indiana, so John Brouhard moved his family to Iowa. He fought for the North in the Civil War. And now Oregon District 4 has Arthur Brouhard Robinson running for Congress.

Iowa is in the heart of middle America. Its people still hold to the culture of our traditional hard-working farmers and small-town businessmen.

There is a story about some retired Iowa farmers, who liked to visit each day down at the local barber shop. One day, one of them spoke up, "Boys, I have a confession to make. I've joined the Democrat Party."

His friends were astonished. "Why would you do a thing like that? You've been a good Republican all your life."

"Well, it's like this. I've been to my doctor. He says I have only six months to live, and I think it's better that one of them should die than one of us."

Today, the farmer wouldn't need to switch. Millions of Americans are rising up to demand a return to liberty. They are Republicans, Democrats, Independents, Libertarians, Constitutionalists, and a mixture of many other groups. I had the nominations, endorsements, and support of all of these in 2010, except the Democrats – and if the law allowed it, I would have tried for the Democrat nomination, too.

The old guards in both major parties don't know what to do. They have been sharing power in Washington for too long. If they had done a good job, this would not be happening. But, they haven't. The people, especially the young people, want liberty. They want their country back, and they are going to get it.

One caution, however, about retired Iowa farmers and businessmen. As a young man, I often visited my relatives in Ames, Iowa. There is an Elk's club there, where the older men play checkers and gin rummy.

Watch out! These seem like simple games, but a mere mortal cannot win, not even one game! These guys played against their grandfathers, who played against their grandfathers. They are unbeatable.

13

CONGRESSIONAL AUTHORITY

In all Cases affecting Ambassadors, other public Ministers and Consuls, and those in which a State shall be Party, the supreme Court shall have original Jurisdiction. In all the other Cases before mentioned, the supreme Court shall have appellate Jurisdiction, both as to Law and Fact, with such Exceptions, and under such Regulations as the Congress shall make.
Article III, Section 2, Part 2

The Constitution protects our freedom. Congress is entrusted with the powers – and **only** the powers –

Congress is the most powerful branch of our national government. Congressmen take an oath to uphold our Constitution. All funds used by government must be granted by Congress. Congress can, by controlling funding, prevent any action by the president. Congress can also, if it wishes, remove an issue from the jurisdiction of the Supreme Court.

The people are responsible for the actions of Congress, since they can replace any representative every two years and any senator every six.

provided to it in the Constitution. The people elect the Congress. Thus, the ultimate responsibility to protect our Constitutional Republic rests with the people. The people exercise that responsibility every two years.

Congress controls the power and resources of the U.S. government. Among the powers of Congress are the exclusive authority to declare war and, most important, the power of the purse. The president can't use the lights at the White House unless Congress gives him the money to pay the electric bill.

> **"Government is not reason, it is not eloquence, it is force, and like fire, it is a dangerous servant and a fearful master."**
> *George Washington*

Since Congress can fund and de-fund any U.S. government activity, it has ultimate authority over almost all government activities. It, therefore, bears the responsibility for those activities.

Most laws require public funds to function. Even if Congress does not have the support of the president to repeal an unwise law, it can still de-fund it and thereby prevent its effects.

For example, the regulatory agencies, which are now stifling our economy and blocking tens of millions of real jobs for Americans, did not exist during most of our nation's history. Since Congress funds these agencies, it can also de-fund any of their activities.

Congress can be credited with most things that the government does rightly and properly blamed for most things done wrongly. The president has far less authority.

Congress and the Supreme Court

Congress can also remove from the Supreme Court and take to itself jurisdiction of almost any issue. This is an infrequently invoked constitutional provision.

There have been occasions where Congress decided that it was none of the Supreme Court's business to interfere with some policy the Congress decided was a good idea, so Congress passed a bill that removed the court's jurisdiction from the issue.

Article III of the Constitution governs this. The Supreme Court has no authority over any matter that has been removed from its jurisdiction by Congress. This does not require presidential approval. The Constitution is clear that the Congress has sole and exclusive authority over the Supreme Court with respect to permitting its jurisdiction.

Article III, Section 2, Part 1 of the Constitution excludes Supreme Court jurisdiction of a dispute between a state and a citizen of that state.

Socialized Medicine

The most recent use of this congressional power to set aside the court jurisdiction occurred in the "Obamacare" bill that my opponent helped vote into law.

This law specifically removed all court jurisdiction over the "Independent Payment Advisory Board," the IPAB. The IPAB has been characterized as a "death panel" because this un-elected board is given power to decide who will receive medical care and who will not – the power to ration medical care individual by individual under any rules it decides to set up.

This gives the IPAB the power to decide who will live

and who will die – and the authority to exercise this power without oversight by any court.

As the law now stands, a specific act of Congress would be required to save the life of any American targeted for withdrawal of medical care by the IPAB.

The Memory Hole

This constitutional provision is rarely used. Americans have been led to believe that the Supreme Court has final jurisdiction, and that the only thing that can overturn a decision by the Supreme Court is either a subsequent decision by the Supreme Court or a constitutional amendment.

This is not true. The Constitution clearly says that the Congress has the power to remove the jurisdiction of the Court in almost every area of dispute. Congress has the power to tell the court "mind your own business," and the court is constitutionally required to do so.

Abdication of Responsibility

Congressman Ron Paul has said that, early in his career as a congressman, he would oppose a particular bill on the basis that it was unconstitutional. Again and again, he said, one of his colleagues would say that it is the job of the Supreme Court to determine whether a law is unconstitutional. They would say that it is Congress's job to pass the law, without worrying about whether it is constitutional or not. Yet, each congressman swears to uphold the Constitution.

A person who is elected to Congress should never assume that it is legitimate for him to hand over to the

> On KPNW 1120 AM (April 1, 2010), Bill Lunden asked Congressman DeFazio, "Do you believe that it is constitutional for the government to tell people that they have to purchase health insurance?"
>
> Peter DeFazio replied,
>
> "Well, um, I'm not a lawyer . . . that's why we have courts . . . Congress often passes laws that are of dubious or questionable constitutionality."

Supreme Court the responsibility to determine the constitutionality of a particular law. The Supreme Court does have jurisdiction, but that jurisdiction can be removed at any time, for most issues, by a majority vote in the House of Representatives and the Senate as specified in Article III, Section 2, Part 2 of the Constitution.

Lobbying Congress

A member of Congress, on average, now oversees the expenditure of about $13 billion in public money every two years, in addition to the regulatory and other legal powers that Congress has assumed.

Yet, it only costs about $1 million per year to keep each Congressman in wages, perks, and amenities and another $1 or $2 million or so in corporate, union, and other special interest campaign contributions to pay for his re-election.

Sure, there is a little more. Congress has exempted itself from many laws. For example, insider trading in the stock markets has been legal for members of Congress. For anyone else this results in prison. Congress is now scrambling to undo this perk. It has gotten too much press coverage.

Consider the leverage. A couple of million dollars in campaign cash and other perks to help a congressman's career along influences more than 13 billion dollars of votes in Congress every two years. This is a multiplier of over 6,000 to 1. No wonder lobbying is such a big business!

Conflict of Interest

Except, that none of this should be happening. It should not be possible to buy congressional influence at any price. The congressional oath to uphold the Constitution of the United States should make this impossible. It does, but for only a meager few in Congress.

This corruption is a result of ordinary human nature as it interacts with the temptations of money and power. Most citizen volunteers, like those who filled our Congress for the first one hundred years, were not there for the perks and power. And they were not there long enough to cultivate a taste for these things.

Career politicians are different. There exists a conflict of interest between their own careers and the best interest of the nation. They act in favor of their own self interest first, and on behalf of the people and nation second. The longer they are in Congress, the worse this becomes.

Part III

ISSUES IN 2012

14

HOW TO BRING JOBS BACK TO OREGON

We the People of the United States, in Order to form a more perfect Union, establish Justice, insure domestic Tranquility, provide for the common defence, promote the general Welfare, and secure the Blessings of Liberty to ourselves and our Posterity, do ordain and establish this Constitution for the United States of America. Preamble

"To promote the general welfare." What did this mean in 1787? It didn't mean the welfare state. There was no welfare state. It did not mean "shovel-ready" jobs funded

---

There is only one way to bring real jobs in sufficient numbers back to Oregon. That is to eliminate the reasons that the jobs went away.

We must end the over-taxation, over-regulation, over-spending and over-indebtedness that Congress has placed on the backs of Oregonians and of people throughout the United States.

This will bring jobs back from abroad, permit Oregon businesses to create new jobs, and allow American customers to afford Oregon products.

by tax money from Washington. There were no such programs.

It meant liberty. The men who wrote the Constitution knew that liberty was the way to create wealth. They knew that wealth and hard work go together. Liberate a man, and he is more likely to work hard than if he is a slave working without freedom.

It still means liberty. Liberty makes jobs possible. To liberty add thrift, foresight, effective planning, tools, profits, savings, and everything else that makes it possible to hire someone – and you have **created jobs**.

Cause and Effect

I'm a scientist. The starting point for any successful scientific investigation is the same as the starting point for any other investigation: you have to ask the right question. If you don't ask the right question, you are not going to come up with the right answer.

So, when we want to solve the problem of high unemployment in Oregon, we first have to ask, "what is the cause of the high unemployment?" If we don't get the cause identified, we are not going to get the solution. It's a question of cause and effect. If we get the cause wrong, we are going to get the effect wrong.

Let's keep this simple. If we keep it simple, we won't confuse ourselves. What does it take to create a job?

It takes capital. Somebody has to have the money to go out and hire somebody else and buy the tools of production that are necessary to produce a final product. This is true in every field. If nobody has saved any money or made any profit, there will be no capital to provide jobs.

"Capital" is accumulated real wealth. It is savings, profits, machines and supplies used to make products. If you or I work for a wage; pay 50% of our wages in federal, state, and local direct and indirect taxes (taxes paid by those from whom we purchase things) as Americans, on average, do today; spend 40% of our wages on living expenses and recreation; and put 10% of our wages in the bank, the 10% becomes capital for us to spend later or invest.

The 50% is also capital, but it is no longer ours. It will be spent by politicians and their friends in Washington and by state and local politicians. Money is just a way of measuring and exchanging capital.

Some people like to refer to "human capital." I do not. It is never a good idea to treat people as objects. Capital is created by people, saved by people, and used by people. People are the ultimate resource, but they are not objects.

Our agreement with our employer is that he will give us capital in exchange for our work. That capital is measured in dollars that we can conveniently exchange with someone else for their capital – food, clothing, fuel, and other things we want or need.

The 10% savings from our wages is our unspent personal profit. We pay all of the expenses of our business (in this case our taxes and personal expenses), and what is left over is our profit.

Most private businesses work the same way, except that they have additional expenses in the form of employees, more taxes, supplies, and equipment. A business pays all of these expenses. What remains is profit.

For legal and tax reasons, many businesses become corporations, especially large businesses, but the process is the same. The corporation pays expenses and taxes. The

> But wait. The statists say that saving is unnecessary. My opponent and his friends say that they will create jobs by taxing the rich, borrowing, and having the Federal Reserve print up some more money. "Saving?" "Capital?" "Profit?" They disrespect these things.
>
> Well, the definition of capital is assets used or available to use – real assets. How can printed money be a real asset? How can taxing one American, taking his assets, and giving them to another American create assets? How can saddling Americans with debt create assets? Capital – real assets – pays for real jobs.
>
> To be sure, Congress can take assets from those who earned them and give them to those who did not. How likely are the recipients – selected by Congress – to use that capital as wisely as those who earned it? **These transfers – this "spreading the wealth around" – just destroys capital and jobs.**

remainder is profit.

The accumulated savings and profit from all sources in our society, personal and business, is the capital we have to start new businesses or expand old businesses. When capital expands, there are more jobs. When capital contracts, there are fewer jobs. Without increased profit or savings, there are no new jobs.

But what about that 50%? Government has capital, too. It has half of all the earnings of the people, businesses, and corporations in America combined. So, it can "create" more jobs. Right? Wrong.

Government, at all levels, is already spending every dollar in capital it receives and lots more besides. In 2011,

Congress spent the entire $2.3 trillion it received in taxes and $1.3 trillion more. If it stops spending, the professors at Oregon universities and the other people who depend upon the enormous flow of government dollars into Oregon are going to be in real trouble. State governments and local governments are also spending more dollars than they receive in taxes.

Where does Congress get that extra $1.3 trillion? It gets part of it by issuing bonds that are traded to Americans and people in foreign countries for their profits. In this way, it borrows private sector and foreign capital. This cannot create net jobs because it uses up capital that would have created jobs elsewhere. It can be used to move jobs around to places where politicians need votes, but this is coming to an end.

Congress has borrowed so much money that lenders are beginning to refuse to lend it more. The national credit rating is sinking. Also, paying interest on this vast public debt is gradually bankrupting the country and endangering those who depend on government payments. Borrowed money does not produce net jobs, unless it is used wisely to create capital in profitable businesses. Congress does not run such businesses.

Congress also gets part of the $1.3 trillion by money printing. Much of this is now computer created rather than printed. A deceptive indirect procedure is used under congressional authority by the Fed to do the printing and then loan the money to the Treasury or to banks that loan it to the Treasury.

Printing money just dilutes the measure of capital. It taxes away saved capital. If you have saved $5,000 and Congress increases the money supply by 10%, the purchasing power of your savings may decrease to $4,500. You still see $5,000 in your bank account, but prices rise, so you actually lose $500. Other factors affect the exact numbers, but this is the essence of the effect. Prices rise later and irregularly because different parts of the economy respond differently. This helps to hide this inflation tax.

Printing money is just a deceptive way of increasing taxes and taking private savings. There is no net increase in real savings or capital, so there are no net new jobs.

So, what about taxing the "rich." My opponent apparently thinks this is great politics. He is stumping for re-election by demonizing the "rich." He must hope that the politics of envy and class warfare will conceal his poor congressional record. Well, what about this? Is the confiscated capital of the rich a source of new jobs?

When one looks at the actual effects of these new taxes on the "rich," they really are, in effect, taxes on almost everyone – with the poor suffering the most.

Higher taxes must be paid. There is only one source. That source is capital. Whether or not capital is in the $100,000 account of an affluent man or in the $100 account of a poor man, the net capital in private hands decreases by an amount taken by the new taxes. Since capital is the only source of jobs, high taxes just transfer jobs from the private sector to the sector that Congressmen think will buy them the most votes. There are no new jobs.

In times past, people kept more of their savings in banks, and banks loaned this capital to private enterprise, where it paid for jobs. Congressional authorization of the Fed to print money, however, steals saved capital, so people now keep more of their savings in "investments."

Increased taxation reduces private sector capital, so as

many jobs are lost as are created. Actually, when capital is transferred to government, there is a net loss of jobs.

Government pays public workers higher wages than are paid in the private sector. This means that there are fewer jobs. If a public employee is paid $100,000 in wages and benefits and a private employee is paid $60,000 for equivalent work, then the destruction of 10 private sector jobs by taxation only creates 6 public sector jobs.

On average, by researched estimates, public sector employees receive about 60% more in wages for the same work than do private sector employees.[20,21] When pensions and other benefits are considered, public employees receive, on average, about 100% more. (There are many estimates of these percentages. They are all qualitatively similar, but vary quantitatively over a wide range. Some show a smaller percentage difference.)

It is also common sense that those who earn capital will be much more careful in spending it than will those who just sit in Congress and collect it by taxation. This turns out to be very true, as the many boondoggles revealed about congressional spending constantly illustrate. Wasted capital is lost capital, and results in more lost jobs.

There is increasing tension in America between public sector unions and the private sector voters who pay their wages. Politicians are fanning the flames of this dispute to get more votes. This is unfortunate and unnecessary.

We need public sector workers just as we need private sector workers. Moreover, liberty and justice require that workers be entirely free to sell their labor for the highest wage and best working conditions they can negotiate. Most people prefer to exercise this freedom personally. Most workers do not belong to unions. Those who decide to negotiate collectively by belonging to unions are entirely within their rights as free men and women to do so.

However, and this is a big "however" at the heart of many disputes today, the Constitution and the principles of liberty and freedom, do not give Congress any authority to pass laws that favor either unions or employers.

Creating Jobs

Let's think about the process of job creation.

Say that there is a fellow named Jones who has an idea for a product that he thinks another fellow named Smith is likely to buy. Smith could use something like this, but nobody is offering it for sale, or at least nobody is offering it at a price that Smith is willing to pay.

So, Jones sits down and develops a plan of action. He has to hire people to produce the product. He may decide to borrow money, so that he can afford to buy the tools of production. He had better have a marketing plan, because if Smith doesn't know that Jones has produced the product, Smith is not going to buy it.

Jones has to go out at this point and convince Brown to go to work for him. Brown is hopeful that the job will be a good one, and a permanent one, which means that he has to trust Jones with respect to the willingness of Smith to buy the product. Jones can't make any money if Smith will not buy the product. Brown can't make any money if Jones does not hire him.

In a sense, Jones, Brown, and Smith are a kind of team. Each of them needs the other in order to get what he wants. Jones wants to make a profit. Brown wants a job. Smith wants a good product at a good price. If the three of them can get together in a voluntary way, each of them is going to be better off.

Why don't they get together? This is ultimately the important question that we have to get answered if we're going to bring jobs to Oregon. If it is profitable for Jones to sell something to Smith, and he needs Brown to cooperate with him in order to sell something to Smith, there ought to be a way to work out an arrangement.

Four of the most important words in America are these: *let's make a deal.* Americans are always trying to find a way to make a deal. *Americans are the greatest deal makers in the world.* If they think there is a profit, they will go to great lengths to earn that profit. That is why many new businesses are started every year.

The question really should not be this: How can we get jobs back to Oregon? The question is this: Why did jobs go away in the first place? If Jones's grandfather hired Brown's grandfather in order to sell to Smith's grandfather, why did the arrangement break down? It was working for a long time. Why did it stop?

When a deal that has done well for a long time stops working, we should look for a reason. People in Oregon still want good jobs. Producers in Oregon still want profits. There are buyers all over the world who would like to buy good products.

So, what happened to the arrangement that used to work, but is no longer working? It's not just that Oregonians are out of work; it's that the system that used to provide them with work is no longer working. The system is not working, so Oregonians are not working. And it's not just Oregonians who are not working. *Americans all over the country are not working.*

Jobs: Strangled by Congress and Bureaucrats

The problem that Americans face today is that the government does not allow Jones, Brown, and Smith to get together to make a deal. There is somebody else in the picture. It is a government official named Williams who tells Jones that he cannot legally hire Brown at a wage that Brown is willing to accept. He tells Jones that he must provide working conditions far more expensive than the conditions that allow him to make a profit. He tells all three, Jones, Brown, and Smith that they cannot produce the product they had in mind and cannot use natural resources they need to make the product.

And, the official has a partner who taxes away a lot of money from Jones, Brown, and Smith, which makes everything more difficult for all three.

The government official doesn't check with Brown. He doesn't ask Brown if Jones' offer is good enough. He pays no attention to Brown. He pays attention to a thick book of rules written by Congress and the Washington bureaucrats they pay and published in a little-known daily publication called the *Federal Register*. [22]

The *Federal Register* now contains more than 80,000 pages per year of federal pronouncements. These are printed in three columns. Only lawyers can understand what is written in the *Federal Register*. But anyone who violates the rules reported in the *Federal Register* and then listed in the resulting 165,000 pages of the *Code of Federal Regulations* is subject to prosecution.

The *Federal Register* reports regulatory activity of the Federal Government. The *Code of Federal Regulations* lists laws and regulations currently in force.

You may never have seen a page from the *Federal Reg-*

ister. The *Federal Register* is the official daily publication for rules, proposed rules, and notices of federal agencies and organizations, as well as executive orders and other presidential documents. On page 141, I have reproduced a page of the *Federal Register* for December 30, 2011. Take a look at the page number. Take a look at the fine print. The *Federal Register* has more than 82,000 pages for 2011. That is for one year. For the last 30 years, it is more than 1,900,000[22] pages, and the *Federal Register* has been published for a lot longer than 30 years.

Most Americans have never seen the *Federal Register*. Most Americans have never heard of the *Federal Register*. But let me assure you, lawyers have seen it. Every day that it comes out, lawyers across the United States rejoice. They know that they will have plenty of business.

> **"It will be of little avail to the people that the laws are made by men of their own choice if the laws be so voluminous that they cannot be read, or so incoherent that they cannot be understood."**
>
> *James Madison*

The companion to the *Federal Register* is the *Code of Federal Regulations*, the contents of which are updated annually. As of December 31, 2010, this Code contained 165,494 pages. It contains more than 300,000 laws and regulations. As an American citizen, you are subject to all of the rules and regulations on those 165,494 pages, as corrected in the 2011 updates.

Are you thoroughly familiar with your duties? Do you know what additional constraints are in your future? By reading the more than 82,000 pages of the 2011 Federal Register you can find out about your new duties and proposed new duties.

It has been estimated that the average American unknowingly commits three crimes a day[23, 24, 25] by violating rules in the *Code of Federal Regulations.*

President Reagan (1981-1989) managed to make a noticeable dent in this process, which had accelerated under Nixon, Ford, and Carter, as seen in the graph that follows. The number of pages in the Federal Register decreased substantially during Reagan's presidency.

As soon as he was gone, however, Congress immediately lost this common sense. The period in which American business and industry began to be truly crushed by federal regulation and litigation began in about 1970. The number of pages in the *Code of Federal Regulations* and yearly additions to the *Federal Register* have increased about 4-fold since 1970.

This is two-thirds of the process that I call **over-taxation, over-regulation, and over-litigation**. It is not just that the government taxes away our earnings. The government also taxes us by restricting the number of products and services that we can make, the conditions under which we are allowed to work, and the natural resources we are allowed to use to make those products – such as the forests and minerals of District 4. Litigation enforces this.

Some people might say that there are bad products and services. Some people say that there ought to be laws against bad products and services. How many laws do they think there ought to be? In Washington, they know. About 165,000 pages worth.

On top of this, the U.S. Tax Code informing Ameri-

82354   Federal Register / Vol. 76, No. 251 / Friday, December 30, 2011 / Rules and Regulations

FEDERAL COMMUNICATIONS COMMISSION

47 CFR Parts 1, 6, 7, and 14

[CG Docket No. 10–213; WT Docket No. 96–198; CG Docket No. 10–145; FCC 11–151]

Implementing the Provisions of the Communications Act of 1934, as Enacted by the Twenty-First Century Communications and Video Accessibility Act of 2010

AGENCY: Federal Communications Commission.

ACTION: Final rule.

SUMMARY: In this document, the Commission adopts rules that implement provisions of section 104 of the Twenty-First Century Communications and Video Accessibility Act of 2010 (CVAA), Public Law 111–260, the most significant accessibility legislation since the passage of the Americans with Disabilities Act (ADA) in 1990. A Proposed Rule relating to implementation of section 718 of the Communications Act of 1934, as enacted by the CVAA, is published elsewhere in this issue of the **Federal Register**. This proceeding amends the Commission's rules to ensure that people with disabilities have access to the incredible and innovative communications technologies of the 21st-century. These rules are significant and necessary steps in ensuring that the 54 million Americans with disabilities are able to fully utilize and benefit from advanced communications services (ACS). People with disabilities often have not shared in the benefits of this rapid technological advancement. The CVAA implements steps in addressing this inequity by advancing the accessibility of ACS in a manner that is consistent with our objectives of promoting investment and innovation. This is consistent with the Commission's commitment to promote rapid deployment of and universal access to broadband services for all Americans.

DATES: Effective January 30, 2012, except 47 CFR 14.5, 14.20(d), 14.31, 14.32, and 14.34 through 14.52, which contain information collection requirements that have not been approved by the Office of Management and Budget (OMB). The Commission will publish a document in the **Federal Register** announcing the effective date of those sections.

FOR FURTHER INFORMATION CONTACT: Rosaline Crawford, Consumer and Governmental Affairs Bureau, at (202)

418–2075 or *rosaline.crawford@fcc.gov*; Brian Regan, Wireless Telecommunications Bureau, at (202) 418–2849 or *brian.regan@fcc.gov*; or Janet Sievert, Enforcement Bureau, at (202) 418–1362 or *janet.sievert@fcc.gov*. For additional information concerning the Paperwork Reduction Act information collection requirements contained in this document, contact Cathy Williams, Federal Communications Commission, at (202) 418–2918, or via email *Cathy.Williams@fcc.gov*.

SUPPLEMENTARY INFORMATION: This is a summary of the Commission's *Report and Order*, FCC 11–151, adopted and released on October 7, 2011. The full text of this document is available for inspection and copying during normal business hours in the FCC Reference Information Center, Room CY–A257, 445 12th Street SW., Washington, DC 20554. The complete text may be purchased from the Commission's duplicating contractor, Best Copy and Printing, Inc. (BCPI), Portals II, 445 12th Street SW., Room CY–B402, Washington, DC 20554, (202) 488–5300, facsimile (202) 488–5563, or via email at *fcc@bcpiweb.com*. The complete text is also available on the Commission's Web site at *http://hraunfoss.fcc.gov/edocs_public/attachment/FCC-11-151A1doc*. To request materials in accessible formats for people with disabilities (Braille, large print, electronic files, audio format), send an email to *fcc504@fcc.gov* or call the Consumer and Governmental Affairs Bureau (202) 418–0530 (voice), (202) 418–0432 (TTY).

Final Paperwork Reduction of 1995 Analysis

This document contains new and modified information collection requirements. The Commission, as part of its continuing effort to reduce paperwork burdens, invites the general public to comment on the information collection requirements contained in document FCC 11–151 as required by the PRA of 1995, Public Law 104–13. In addition, we note that pursuant to the Small Business Paperwork Relief Act of 2002, Public Law 107–198, *see* 44 U.S.C. 3506(c)(4), we previously sought specific comment on how the Commission might further reduce the information collection burden for small business concerns with fewer than 25 employees.

In this proceeding, we adopt new recordkeeping rules that provide clear guidance to covered entities on the records they must keep to demonstrate compliance with our new rules. We require covered entities to keep the

three categories of records set forth in section 717(a)(5)(A) of the CVAA. We also require annual certification by a corporate officer that the company is keeping the required records. We have assessed the effects of these rules and find that any burden on small businesses will be minimal because we have adopted the minimum recordkeeping requirements that allow covered entities to keep records in any format they wish. This approach takes into account the variances in covered entities (*e.g.*, size, experience with the Commission), recordkeeping methods, and products and services covered by the CVAA. Furthermore, this approach provides the greatest flexibility to small businesses and minimizes the impact that the statutorily mandated requirements impose on small businesses. Correspondingly, we considered and rejected the alternative of imposing a specific format or one-size-fits-all system for recordkeeping that could potentially impose greater burdens on small businesses. Moreover, the certification requirement is possibly less burdensome on small businesses than large, as it merely requires certification from an officer that the necessary records were kept over the previous year; this is presumably a less resource intensive certification for smaller entities. Finally, we adopt a requirement that consumers must file a "Request for Dispute Assistance" with the Consumer and Governmental Affairs' Disability Rights Office as a prerequisite to filing an informal complaint with the Enforcement Bureau. This information request is beneficial because it will trigger Commission involvement before a complaint is filed and will benefit both consumers and industry by helping to clarify the accessibility needs of consumers. It will also encourage settlement discussions between the parties in an effort to resolve accessibility issues without the expenditure of time and resources in the informal complaint process. We also note that we have temporarily exempted small entities from the rules we have adopted herein while we consider, in the Accessibility *FNPRM*, whether we should grant a permanent exemption, and what criteria should be associated with such an exemption.

Synopsis

I. Executive Summary

1. In this *Report and Order*, we conclude that the accessibility requirements of section 716 of the Act apply to non-interconnected VoIP services, electronic messaging services,

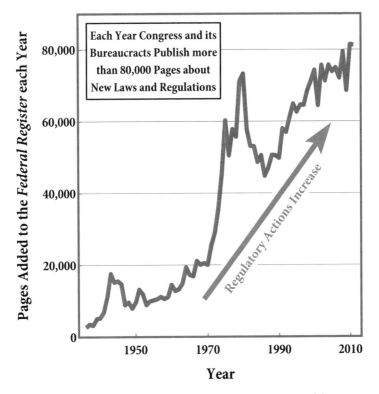

Pages Added to the Federal Register per Year

This measures the Congressionally funded growth of govern-ment operations and regulations. The number of pages doubled between the 1950s and 1970 and then quadrupled again by 2010. Thus, government, by this measure, is costing 8-fold more than in 1950. This takes money away from its intended recipients, includ-ing our seniors and veterans – and destroys private-sector jobs.

cans about the rules and regulations they must conform to when paying their taxes is now more than 60,000 pages.

If you wonder why Jones, who has spent all his life in Oregon, is not willing to hire Brown, who has spent all of his life in Oregon, it may be because of Williams, who

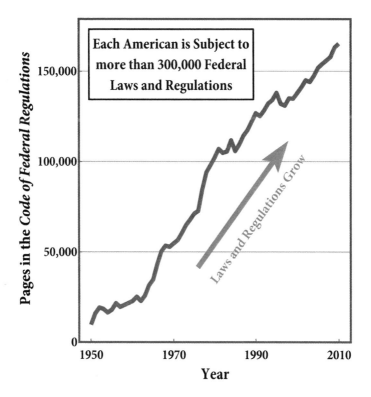

Pages in the Code of Federal Regulations

This measures the Congressionally funded growth of Big Government intrusion into our lives. There are now more than 300,000 laws and regulations on the backs of all Americans. Thus, by this measure, we are 8-fold less free than in the 1950s. This has diminished liberty, damaged our economy, and destroyed jobs.

grew up in New York City, went to college at a New York university, went to law school at Harvard, and went to work in Washington 30 years ago.

Williams has never been in Oregon. He may never have been west of the Mississippi, except in a hotel to attend a conference. But he has control over Jones and Brown. He writes rules making it illegal for Jones and Brown to get together and work out a deal with Smith.

Oregonians Are Competitive

Do you ever order things on Amazon? Do you ever shop at a local store that buys goods that are made out of state? You probably do. Most products are made out of state. That's what freedom is all about. The buyer gets to decide what he wants to buy on his terms. Jones cannot dictate to Smith. Brown cannot dictate to Jones.

But Williams can dictate to Jones, and if Jones cannot afford to satisfy Williams, he does not start the business or manufacture the product. This means that Smith, who would have been willing to buy the product, buys from somebody else. Or maybe he doesn't buy anything like it at all.

There are some products that people in Oregon can produce at a competitive price. But most things that Oregonians buy, they cannot produce at a competitive price. This is true of every state in the union. It is true of every country in the world. People in each region have competitive advantages in the free market. They have an advantage that they want to use to make a profit, get a job, and pay for the kind of life they want to live.

I don't think anybody in Oregon wants to blame Smith if Smith decides to buy a product that was made somewhere else. America has had freedom of choice on a broader scale for more people for a longer period of time than any country in the world. That was what gave Americans the greatest opportunities in the world until about 1970.

Jones should not blame Smith for not buying whatever

it is that Jones and Brown together used to produce, but which some other company now sells to Smith. Nobody likes to lose business, but every businessman knows that the only way to get an honest profit is to remain competitive. Brown knows the same thing.

The problem today is Williams. The problem today is the United States government – run by the U.S. Congress. The government has placed so many restrictions on the production of goods and services all over the United States, and has done so without regard to the freedom of Jones, Brown, and Smith to make a deal, that the United States has ceased to be as productive a nation as it was in 1970.

The way to get jobs back to Oregon is to get the Washington bureaucracy out of the lives of the American people. The bureaucracy in Washington is carrying out the will of Congress, and Congress must stop passing laws that interfere with Americans in their quest to build better lives for themselves and their families.

Are We Children?

Congress pretends that Americans are not reliable, not trustworthy, and not competent enough to make decisions in their own lives about where they will work, what wages they will be paid, what work environment is best for them, what price they should pay for the goods they buy, and how to plan for their retirement.

Congress acts like Americans are children. They believe the children have a right to vote, but they do not believe that the children have a right to work out deals with each other. Why is someone competent to exercise the vote over who will go to Washington, yet incompetent to decide what product to buy, what price to pay, where to work, what to offer an employee, who should be hired, who should be fired, who should be promoted, and when to quit? This defies common sense.

Americans send 535 people to Washington to serve in the House of Representatives and the Senate. These people get together with each other to decide how other Americans will live. Then they work out deals with the President.

After all the details are worked out and the laws are passed, federal bureaucrats decide how to interpret these laws, and they publish them in the *Federal Register* and the *Code of Federal Regulations.*

No one in Congress has read the rules and regulations that the bureaucrats have imposed on the American people on the authority of Congress and the President. No Representative or Senator has time to read 80,000 pages a year.

A major bill is often 1,000 pages, and sometimes 2,000 pages, and the Congressmen who vote for those bills do not read them either.

In some cases, Congress votes for or against a bill before the text of the bill has been completed. This seems hard to believe, but it is true. Furthermore, most bills also involve thousands of pages of testimony from "experts", and Congress doesn't read the testimony, either. Moreover, a major bill that is "moving" as they say in Congress is larded up with hundreds of unrelated laws that the members have agreed to tack onto it in return for special favors for themselves and the special interests that they serve.

How is it possible that 535 people in Congress, plus a President, think they are capable of regulating the lives of 310 million Americans? They do not have time to read the

> I will read the bills. Moreover, if a bill is too long for a Congressman to read and fully understand in the time between its presentation and the vote, I will vote against that bill – every time.

bills. The bills are put together by lobbyists, special-interest groups, and other federal agencies, and committees and political staff members. Together, they draft these bills, that nobody in Congress reads.

I will tell you who reads the bills. Lawyers read them. Some of them are government lawyers, and some of them are hired by businesses, and they together determine whether the business established by Jones has broken the law. They establish whether Jones is going to be allowed to offer a job to Brown. And that confrontation between government lawyers and private lawyers will determine whether or not Brown has a job.

Oregon in 1970 and Today

To argue that it is not the government which has created unemployment is to argue that Americans are no longer productive. It is to argue that the businessmen like Jones, who for 200 years found out how to make a profit by hiring people like Brown to serve people like Smith, somehow lost a lot of this ability sometime around 1970 and have lost a lot more since. I wonder why that was?

Why was it that Oregonians sometime around 1970 began to lose their ability to compete? Did they become less intelligent? Did they become lazy? Did they forget how to run a business?

A major export from Oregon is lumber. There was a housing boom from 1945 until 2007. Why was it that the lumber companies began to lose money? Why was it that workers who were among the most skilled people in the world in the field of lumber production could no longer make a profit? The demand for lumber continued to rise. Yet the lumber industry in southern Oregon went into a slump that has yet to be reversed.

The cause of this decline did not originate in Oregon. It originated in Washington. The environmental movement, empowered by Congress, got its hooks into Oregon, so that the lumber industry could not use the trees.

We get back to the same three causes: *taxation, regulation, and litigation*. There are too many lawyers in Congress, too many lawyers working for the bureaucracies, and too many lawyers having to be hired by businesses to defend their ability to produce goods and services that people like Smith want to buy. We are a nation run by lawyers, who have gained their power by means of unwise and unconstitutional actions by Congress.

There is an old story of a lawyer who couldn't make a decent living. He lived in a small town. He did not know how he could ever make a decent living. Then, one day, another lawyer moved into town, and now they both make excellent livings.

In Iowa, they tell another story. Two neighboring farmers got into a fight. One farmer's pigs had gotten into the other's field. So, one of them stormed into town to see his friend, a lawyer. "I'm sorry, we have been friends for years, but I can't represent you," said the lawyer. "Your neighbor has been here before you, and I am already representing him. There is, however, a very good lawyer across town. I'll give you a recommendation to him."

The recommendation was in a very nice envelope, and, as he walked across town, the farmer got to wondering what it said. So, he opened the envelope. The recommendation read, "Two fat geese come to town. I'll take one. You take the other."

I am not a lawyer. I am on the side of Jones, who has a right to hire Brown so that together they can make a profit by selling something to Smith. I am also on the side of somebody named O'Brien who wants to hire O'Malley to sell something that Schwartz would like to buy.

Congress does not agree. Congress even wants to decide which light bulbs we can buy. If Jones wants to make a better light bulb, he needs permission from Congress or the bureaucrats who work for Congress. If he doesn't have enough money to hire lobbyists to outbid the lobbyists of his competitors, he is not allowed to make the product. So, Congress decides what we can buy.

The problem is Williams back in Washington, who is working reasonably hard, and I wish a lot less hard, to figure out ways to keep Jones, Brown, O'Brien, and O'Malley, from working.

> Peter DeFazio voted to ban the Edison light bulb. He later voted against repealing the ban.
>
> Do we really want so much of our liberty taken away that we can't even decide which light bulb to buy?
>
> The light bulb ban was primarily a creation of special interest lobbyists. Corporations that make light bulbs lobbied for the ban. They make much greater profits from mercury-containing fluorescent bulbs.

No More Subsidies

The way to get jobs back to Oregon is the way to get jobs back to America. It is to make it easy for entrepreneurs to expand businesses and start new businesses.

Economists know that the main source of new employment is small business. It is not just small businesses that create jobs; it is new businesses that create the most jobs.

What we need is the freedom for Americans to become small business owners. Small business owners are those, more than anyone else in America, who offer jobs to other Americans. If we do not have small business growth, then we will not have anything like full employment.

I am not calling for government subsidies of small businesses. It is time to stop subsidizing businesses. We should not subsidize big businesses, middle-size businesses, export businesses, import businesses, or any other businesses. The best people to decide what other people want to buy are the businessmen who put their own money and reputations on the line.

If they are correct in their ventures, they will earn money. If they are incorrect, they will not. What I am convinced of is this: some bureaucrat in Washington should not make decisions for American business.

After I am elected to go to Washington to serve in Congress, I am going to vote against every business subsidy that comes up for vote. I am also going to vote for almost any bill that proposes to reduce the regulatory burden on American businesses. (There are some regulations, of course, that make common sense.) Unfortunately, I don't expect to see many proposals of the latter variety. I expect to see lots of proposals of the former type.

I am not going to Washington in order to vote for laws

Politicians, predictably, blame foolish government expenditures on everyone but themselves. For example, the $527 million lost in the Solyndra solar electric subsidy [26,27] is being blamed on President Obama, the Energy Department, and the Secretary of Energy. Republicans are up in arms about this.

Yet, it is Congress – Republicans and Democrats – that gave this money to the Department of Energy. It is Congress that has funded the Department of Energy ever since the Carter Administration, while it predictably wasted vast amounts of money and actually inhibited our energy industries.

Congress is entirely responsible for Department of Energy wastefulness. Congress appropriated the money.

Surely, President Obama and his Secretary of Energy actually wasted this money, but Congress had plenty of warning that they would. Congress appropriated the money, so that voters would think they were pro-alternative energy. Political credit was their goal. When the thing blew up, of course, they blamed others.

Congress controls the purse strings of the government. Where expenditures are concerned, the entire responsibility rests with Congress.

that will extract money from people outside of Oregon to create subsidized jobs in Oregon, and I am also going to vote against laws that would tax Oregonians to pay for subsidized jobs in other states.

I will vote against legislation that interferes with the ability of businessmen and workers to come to an agreement with each other about the terms of their employment. I trust businessmen and workers to come to an agreement on mutually beneficial arrangements about what kinds of products and services to produce.

If Oregonians look to Washington to bring jobs to Oregon, they are going to be disappointed. Oregon District 4 has been in decline for decades in the very industry in which it has the greatest competitive advantage in the United States: wood products. That is what Washington regulations have done to residents of District 4. Those who have looked to Washington to bring jobs to Oregon have instead found that Washington has, over all, killed jobs in Oregon.

The Secret of Job Creation: Liberty

The secret of job creation is really very simple. It is called Liberty. The power to create jobs is in the hands and minds of people with capital and workers with skills. What we need is for government to get out of the way of people with capital and workers with skills, so that they can sell goods and services to people with money. This is how America became the richest country in the world between 1800 and about 1970.

The liberty of action that made possible the enormous wealth of America was the result of voters' commitment to the Constitution of the United States. When voters sent people to Washington who were committed to restricting the federal government from expanding beyond the limits established by the Constitution, Americans became the richest people in the world. The restrictions on government that were imposed by the Constitution kept Congress out of the lives of most Americans.

There are a few people still alive in the United States who were born before 1913 – before the beginning of the income tax. Back in 1913, the only contact that the average American had with Washington was the United States Post Office. The friendly mailman who dropped off the mail in people's mailboxes was the only federal official that most Americans saw.

Government was not a threat to the average American in 1913. But, after 1913, the government began to expand, relentlessly. Step-by-step, the freedom of individual Americans was taken away and transferred to Washington. It was transferred to Washington bureaucrats. Decade by decade, Congress has expanded its control over our lives.

For many decades, the wealth and vibrant free economy of the United States stayed ahead of the bureaucrats and career politicians, but gradually and relentlessly they expanded their power until the great engine of America weakened and slowed to the shadow of itself that remains today.

Many voters may not realize the extent to which our freedoms have been taken away. They have been taken away slowly but surely by Congress, by the president, and by the army of bureaucrats who work under their authority. *The goal of most bureaucrats in Washington is to remake America in the image of the Washington bureaucracy.* They want everything done by forms. They want everything done by permission in advance. They want to control businessmen and workers.

It is possible to bring jobs to Oregon by passing laws that favor special-interest groups in Oregon. But the price of that legislation is the loss of freedom and jobs of

Oregonians and other Americans who are not part of the special-interest groups that are subsidized and favored by the government.

If we want to bring jobs to Oregon, then as Oregonians, we have got to get together to make more deals. Businessmen must get together with employees to see what kind of deals they can work out, so that together, they can work out deals with buyers. If the buyers do not want to buy the goods and services produced by Oregonians, then Oregonians must figure out better ways to make products that other people want to buy. That is the American way. It is the Oregonian way.

The American way is not to subsidize the creation of jobs; the American way is to restrict the federal government, as well as local and state governments, so that Americans can get together with each other to work out profitable arrangements.

I want to stop the growth of the Washington bureaucracy and then reduce its size.

If the voters do not elect representatives who systematically cut congressional funding to federal bureaucracies that interfere with the lives of Americans, then we are going to suffer more and more in coming years. We will see the further strangulation of businesses and further loss of American jobs.

I am pro-business. I am a businessman. I built a research laboratory, a sheep farm, and an education business. I know the limitations that are placed on us by the free market. I know all about profit and loss. I am in favor of American business.

I am also pro-labor. I am in favor of a laborer's right to quit and get a better job at any time. I am even in favor of laborers getting together and quitting their jobs at the same time, if they think they are being misused by an employer.

What I'm not in favor of is for the federal government to send bureaucrats out to tell either businessmen or laborers how to work and live.

If we want to bring jobs to Oregon, we must look at the reason the jobs went away. That reason is the government. That reason is Congress. As the government has grown, the job market has shrunk. As the government has increased its authority over business and labor, people who want good jobs find that these jobs are not available.

It's not that Washington should bring jobs to Oregon. It's that Washington should stop making it difficult for Oregonians to create jobs in Oregon. The government does not "create" jobs without killing jobs somewhere else.

If the over-taxation, over-regulation (and over-litigation that enforces the over-regulation), and over-spending by Congress stops, the rural residents of Oregon will see their prosperity and freedom rise. If it is not stopped, our economy will continue to erode and our children's futures will be grim. The rural citizens of District 4 are used to this. They will continue to "make do" with less and less.

The really spectacular changes, however, will come around Eugene and Corvallis. These areas depend upon large amounts of government capital that floods into the universities and other enterprises. When this capital stops coming – and it will stop coming if common sense does not return to Washington – these areas could very quickly be economically destroyed. We must not let this happen!

"Progressive" Government

Back to the Future?

It is natural for people to desire progress. We all want the future to be better than the past. For this reason, liberal statists and corporatists, including the 25-year career congressman in District 4, have taken to calling themselves "progressives."

The word "progressive" sounds very forward looking. Words, however, can be used in misleading ways. "Liberal," for example, historically referred to those with a dedication to individual liberty. Now, however, it generally is used to represent the opposite - to mean those who advocate that liberty be greatly curtailed in favor of governmental power.

Unfortunately, well-meaning people, including many who are actually personally in favor of the cause of liberty, now erroneously think of themselves as "progressives."

Nothing could be further from the actual political situation because "progressive" groups, such as the congressional Progressive Caucus (of which DeFazio is a member), are foremost in the advocacy of high taxation, overbearing regulation, and centralized governmental power in Washington. They consistently oppose liberty in favor of big government.

Overwhelming power in the hands of central authority has been the rule during most of recorded history. Kings, queens, conquerors, feudal lords, ecclesiastical authorities, and other power-driven people have wielded authoritarian power over ordinary people in most governments and empires during thousands of years.

Centralized governmental power, both ancient and modern, has always led to poverty, lack of individual freedom, and war. Where larger countries were involved, those in control sought world empire. These efforts toward empire have resulted in vast human suffering from war, economic misery, and the boot of oppression upon the backs of ordinary people.

When America was born and dedicated to small government – to liberty and justice for all – to a nation where the rights of the individual stood above the state, mankind took a giant step forward. The great influx of immigrants to the United States was drawn to our shores by liberty and justice, and the prosperity and charity that liberty and justice make possible. For the first time in history, a great people was freed of governmental power and oppression - in a country so vast, rich, and well formed that liberty and justice were likely to endure.

The founding of the United States was primarily the throwing off of centralized authority and tyranny.

Today, the political battle lines are drawn between those who want to continue this great experiment in human freedom – in individual liberty and justice – and those who want to turn back to the past and change America into yet another failed example of centralized governmental power and empire.

We are today at a crossroad between these two visions of the future. Half of our economic freedom has been transferred to government through over-taxation; much of our personal freedom has been transferred to government by over-regulation; and central government power is enslaving us.

It is our duty – to ourselves, to our fellow Americans, to our descendents, and to people everywhere for whom American success serves as hope and an example of liberty – to turn our country away from its slide back toward centralized power and big government tyranny. Big governments have enslaved people for thousands of years. We must return to the system of liberty and justice that made our country exceptional for 200 years.

This is the real political issue in 2012. It is the central issue in the District 4 congressional campaign. The incumbent has consistently voted for centralized big government power during his 25 years in Congress.

He and congressmen like him are responsible for our current lost jobs, lost freedom, difficulties abroad, centralized education, centralized regulatory power, and all the problems that arise as a result. Of course, when things go wrong they deny responsibility, but these denials ring false.

> **"I have sworn, upon the altar of God, eternal hostility against every form of tyranny over the mind of man."**
>
> *Thomas Jefferson*

Their policies are not "progressive" at all. These policies are regressive, and their effect is to turn America back toward a previous age – the age of centralized governmental power – an age-old tyranny that our country escaped 250 years ago. Centralized government gives power and wealth to an elite few, and our current crop of congressmen surely intend to be among that few.

We need not worry about each other, whether or not we are in the "99%" or the "1%." Our danger lies in the 0.001% – the few corrupt people who seek power over us all through their misuse of our Constitutional Republic.

Welcome to George Orwell's *1984* where the meanings

of words on the road signs are inverted – they mark roads back into the past – roads that we must not travel.

Foreign Competition

Some say that low wages in other countries and foreign trade have caused Oregonian jobs to move abroad. This is misleading. **Americans were once known as producing the highest quality goods at the lowest prices in the world. At that time, American wages were the highest in the world.** We had nothing to fear from foreign workers, foreign trade, or foreign industries.

Current "trade" agreements are just more of the same regulation and government meddling that is reducing our prosperity at home. They are the same sort of job-killing things that Washington politicians and bureaucrats do elsewhere within our nation.

Free trade has always been a hallmark of American Exceptionalism. Americans have always been ready and able to go up against any competitor anywhere in the world and to benefit from the products made by people everywhere. "Free trade" agreements are unnecessary. Why should we need laws to trade freely? (Please see the chapter *Foreign Trade* later in this book for more about this.)

When federal, state, and local government, on average, tax away half of the capital that Americans earn; when governmental regulations cause the further waste of much of the capital that remains; and when, therefore, Americans must support their families and capitalize their businesses with a small fraction of their actual earnings; it is just impossible for them to compete with those who have greater economic freedom.

This is the truth. We all know now about the deals that congressmen make with the lobbyists of some industries, banks, and other large enterprises. These banks, industries, and enterprises obtain money and advantages over their competitors by inducing congressmen to give them unconstitutional advantages. You may wish to look over my opponent's campaign financing report to see some of those enterprises for which he does such favors.[5,6]

Trade "agreements" involve the same sorts of favors. They are not in our best interest.

Special interest favoritism actually only benefits a select few. The special interests, however, can pay for a lot of campaign advertisements. See my opponent's television ads this coming October to view such advertisements.

Win or lose, everything worthwhile should be based on the truth – even a political campaign.

Job creation does not come from Washington. Job creation comes from creativity and capital and hard work by individual citizens. That's it. That's how we bring jobs to Oregon. We get the government off our backs, and we create jobs by making products that people want to buy. That's the American way.

15

BAILOUTS, STIMULUS SPENDING, AND DEFICITS

The Congress shall have Power To lay and collect Taxes, Duties, Imposts and Excises, to pay the Debts and provide for the common Defence and general Welfare of the United States; but all Duties, Imposts and Excises shall be uniform throughout the United States; To borrow Money on the credit of the United States; . . . Article I, Section 8, Parts 1,2

Bailouts, stimulus spending, and deficit spending all involve congressional spending of money that Congress takes from those who earned it.

This money is spent to subsidize enterprises chosen by Congress and its bureaucrats and friends.

The taking and political spending of this money is ethically wrong. Moreover, this money has been spent so unwisely that it has actually hurt our economy and destroyed jobs.

The earnings of the American people should remain in their hands. They will spend in common sense ways that increase prosperity and create jobs.

Congress is in charge of taxing, spending, and borrowing. It cannot escape this responsibility. But what about using public funds to bail out failed banks? And it's not just banks. Many businesses want subsidies. After the subsidies prove to be too little, they want bailouts.

Lobbyists are the primary facilitators of bailouts, subsidies, and special favors. Jack Abramoff's book *Capital Punishment*,[56] written after he served time in prison for doing the same things that are still going on in Washington today, describes the system that lobbyists use to get favors from Congress. This is a pervasively corrupt culture in which congressional votes are bought and sold for personal perks, traded votes, and campaign cash. This culture results from "careers" in politics. It should end.

Big Business Bailouts

Bailouts work, if you are the person getting the bailout. The question is this: Do bailouts work for the taxpayers who have to come up with the money to pay for bailouts?

In the debate over the huge bailout and stimulus packages, the public was overwhelmingly opposed.

The public had no say in the matter. The politicians didn't care what the public thought was the right thing to do. The politicians took this approach: We are going to do exactly what we want to irrespective of what our constituents want us to do because we think this is the best thing for us – personally – right now. And so they did.

Shortly after Obama took office, my opponent bragged about his support for a stimulus program and voted "yes" on four bailout, stimulus, and debt increase measures. On one such measure, his only "no" vote, he voted "yes" first and then "no" when the bill came up again. He voted "no" on that one because it gave less money than he wanted for the special interests that fund his campaigns and it lowered taxes.[11] He now advertises that he voted "no" on stimulus.

Who Is to Blame for Congressional Corruption?

The lobbyists ask Congress for things they should not receive, and Congress provides these things to them in exchange for campaign contributions and other perks. Who is the most to blame, Congress or the lobbyists and their clients? Lobbyists do not take an oath of office.

Congress is, by far, the most to blame. It is Congress that has been entrusted by voters with the money and power of government. It is congressmen who misuse this trust to serve their self interests. There will always be people, institutions, corporations, banks, and others who ask for things they should not receive. It is the job of Congress to say, "No."

After I am elected to Congress and a lobbyist comes to my office to make an inappropriate request, I will just politely turn him away.

After a few such sessions, the word will get around. Lobbyists will stop coming to my office. We will have more time for the people's honest business.

If you look over contributions to my campaign in 2010[5,6] and contributions to my opponent's campaign,[5,6] you will see that all of my support came from the contributions of private individuals and that the largest part of my opponent's support came from lobbyists, corporations, and other special interest sources. My opponent is a typical career politician in this regard (please see the earlier chapter on *Campaign Finance*). He improperly gives our money and governmental power to the clients of lobbyists, and they reward him with campaign contributions. His favors are to special interests that do most or all of their business outside Oregon.

Now, he is calling for higher taxes to pay for the stimulus, bailout, and deficit spending programs that he supported.

He is certainly not "independent as Oregon" as he claims. He is up to his ears in debt to the lobbyists.

Taxpayers Pay, Government Skims

Bailout and stimulus programs are not fair and, moreover, do not work. Under these programs, government spends money that it takes – now or later – from the private sector. Private economic activity therefore shrinks by an amount equal to increased government funded activity plus the costs of government.

> **"I contend that for a nation to try to tax itself into prosperity is like a man standing in a bucket and trying to lift himself up by the handle."** *Winston Churchill*

Bailout and "stimulus" activities are like taking a lot of water out of a swimming pool at one end, spilling some, and pouring the rest in the other end. The level of the water does not rise. The level – economic activity – actually falls by the amount lost to government waste and inefficiency.

Then there are the special-interest payments called "earmarks." An earmark is a grant of money to some project in a congressman's district. It does not require a separate law of its own. It is attached to a bill that may have little or nothing to do with the project.

Earmarks and "requested" earmarks are used by incumbent congressmen to buy votes by taking money from all of the people and giving it to a select few.

"Requested" earmarks are especially interesting. Only a very small percentage of the requested earmarks are actually funded, but voters for whom a congressman makes such "requests" (requests that are easily granted, since they cost nothing) – hoping that theirs will be among the funded – give him their support at election time.

Stimulus, bailout, pork barrel, and earmark appropriations are used to award taxpayer money to special interests in return for political favors. The current Congressman from Oregon District 4 receives large amounts of campaign cash from such businesses and special interests.[5,6]

Most people know little about this process. The recipients surely do. The recipients think, "It's free money from Washington." How do people expect these projects to be financed? There are three principal ways:

1. **Taxation**, which destroys private jobs

2. **Borrowing**, which raises debt and destroys jobs

3. **Money printing**, which destroys savings and jobs

Taxes on the Poor

Politicians are insisting that any new taxes will fall only on the "rich." They have been saying this for about a century. The income tax began in 1913, but a funny thing happened on the road to wealth redistribution. The rich are still rich. The great equality has not come to pass – not in the United States, and not anywhere else, either.

Here we are in 2012. If Congress could or wanted to really eliminate inequality, it would have done it – in 1970 or 1930. It hasn't. In fact, the inequality has increased. The prosperity of all income groups has increased with technological advance, but not because of Congress.

Taxing the rich to pay for the needs of the poor has been a popular promise for over 70 years. It is like Lyndon Johnson's war on poverty. Poverty is still around, isn't it? Yet in 1964, he promised to defeat poverty.[29]

We're still waiting.

In order to pay higher taxes, taxpayers must sell shares of their ownership of productive capital. As a result, there is less capital than before taxes were imposed even on the "rich." Actually, these taxes are imposed on just about everybody. Not only do they destroy jobs, but they are passed on to the public in higher costs of the things they buy.

The "rich" do not keep their money as piles of currency under their beds. Their wealth is invested in stocks, bonds, and other productive assets. The rich provide the capital necessary to build, maintain, and operate many of the businesses and industries that fund jobs for Americans. If there is less capital, then there are fewer jobs and businesses must raise their prices.

Do we want able-bodied workers on welfare or working in fulfilling careers? I prefer the latter. So do they.

Because politicians are generally unsuited to the wise use of money, a substantial part of government revenue is wasted, so there is a net loss of jobs – especially jobs for

> "Property is the fruit of labor . . . property is desirable . . . is a positive good in the world. That some should be rich shows that others may become rich, and hence is encouragement to industry and enterprise. Let not him who is houseless pull down the house of another; but let him labor diligently and build one for himself, thus by example assuring his own shall be safe from violence when built."
>
> *Abraham Lincoln*

poor and middle class workers. If left in private hands, that money would have supported more jobs.

The government can still borrow from abroad, although foreign countries are increasingly surly about this. They suspect the money will never be repaid.

Do we want the Chinese and other foreigners to own lots of our government's debt?[30] Do we want Chinese officials to dictate policy to our leaders, on threat of dumping these U.S. government IOUs?

Higher taxes, borrowing costs, and money printing all cause prices to rise. Price rises are far more harmful to the poor and middle class because their fewer dollars are more precious to them. The result is fewer jobs and higher prices, further impoverishing poor and middle class Americans.

It is especially cynical for millionaire career politicians like my opponent to proclaim, as he did at a Portland "Occupy" rally, that they are among the "99%." His political spending and borrowing is crushing the middle class and the poor. He is actually in the 0.001%, who seek to enslave the entire 100% in their quest for political power.

Big Spending, Big Deficits

Deficit-spending in Washington is putting the national budget in the red by about $1.3 trillion dollars *per year*. American voters favor a balanced budget.

Do congressman DeFazio's votes balance the budget? No. Instead, at taxpayer expense, he sends fliers to voters saying that he supports a Balanced Budget Amendment to the Constitution [31] – and then he votes for more deficit spending.

He knows that, even if such an Amendment is passed, the amendment process will take many years, until long after he has left Congress. He also knows that Congress already often ignores the Constitution. While a Balanced Budget Amendment, if carefully written, would be useful, it will surely not be passed in time to affect budgeting during the 2013-2014 congressional session.

The federal budget must be balanced, but it should not be balanced by imposing additional burdens on the backs of American workers. And, it should not be further unbalanced by vast political slush funds represented as "stimulus" and "bailout" programs. Neither should the budget be balanced by lowering payments to those who depend upon Social Security and other critical programs. (Please see the Chapter on *Balanced Budget and Taxation*.)

Government Grants

We all have our stories about the ill effects of government grants. In my world of science, there are many stories. Since the federal government has taken over most academic research in the United States, even our best scientists are now forced to rely primarily on federal grants.

This has followed a familiar pattern. Americans already had the finest scientific research system in the world. It was funded largely by private money. The government taxed away the private money and moved in to fund scientific research itself. Now government brags that, without its funding, scientific research would not take place.

Government funding causes research to be influenced by bureaucrats and research trends to be directed politically instead of by the best efforts of independent scientists.

Moreover, the scramble for grant funding resembles to a great extent the scramble for other funds from Congress, an increasingly dishonest and unethical activity that is not healthy for science, which must be based on truth.

Scientists are better off if their work is funded by private enterprise and by private contributions, as was generally the case prior to World War II. At the Oregon Institute of Science and Medicine, my colleagues and I do not apply for government grants. We are entirely funded by individual private contributions.

After the war, seeing the success of the Manhattan Project, many scientists thought more such funding might make possible great advances. This, with few exceptions, has not turned out to be the case.

Surely, one can point to many scientific discoveries that have since been made with funding from government grants because government has co-opted almost all nonindustrial research funding.

Research is now so heavily dependent on government funding that changing back to private support would be a long process. So, any changes must be carefully done.

The problem is that Congress has essentially bankrupted the federal government. This has plunged our nation into a series of financial crises, with no end in sight. So, one day soon, our scientists may wake up to find that they have no funds at all.

When I was a young scientist in the 1960s, most academic scientists were very conservative. This is the common sense attitude of people in science. Now, however, academic science has been largely dependent on government money for 50 years. So, most academic scientists are now liberal – and they are in a very precarious position.

If the academics are wise, they will start voting for more conservative congressmen because, if the financial mess in Washington is not soon fixed, their checks from Washington may abruptly stop coming.

Here is an example in which government grants almost improved your medical care, but then impeded it.

Beginning in 1968 and extending through 1978, my colleagues and I, including Linus Pauling, invented a field of research called "metabolic profiling" which holds enormous potential to improve both preventive and diagnostic medicine. This work was ahead of its time, so we had to build almost all of our own apparatus and use methods that were very difficult. The immediate practical use of our discoveries in medicine was impeded by this difficulty.

One day in 1971, a scientist from Stanford Research Institute, Dr. Bill Aberth, visited our laboratory at Stanford and told me that he and his colleagues had invented a new way to ionize molecular mixtures, which should make possible the first practical molecular ion mass spectrometer. He wondered if I knew of a use for such a machine that would justify funding to build it.

A molecular ion mass spectrometer ionizes, separates, and measures the amounts of substances in a sample, without breaking the molecules. It is a very fast and eco-nomical means of measuring the amounts of substances in complicated mixtures.

I suggested that we use Bill's machine as a metabolic profiling device. It would be much faster, more economi-cal, and perhaps far better than the methods we were then using. It might be so much better that our work could be of immediate use in practical medical applications.

Unfortunately, Linus and I were then still funded pri-marily by government grants, so that was the only source we could turn to for this money. Fortunately, however, there was an excellent scientist at the National Institutes of Health, Dr. Robert S. Melville, who arranged for us to receive the necessary government grant.

All went well. Bill built a superb spectrometer. But then difficulties developed with Bill's superior at Stanford Research Institute, Michael Anbar. Anbar wanted to dis-honestly take credit for our medical project, so he ruled that we could not run samples on Bill's device, which was located at SRI. Bob Melville intervened, however, so we were able to run 200 samples.

These samples tested the mass spectrometer's capabil-ity to diagnose breast cancer, multiple sclerosis, muscular dystrophy, and several other things. I designed the experi-ment with tasks that were so easy I knew it would succeed, but also with more difficult and more important examples.

After the samples were run, Laurelee and I spent about two months calculating the results. It took this long because the experiment completely failed. We knew this couldn't be true, but there it was. We had 200,000 data points that were no more valuable than random numbers.

Although we worked very hard, there was just no

Laurelee Robinson Works with Her PDP-11
Computer in the Linus Pauling Institute

information in the data. So, we abandoned the method. I was most surprised when Dr. Melville arranged generous funding for our later work on other research. The earlier failure had wasted a lot of money.

Years passed; work on profiling at the Pauling Institute ended; and we were working in Oregon. Dr. Melville, who had now retired from government, invited me to dinner at the Cosmos Club in Washington, D.C.

After dinner, when we were in his car, he hesitated; did not start the engine; and then, on that dark street in Washington, told me a remarkable story. He prefaced this by saying he considered it the only black mark against his career in Washington (where he had done excellent work).

He told me that, a little while after our 200-sample experiment failed, he received a letter from Michael Anbar admitting that he had secretly entered the laboratory and scrambled the labels on our 200 samples, thus destroying the experiment.

Further, Anbar's letter contained a code for unscrambling the samples. At about that time, Anbar had submitted a research paper using the spectrometer for a medical profiling experiment. He apparently wanted to slow us down, so that his work (pirating ours) reached the literature first.

Anbar acted very unethically. Scientists are people. There are more sad instances of their ethical failures than you might imagine. But he did write to Melville intending later to mitigate the damage. Neither of them, however, anticipated our government.

Dr. Melville said that, since the event was highly unusual, Anbar's letter was forwarded to his superiors, and, from there, it went to the very top of the National Institutes of Health bureaucracy. And, the bureaucrats ruled in their own self interests. Frightened that the incident might reflect poorly on them, they ordered Melville to destroy Anbar's letter and not tell us why our experiment failed.

"Did you destroy the letter?" I, of course, immediately asked. He replied that he might still have it. A year later, at his home, Bob Melville handed me a copy of Anbar's letter, including the code to unscramble the samples.

So, did we then unscramble the data and finally learn the results of the experiment? No, we couldn't. Therein lies another tale. An individual at the Pauling Institute had apparently intentionally destroyed all of the 250 magnetic tapes, many disk drive records, and 15 file cabinets of printed data from the entire 10 years of our work on metabolic profiling. Besides the mass spectrometry data, also destroyed were metabolic profiles of 1,000 newborn infants in which we discovered distinct types of individuals with potentially preventable health problems.

Several efforts were made in later years to investigate this in the hopes that some data still remained, but an administrative employee, with the help of lawyers, thwarted those efforts.

At present, in our research on metabolic profiling, we use exclusively a molecular ion mass spectrometer. This spectrometer is so advanced from the earlier model that I refer to it as a "miracle in a box." I am certain this technology will eventually make a great contribution to medicine.

The mass spectrometer we now use has a newer and better method of molecular ionization than the one that Bill Aberth and his colleagues invented. A Nobel Prize was given for its invention.

Had Bill's work not been lost in this remarkable series of events, Bill Aberth might have shared a Nobel Prize. There is no doubt that, had the experiment not failed, we would have devoted a major effort to improving Bill's technique. Who knows how far we would have progressed?

These events caused a great setback for research on the use of molecular ion mass spectrometry in medicine. Actions have consequences. Had mass spectrometric metabolic profiling developed as it should, it could have saved Laurelee's life in 1988, by getting her to surgery in time, and the lives of countless other people.

She died of a sudden illness that profiling could easily have detected and immediate surgery mitigated.

Deficit spending, bailouts, and stimulus spending should not be authorized by Congress. Congress should exercise common sense in its spending and should balance its budget.

16

ACADEMIC EXCELLENCE
IN PUBLIC SCHOOLS

*The powers not delegated to the United States by
the Constitution, nor prohibited by it to the States, are
reserved to the States respectively, or to the people.*
Amendment 10

If we do nothing else in America during the next two
years, we ***must*** get our education system back on track.
With the futures of the 50 million children now in school
at stake, this problem just will not wait!

Yet, everywhere we look the fat cats of "Big Education"
stand in the way of improving our schools.

> **I support state and local merit pay for teachers,
> teacher testing, tenure reform, vouchers, charter
> schools, education savings accounts, state waivers
> from federal rules, and getting the nose of Congress
> and its bureaucrats out of our local schools.**
>
> **Peter DeFazio voted against every one of these
> efforts to improve our schools except the last, which
> has not yet come up for a vote.**

Why did my opponent vote against state and local merit pay for teachers, teacher testing, tenure reform, vouchers, charter schools, education savings accounts, and state waivers from federal rules? He voted to please the congressionally-empowered education monopoly that controls American education. Their political power strongly influences congressional elections.

Fortunately, Congress passed the voucher measure for students in Washington, D.C. schools, the majority of whom are African American. The measure passed regardless of his "no" vote. As a result, high school graduation rates in D.C. increased among those students in the voucher program, while per-student costs were cut in half.[71]

Now, President Obama's new budget proposes to cancel this voucher program,[72] while raising the federal subsidy paid to buyers of General Motors "Volt" cars to $10,000.[73] Why are the educations of D.C. minority students less important than tax subsidies to wealthy buyers of "green" automobiles?

All across the United States, students attend schools that are, on average (based on standardized student exams), academically inferior to those in most of the developed world. This – in a nation that spends more than any other on education and once had the finest schools on earth!

I know education. I have been an educator all my life – tutoring other kids when I was in high school; teaching chemistry to 300 undergraduate students each year at the University of California at San Diego; teaching graduate students; educating my own six children – Zachary, Noah, Arynne, Joshua, Bethany, and Matthew Robinson – after my wife died; and originating an award-winning home school curriculum now used by more than 60,000 American students.

In 2008, our curriculum won an unprecedented seven first places in the most prestigious national home-school curriculum competition – based on the votes of mothers using it.

We have a scholarship program that has given away more than $600,000 dollars in educational materials to families with low incomes. Many other lower income families have benefited because our curriculum for an entire 12 years of education costs only $195 per family.

I know that our public schools can return to the world-class excellence that they once enjoyed. All we need to do is get big government off our teachers' and students' backs and out of our classrooms. Our public schools need to be returned to local control and to the excellence that mothers, fathers, and teachers want for children.

Our schools and our students need to be freed from Big Education – the self-serving national "teachers" unions, big businesses with whom they collaborate, and micromanaging congressionally-paid bureaucrats that now cause ever lower test scores and ever lower quality academic educations of our young people.

The Robinson Students and Education

In most home schools, the mother serves as a teacher. When Laurelee died, our six children were left without their teacher. We were fortunate to live on a wonderful Oregon farm, and I was able to be with them because I make our living in our research facility here. But, I did not have time to be their teacher.

So, together we worked out methods by which they

could teach themselves. These worked so well that we eventually made a rule that I would not teach at all.

Matthew says that I exaggerate this. He reports that I did help him – about once every two years. Since he was 18 months old when his mother died, he never experienced any academic education other than in this self-teaching home school.

Zachary: I was aware that the children were doing well, but this became especially evident when the oldest, Zachary, was about to enter college as a chemistry student at Oregon State University. Zachary learned about Advanced Placement exams shortly before the deadline and took a battery of these tests without preparation.

His scores were so high that he was admitted to OSU as a junior, skipping the first two years. Zachary attended OSU for one and one-third years over a two-year enrollment period and earned a BS in chemistry. Zachary then enrolled in Iowa State University, earning an MS in chemistry and a doctorate in veterinary medicine.

Noah: The second oldest, Noah, also skipped two years with advanced placement exams and entered the chemistry program at Southern Oregon University as a junior. He earned his BS in two years. He then entered Caltech as a graduate student and earned his PhD in chemistry from Caltech in the unusually short time of three years.

While they were going through school, both Noah and Zachary also did original research under the direction of Nobel Laureate R. Bruce Merrifield. Noah published a research paper with Merrifield, and Merrifield thought so much of him and his work that he bequeathed his laboratory equipment to Noah. It is now a part of our laboratory.

Arynne: The third oldest, Arynne, attended SOU

and then Bethel University in Minnesota, earning a BS in chemistry. She then earned a doctorate in veterinary medicine at Iowa State University. Like Zachary, she is now a practicing veterinarian.

Joshua and Bethany: Twins Joshua and Bethany earned BS degrees at Southern Oregon University, Joshua in mathematics and Bethany in chemistry. They then entered graduate school at Oregon State University, working to earn PhD degrees in nuclear engineering.

Both have excellent grades, have excellent examination performance, and carried out superb research at OSU.

Matthew: The youngest Robinson, Matthew, earned a BS in chemistry at Southern Oregon University in just two years and carried out published research at Caltech. Matthew was then offered $57,000 per year by MIT to support graduate work by him in chemistry at MIT. He decided to join his brother and sister in nuclear engineering at Oregon State University instead.

The six: The college and graduate school grades of these students have been truly exceptional, as have their SAT and GRE (SAT for graduate school) scores.

Noah's GRE scores were two perfect 800s and a 99th percentile in the third. Although he decided to attend Caltech, when he applied for graduate school, MIT told him that he was their top ranked applicant in chemistry. During his three years at Caltech, he published four papers in the *Proceedings of the National Academy of Sciences, USA.*

Matthew's GRE scores were higher than any other student who has ever attended the nuclear engineering graduate school at OSU.

Yet, none of the Robinsons, including their father and mother, are geniuses. These six students are all just ordinarily smart and very hard working students, who have been privileged to have an excellent environment in which to work and good instructional materials and examples.

Moreover, their six college educations and graduate school educations were paid for by money these six students earned themselves. They put each other through college and graduate school.

I have been delighted to watch as these six young people – in their farm and business work and in their academic accomplishments have exceeded my own. I wish that every American student could do similarly.

Every American child and young adult deserves the best educational opportunities our communities can provide. Our public schools must return to academic excellence. Home schooling is helping those families that can use it, but most American children are being left behind.

In Congress, I will work to overcome the power of the self-serving monopoly that has taken over our public schools, reduced their quality, and deprived most American young people of the opportunities that I enjoyed when I attended public schools.

The Founding Fathers and Education

What does the Constitution have to say about education? Nothing. Does this mean that the men who wrote it did not care about education? Hardly. Many were highly educated men – far better educated than those who occupy seats in Congress today. And, the Founding Fathers insisted that the young people for whom they were responsible be likewise.

In 1781, John Quincy Adams (who became the sixth

American president) received the following[65] in a letter from his father John Adams (who became the Second American President):

"I want to have you upon Demosthenes. The plainer Authors you may learn yourself at any time. I absolutely insist upon it, that you begin upon Demosthenes and Cicero. I will not be put by. You may learn Greek from Demosthenes and Homer as well as from Isocrates and Lucian – and Latin from Virgil and Cicero as well as from Phaedrus and Nepos.

"What should be the cause of the Aversion to Demosthenes in the World I know not, unless it is because his sentiments are wise and grand, and he teaches no frivolities. If there is no other Way, I will take you home and teach you Demosthenes and Homer myself."

John Quincy Adams *entered* Harvard four years later in 1785, already an accomplished classical scholar.

Even the Founding Fathers who had little formal education wrote such erudite letters that they cannot be equaled by most of our modern scholars.

The Founding Fathers did not write anything about education into the Constitution for a reason. Education was a personal and local matter, with colleges funded by donations and student tuition in most cases.

Education was obviously the responsibility of parents and the local communities. The Founders did not think that the federal government should have anything whatever to do with education. The 10th Amendment applied. This is not a federal concern.

Until recently, K through 12 education was still a local matter and American schools were excellent, as they had been for 200 years. But then Congress unconstitutionally put its nose under the schoolroom door. Not only did Congress create a federal bureaucracy under a "Department of Education," but it also passed legislation giving control of American schools to public employee "education" unions and associated corporate and other special interests.

In return, these special interests make sure that incumbent congressmen have plenty of campaign cash and plenty of campaign workers to keep them in office.

A good time was had by all, except for one thing.

They forgot about the students.

Academic standards began to plummet. The unions grew in power and membership – membership that includes so many administrators and non-teachers that less and less school funding actually reaches the classrooms.

Big Education took control, and local school boards found that they no longer controlled local schools. Moreover, this congressional-special interest partnership has invited in a third partner, corporations that supply "approved" text books and otherwise profit from this system.

> **"The contest for ages has been to rescue liberty from the grasp of executive power."**
> *Daniel Webster*

Today's big-government-empowered Big Education unions have hundreds of millions of dollars per year in dues with which to project their political power; to lobby congressmen; to advertise reasons why the unions should continue to run American schools; and to oppose efforts to improve the schools. DeFazio votes with the unions. They ignore the Constitution and even do their best not to teach it in the schools. Politically, they attempt to crush any candidate for office who does not toe their line.

Education is, however, a matter where results are the most essential aspect. The educational performance of 50 million American children and our country's future are riding on the academic quality of American schools.

Regardless of whether this congressional-union-corporate "Big Education" monopoly is appropriate; regardless of our views on big government; regardless of whether these people are politically corrupt; regardless of whether they empower literal armies of grossly overpaid administrators; and regardless of whether they use their power to promote a leftist political agenda – if those 50 million students were still scoring the highest in the world on academic tests, I would be very slow to challenge the current situation.

Meddling with the successful educations of 50 million children is not something that should be lightly done.

The problem is that these schools are academically failing. Since we lost our locally controlled schools – schools that have served our children well for many generations, we have seen the average academic quality of these schools collapse. This cannot be allowed to continue.

Surely, here and there across America there are still good public schools. Most people who go into teaching have idealistic objectives, and some of them succeed regardless of impediments. The problem is that, on average, American public schools are failing those 50 million students.

When I attended public school, American public schools were the best in the world as measured by student academic performance on standardized examinations. Those schools prepared me for Caltech, and Caltech prepared me for a wonderful life in science. I owe a great personal debt to the public schools.

Yet, the schools I attended no longer exist in most places. Now, average American schools, based on standardized academic tests, are among the worst in the developed world, and Oregon schools are among the worst in the U.S.

To be sure, our schools are more than just academic institutions. They are centers of social life, sports, and a cornucopia of other community activities. But public enthusiasm for these activities masks a terrible flaw.

These schools are cutting our young people off at the knees academically just at a time when they need the best education they can get in order to compete with young people in other countries who are rising technologically and economically.

Real educators throughout America are not just worried about this – they are furious!

There is nothing that enrages a true educator more than the waste of a single student mind, and American educators are watching in horror while literally millions of young minds are wasted.

Michael P. Farris in *The Wall Street Journal*,[57] reported that, on a battery of tests in reading, listening, language, math, science, social studies, and study skills, where public school students scored an average of 50th percentile, home schooled students scored between the 80th and 87th percentiles, with an overall score of 85th percentile.

On reading tests, the home schooled whites, Hispanics, and African Americans all scored at the 87th percentile, while in math, home schooled whites were at the 82nd percentile and the minorities at the 77th percentile.

In the tax-financed public schools, however, in reading tests whites scored 57th, while African Americans

Dr. Zachary, Sarah, and Lydia Robinson

Zachary earned a BS in chemistry from Oregon State University in just two years and a DVM (doctorate) in veterinary medicine from Iowa State University. He and his wife Sarah now provide veterinary services in Josephine County, Oregon.

and Hispanics both scored 28th. In math, whites scored 58th, while Hispanics scored 29th and African Americans scored 24th. There have been other batteries of such tests, with different numbers – but the overall qualitative results are similar to these.

So, in home schools, the white students and the minority students all did equivalently well. There was no difference between the races. But in the public schools, minority students were badly left behind, and even the majority students performed far below the home schooled students.

Imagine the howls of racism and child abuse that would be heard from the public schools and their unions if these scores for home schools and public schools were reversed. They would demand that home schooling be ruled a racist, child abusing felony. When I read this, my reaction was more mild. I wrote that these failing schools should be abolished.

This situation is child abuse, and it should be abolished – not by closing the schools, but by removing the federal and special interest influences that have made our schools this way. In the 1960s and 1950s and before, America had the best schools in the world. On academic tests, American students always scored, on average, at the top. Now, American scores are consistently at the bottom.

And the cost? Public school costs in 1997 were $5,325 per student year compared with $546 per student year in home schools, excluding, in both cases the capital costs of the buildings where the students were taught. In 2012, the average public school cost is more than $10,000 per student year; the federal government is far more involved; and the educational situation is, predictably, even worse.

Over the past decade, I have spoken with a great many African American and Hispanic mothers who use our curriculum for their children. Their children do as well as white children. These mothers are absolutely determined that their children will have the best possible education with which to rise above their, on average, poorer economic circumstances. These mothers make many sacrifices to keep their children away from the public schools.

Other minority parents try to get their children into better schools. They want school choice and vouchers that allow their children to select their school. Yet politicians,

Dr. Noah Robinson

Noah earned his BS in chemistry at Southern Oregon University in two years and his PhD at Caltech in 3 years. He is a very brilliant scientist. His research work is widely respected throughout the world. Noah has also led his family's work to produce curriculums and books for elementary education – family businesses that earned the money needed for their university educations.

including my opponent,[28] pandering to the education unions, even vote against school choice and vouchers for minority students in Washington, D.C. in order to get Big Education support at election time.

Many voters have seen my opponent's TV advertisements from the 2010 election that feature an out of context video clip of me saying that the schools should be abolished. This video is taken from a luncheon presentation that I co-presented with astronaut and former Senator Harrison Schmitt, a Caltech educated scientist like me.

When Dr. Schmitt spoke with alarm about the lack of

well-educated U.S. engineers for future space programs and the academically failing public schools that have arisen from unconstitutional congressional actions, I then told the audience about an experience I had 10 years before. In answer to a question when I was speaking to a large audience of Maine state legislators on a different subject, I said that these failing schools should be abolished.

The response of these legislators was electric – a long standing ovation. An outside observer might have concluded that all of the people in the room were ready to vote to close the schools. I went on to say that, of course, no one in that room in Maine would have voted to close the schools – but the incident showed how furious we all were about this seemingly intractable problem.

So, the DeFazio advertisement is actually an out-of-context clip of me quoting myself from 10 years earlier. I have made other similar strong statements about the tragic academic state of many U.S. schools. If, however, my life's work in education and my writings and speeches are reported in context, one could only conclude that I am very, very concerned about the problems in our schools, and I want these problems fixed.

What I want abolished is the current reprehensible monopolistic Big Education system in which people seeking power, money, and position have converted America's wonderful locally controlled public schools into bureaucratically and politically controlled big government schools that academically neglect the students.

If I am elected to Congress, I will work to return public schools to local control, to take away the power of the special interests that have academically ruined our schools, and to make sure that every student who attends

Dr. Arynne Robinson and Friend

Arynne earned a BS in chemistry from Bethel University and a DVM (doctorate) in veterinary medicine from Iowa State University. She is shown here with one of her sheep, before attending veterinary school. She is now a practicing veterinarian.

our schools is better prepared academically than students anywhere else in the world. Anyone who studies my work in education would expect nothing less.

School Costs in Oregon

Tax funding for Oregon schools costs, on average, about $10,000 per student per academic year. Do the math. A classroom of 30 students costs $300,000. That is for eight to nine months of actual classroom instruction.

Question: Do you know a teacher who has a salary of $300,000? No? How about $150,000? What's that? The typical school teacher doesn't even earn $150,000 a year? Are you sure? Question: If not, where did the rest of the money go?

A large part of the $10,000 per student is not reaching the classroom. It's going for administration and the enrichment of government-empowered special interests.

What if all of that money went directly to the teacher?

Imagine handing one of our thousands of good teachers a check for $300,000 and 30 students, with the request that she teach them for a year.

The teacher could rent the best room in town, hire an assistant, buy everything the students need, fully fund all extracurricular activities, raise her own salary, and have lots of money left over.

The teacher could, of course, do this more efficiently in a school with other teachers. Maybe she would decide to pool her money with a few other teachers and start one.

This single-teacher example merely illustrates that education resources are more than sufficient – if the resources go to the classroom. I don't propose that it be done in this way.

If the schools were under local control, rather than central government and special interest control, the local school board would assure that the resources do go to the classroom. The local school boards would also provide reasonably paid administrators.

After World War II, my uncle taught school in Iowa. In addition to teaching a full load of classes, he was given a few dollars extra to be the superintendant of schools. The local farmers made sure that their taxes went directly to

Joshua and Fama Robinson with their sons Joseph,
Jonathan, Daniel, and Caleb

Joshua earned a BS in mathematics from Southern Oregon University and then entered Oregon State University to earn a PhD in nuclear engineering. His MS, pre-PhD work at OSU was recognized by the Distinguished Master's Thesis award, for the best MS work in his class.

the classrooms and that activities in the classrooms were those that they wanted for their children.

My mother was a public school teacher in Iowa in the 1930s before the government and union enforced "credentialization" we have now prevented many superb teachers from teaching in the schools. She had just a two-year college education at Iowa State University.

I benefited from her teaching in a special way. After I started school in the first grade when I was five years old, she checked my developing reading skills by having me read to her from my school books. One day, however, her gentle voice said, "Arthur, today let's read from another book I have that is at about your level."

Caught! I couldn't read at all. I had been memorizing the books instead of learning to read. You can probably imagine that life for the next few weeks was a little different in our home, while she made certain that I could read.

Looking through the books and examinations used in my mother's classrooms during that era provides a depressing contrast to the present. It shows how far school academic standards have fallen.

I have a keepsake. It is *A Child's History of England* by

Zelma Robinson

Photograph of my mother when she was teaching school in Iowa.

Bethany Robinson and Misty with Nephew Joseph.

Bethany Robinson completed her home school education, including calculus, at the age of 14. She earned a BS in chemistry from Southern Oregon University and then entered Oregon State University to earn a PhD in nuclear engineering.

Charles Dickens. It is inscribed "Zelma Brouhard, January 6, 1924" in my mother's childhood handwriting. She was then 12 years old.

I doubt that there are many high school students in Oregon, much less 12-year-olds, who would be willing to read this book and stand examination on it. I would have trouble doing so myself. Yet, this was the educational standard of the ordinary people who built our country.

We must restore our schools to excellence, no matter how difficult, no matter how painful, no matter what personal sacrifices that we need to make!

Reversing Educational Decline

We tend to forget what went on in the classroom back when we were children. We remember the highlights of our extracurricular activities, but we do not remember much about the day-to-day activities in the classroom.

U.S. scholastic aptitude test performance has dropped substantially since the 1960s. The administrators of the test redesigned it several times in order to make performance look better. It didn't work. The students do not perform as highly as students did 20 years ago or 30 years ago. They surely don't perform as they did 40 years ago.

The school teachers do their best with the resources and rules available, yet performance declines as resources increase. Is this peculiar? The more money put into the schools, the poorer the performance of the students.

It is not my business to tell school boards what to do to solve local problems – and it surely will not be my business after I go to Congress. Nor would I be obeying my oath of office if I used the authority entrusted to me to empower unions and other special interests to run local schools.

The 10th Amendment of the Constitution prohibits congressional involvement in the schools.

A vast federal bureaucracy and the numerous special-interest organizations Congress empowers now stand between our students and our teachers. This should end.

All aspects of a student's upbringing are the responsibility of the student's parents and any professional the parents engage. Discipline in schools is a local matter.

Together, parents and their community should provide the students with the best possible academic opportunities. This effort must not be imperiled by those who use education for their own purposes, rather than for the students.

Matthew Robinson

Matthew earned a BS in chemistry from Southern Oregon University in just two years. He worked at Caltech and the Oregon Institute of Science and Medicine, carrying out now-published research on Alzheimer's and Parkinson's diseases. Then, turning down a $57,000 per year fellowship to MIT, he entered Oregon State University to earn a PhD in nuclear engineering.

Americans have responded to the deterioration of their schools by providing more and more tax money, but more money has not worked. Much of their money never reaches the students or the teachers. It funds a literal army of non-teachers, administrators, and federal, state, and local bureaucrats (and the corporate interests they favor), who generally spend their time making life miserable for the teachers and interfering with their efforts to teach.

American schools should be returned to local control and to the high standards that prevailed in the past.

Home Schooling

In the 1950s when our schools were under local control, there was very little home schooling in America, because there was no demand for it. There are now an estimated 3 million young people being home schooled in the U.S. This is about 6% of American K through 12 students.

Home schooling is not new. Many outstanding people have been home schooled, including Thomas Edison and Abraham Lincoln.

While home schooling was rare in the 1950s and 1960s, it began to grow as local and parental control of public schools was pushed aside; Big Education took over; and the quality of public schools began to deteriorate. Regardless of the best efforts of hundreds of thousands of good teachers in the schools, this trend could not be reversed.

Two things have driven the rise of the home school movement. First, academic quality. Parents, finding that they could no longer obtain a good academic education for their children in many public schools, moved their children's education into their homes.

Second, as the schools have fallen under political control, classrooms increasingly are used for political purposes. The three R's, reading, writing, and arithmetic, have begun to take a back seat in favor of all sorts of political and social engineering.

As part of "social" education and using the "separation of church and state" as an excuse, some public schools have moved from a neutral stance on Christianity to an openly hostile stance, which many parents do not want for their children.

Indeed, those in Big Education who control the public schools constantly claim that home schooled students lack "socialization" skills. Yet, home schooled students have excellent social skills, especially since they spend much more time with their families and adults.

By "socialization" skills, the Big Education controllers of our public schools mean social skills subservient to their own political and social agendas. These agendas are hidden in all sorts of ways. For example, the learning of so-called "critical thinking" skills is currently popular. Much of this is actually the teaching of "group think" habits and a selected political outlook.

As public schools return to local control, academic quality will improve, the local values of parents and communities will return to the schools, and home schooling will probably diminish.

Restoring Local Control

In Congress, I will support the elimination of congressional influence on public education. It is unconstitutional and unwise for Congress and the special interests it empowers to influence our schools. I support local control of public education. The 10th Amendment to the Constitution leaves education entirely to the states and the people.

But what about funding? The schools currently depend upon federal, state, and local funding. Harm might be done by changing this abruptly. Obviously, any change in sources of funding should be as gradual as necessary to avoid disruption.

What will happen to Oregon's schools if federal control diminishes? I have an answer: they will get better. Local control will guarantee this.

Local control is close to the parents, where real concern

for the student lies. Also, local control places our school districts in competition with each other for academic excellence, so students benefit.

Improvement of our public schools can't wait. It cannot be neglected in hopes that some new government plan will gradually improve the schools over the coming decades. The 50 million children in these schools now will not have a second chance at some future date.

The schools must markedly improve. These improvements must be immediate. Schools must improve. Now!

Higher Education

Beyond high school, U. S. private and public universities are functioning far below their potential.

Our universities have compensated for deterioration in the public schools by watering down their own curricula. The colleges must also compensate for the lowered work ethic taught in the federally controlled public schools.

Americans tend now to say that the students who do well are "smart." Asians, by contrast, say that the students who do well "work hard." Guess which students, Americans or Asians, have the highest average academic performance?

When Matthew was taking his Advanced Placement examinations at a local public high school, he was something of a phenomenon. He took exams in most of the available subjects and had high scores. When I was waiting for him there one day, a school administrator noticed me and asked if I needed help. When I told her I was waiting for Matthew, she responded, "Oh yes. He is the smart one."

Matthew is a talented young man as are most American young men. His AP scores were the result of 12 years of academic hard work. Too many young Americans never realize their potential because of the – reversible – deterioration of their schools. This *must* be corrected.

And, as in the public schools, our minorities suffer hidden discrimination in the watered down university environment that is claimed to be there to help them. When they enter the universities from inferior public schools, they find academic standards that keep them behind.

When I was teaching a class of 300 chemistry students at the University of California at San Diego, one evening several graduate students and I were eating in a local restaurant. During our meal, a tall, formidable African American man joined us at the table. He knew some of the students.

As the conversation commenced, it was clear that he and I were from very different worlds. His "Black Power" "Third World" rhetoric dominated the discussion. It turned out that he also was a professor at UCSD – in the "Third College" that had recently been opened for minority students. (It did not yet have a name.)

Eventually, the talk turned to education. I stated that I paid no attention whatever to the races of my students and not much to their educational backgrounds. My goal was for all of them to thoroughly learn chemistry, which they must know for the science majors they had declared.

In addition to directing the laboratories and course content, I gave 3 lectures per week to the 300 students. Also, after dinner every evening 5 days per week, I went to the lecture hall and answered questions for as long as the students wished. These nightly tutorials were usually attended by about 50 students and lasted about 3 hours.

Mine was the rigorous course. There was also another chemistry course that the students could take. This one was advertised as adapted to the "special needs" of students from poorer quality academic backgrounds.

At the mention of my course, the African American professor became immediately agitated.

He said, "That's right. Yours is a very tough course. I know because I'm tutoring two students in your course. You are exactly right!

"Our worst enemies are these white liberals who come over to the Third College and teach watered down courses to our students – and turn them into permanent second-class citizens!"

Things have gotten worse since then. Now, beginning with government-controlled public schools and extending through the colleges that cater to them, American education is turning too many American students of all races into "permanent second-class citizens."

Our university graduate schools are therefore filling up with foreign students who are better prepared. I even know of one top scientist at a major university who does not take on American graduate students at all. He finds that they don't work as hard and are more poorly prepared.

One part of the immigration debate involves American high-tech companies that want immigration quotas eased for well-educated foreign students. There are not enough qualified American students to fill their needs.

Americans can no longer live on the momentum of our nation's past accomplishments. In part by following the earlier American example, billions of the world's people are lifting themselves from poverty and joining in world competition at all levels – including academic excellence.

Young Americans must compete in this new world. It is a tragic irony that, just as hundreds of millions of competitors using our methods of excellence are arising, our own educational system is abandoning those methods.

Funding Our State Universities

Oregon State University, located in Oregon District 4, serves as an example of government control. This university receives more than $180 million in federal research dollars each year,[66] including approximately $30 million as direct earmark funding from the incumbent congressmen during the last 2-year congressional session. By comparison, OSU private funding for research is now less than $6 million.[66] The school also gets money from politicians for education.

Is it any surprise, therefore, that in the 2010 election, OSU facilities and personnel were used in favor of the incumbent congressional candidate in District 4 and against the challenger? OSU courses often contain partisan political content, even in science courses. OSU has become a partisan political institution, which can lead to serious injustices to students.

By contrast, the California Institute of Technology receives only about half of its funds from public sources. The other half is supported by income from Caltech's endowment, which partially mitigates the political effects.

Oregon State University and the University of Oregon, which are both in Oregon District 4, are very important institutions. Both universities would, however, be much better off if they were not completely dependent upon politicians for their immediate existence.

Very large independent endowments should be built for both universities. These could be built with both public and private funds, but then be administered by the universities without political control.

Oregon State University and the University of Oregon will not be free of partisan political influences until they are independently endowed. Independent endowment from private and public sources should be their principal financial goal.

Public education, from first grade to university graduate schools should be independent of political influence.

I advocate the restoration of local control over public education. I am sure that this will restore the high-quality education that existed when I attended school. I also support merit pay for teachers, teacher testing, tenure reform, vouchers, charter schools, education savings accounts, state waivers from federal rules, curriculum reform, and all other common-sense ideas to improve the schools.

To be sure, not all localities will immediately achieve excellence. Those that do will win out in the competition, and the others will emulate their ways. This will be much better than central control from Washington, whereby the mediocrity and failures of those who control the schools harm the academic educations of all the students.

Robinson Students at OSU

Our family can certainly attest to political influence in schools. The "mind set" of many "educators" has drifted far from traditional goals.

The academic accomplishments of my six children became an issue in the 2010 campaign for Congress. It was more difficult for my opponent to misrepresent my educational credentials when all of my children were academic successes.

Everywhere DeFazio looked, there were Robinsons with doctorates from Caltech and Iowa State University or earning doctorates at Oregon State University.

At first, some OSU public resources were improperly used in minor partisan attacks on my candidacy.

Later, however, the educational experiences of Joshua, Bethany, and Matthew, the three Robinson graduate students at OSU, were turned upside down. All three Robinson students were targeted in highly unusual ways. They were all working independently. The only thing they had in common was that all three had the same father. Their last names were all Robinson.

All three, regardless of their excellent course work, examination, and research performance became the targets of a dishonorable and unprincipled effort by a few people to stop their work and deny them their PhD degrees.

Moreover, senior nuclear engineering professor and President of the OSU Faculty Senate, Professor Jack Higginbotham, was blackballed at OSU as a result of his efforts to rescue them.

The actions against these students have diminished somewhat, but they are still being treated more shabbily than I have ever heard of students being treated in any other American academic institution.

For example, Joshua is now completing his thesis work, in which he has built a unique, award-winning addition to the OSU nuclear reactor facility. Yet, all of his OSU financial support has been cut off, access to his equipment is continually interfered with by a hostile administrator, and he has had to find his own funding for expensive parts that he is installing to improve the reactor facility.

Some progress has been made as a result of very unusual actions on the students' behalf by Professor Higginbotham and by the new Dean of the OSU Graduate School.

An outpouring of public support for the students and Professor Higginbotham made the rescue of the students possible. I was sorry to have to make these matters public, and only did so when I learned that Joshua and Professor Higginbotham were in immediate danger of permanent dismissal without cause from OSU.

A Return to Excellence in Public Education

The 10th Amendment of the Constitution clearly leaves all authority over public education to the states and the people. There should be no federal control over public education, and Congress should not pass laws that give powers to special interests, so that those interests can improperly influence public education.

American public schools were once the best in the world. These schools were under local control, as had been traditional ever since the advent of local one-room schools.

The decline of local control of the schools has caused a decline in the academic quality of the schools. Full local control should be re-established, and all involvement of Congress should end.

Our schools *must* be returned to their former academic excellence.

17

BALANCED BUDGET AND TAXATION

All bills for raising revenue shall originate in the House of Representatives; but the Senate may propose or concur with Amendments as on other bills.
                                        Article I, Section 7

We are constantly told that our country is a "democracy." Actually, it is a Constitutional Republic that uses the method of democracy in a special way. While we choose our representatives by democratic vote, the things that

> Congress must balance the federal budget. The budget can be balanced and taxes lowered, while still meeting our obligations to key federal programs.
>
> We must end over-regulation and over-taxation, so our economy improves and federal income rises; see that funding goes directly to Social Security, Medicare, the Defense Department, Veterans, and other essential programs without depletion by agencies, bureaucrats, and other middlemen inside and outside government; avoid lavish new government programs; end inflation of the currency; and conduct all federal expenditures with common sense.

those representatives are permitted to do are sharply limited by the Constitution. This is designed to give us a small government, where liberty and justice for each individual citizen stand above government.

The Founding Fathers greatly feared unbridled democracy, which had failed in every historical instance in which it had been tried. It had always led to big government tyranny. So, they gave us a Constitutional Republic, which incorporates democracy, but prohibits the use of democracy to destroy liberty and justice.

Congress has damaged liberty and justice by misuse of congressional power. Politicians establish different advantages for different special interests. They are not bashful about this. Career politicians say that they "pick winners and losers." Guess which group sends them money at election time.

> **"When the people find that they can vote themselves money, that will herald the end of the republic."**
> *Benjamin Franklin*

Many of our nation's problems are the result of Congress acting beyond its constitutional authority to create a government with powers not granted to it in the Constitution.

When you go to work, you trade your time and labor for capital. The capital is paid to you in money. Corrupt politicians trade favors and public money for capital. They favor those who pay the most.

Career Politicians Buy Votes

When a career politician goes to work, he buys votes. Yes, he is paid a wage, but if he is not re-elected, he loses his job. So, he buys votes. How does he buy votes? With our money.

> **"Government is the great fiction, through which everybody endeavors to live at the expense of everybody else."**
> *Frédérick Bastiat*

The career politician votes to collect taxes. We pay these taxes. The money flows into the government's bank account. Then the politician votes to spend our money in such a way as to maximize his votes at the next election. Citizen legislators, who do not seek "careers" in politics, are much less likely to do this. I will never do it.

Congress buys votes. The president buys votes. Some voters vote in order to elect politicians who promise to take property from others and give it to them. They often do not think about the fact that their property is no safer than that of everyone else.

Most Americans, if they understand the issues, will vote to retain constitutional liberties. They will not vote to get benefits for themselves at the expense of others.

We do vote for many useful things, such as police to protect us from criminals who would take our lives, liberty, or property and a military to defend our country. Congress, however, has developed out-of-control spending habits now far beyond the realm of common sense.

Spending tax money to buy votes has become a way of life for those who build personal power in Washington.

Our career politicians have drifted into a strange world in which they spend money we do not have – on our "behalf."

In the real world, those people who do not live within their budgets eventually go bankrupt. Big-spending politicians have taken our country to the brink of bankruptcy. The money they spend doesn't belong to them – except for the high salaries, lavish benefits, and ultra-comfortable retirements that they have voted for themselves.

Government has no capital that it did not take from the people. Governments obtain their wealth from people who produce things. This involves taxing, borrowing, or, in this age of fiat currency, printing money – another form of taxation that targets those who save by reducing the value of their savings.

With taxes so high that they are already choking our economy and destroying our jobs, Washington politicians continue to borrow and spend enormous sums of money. They have actually borrowed, in our names and using us as collateral, about $15 trillion and accumulated promised obligations exceeding $50 trillion more.

This amounts to about $650,000 of debt for every American family. How long will it take the average American family to save $650,000 in order to repay this money? Our children and even our grandchildren will need to work, save, and go without for their entire lives to do so – yet Congress is still borrowing more.

These debts are so high that our creditors no longer believe that they will ever be repaid and are becoming unwilling to continue lending. Already, the United States has lost its top credit rating and has a long way to fall.

Yet, the federal budget can be balanced without incurring more debt, while still paying for national defense,

Social Security, Medicare, veterans' benefits, and other essential programs. Social Security payments and the Veterans Administration budget should actually be increased, since both have lagged behind price inflation.

This situation is not hopeless, but it will not be corrected by the same people who caused the problem. They are simply unable to change their ways. Incredibly, Congressman DeFazio is now, in the middle of an ongoing economic crisis, calling for higher taxes, more borrowing, and more spending – the very policies that have caused this crisis and destroyed millions of American jobs.

> **"No pecuniary consideration is more urgent than the regular redemption and discharge of the public debt; on none can delay be more injurious, or an economy of time more valuable."**
> *George Washington*

The budget can be balanced. We can even *increase* Social Security payments, which have fallen far behind inflation, provide good medical care for seniors, and *fully fund* the Veterans Administration, which is now underfunded. These programs lag far behind the increased cost of living. We can do this while at the same time becoming once again a fiscally responsible nation.

Instead of balancing the budget, however, big-spending politicians claim that their opponents will cut funding to the elderly and veterans if we don't allow them to remain in office and tax, borrow, and spend more – a tactic they use during every election in order to frighten voters.

Remove the Government's Middlemen

The budget can be balanced by reducing and, where possible, eliminating a large part of the vast government bureaucracy and numerous federal agencies that are attached to the federal budget. These agencies – which were not present during most of American history – do not create or produce anything. The legitimate duties of these agencies can be met by new, much smaller entities.

The current agencies take resources and wealth away from the American people, including workers and employers, while creating road blocks to businesses who want to create jobs and companies that are struggling to remain in America and still be financially viable.

The vast government bureaucracy and its favored special interests waste enormous amounts of money needed to protect our senior citizens and other essential programs.

With the money now allotted to Social Security, Medicare, and other programs for seniors, a lot more money could be sent directly to every senior. Seniors could then buy better health insurance and have much better lives. The bureaucracy that wastes their money is not needed.

Americans have varied opinions about how their children should be educated and their seniors cared for in the distant future. There is no disagreement, however, about the present and immediate future. Our 50 million school children and 50 million seniors have been promised certain benefits. Today's citizens have adjusted their plans in terms of these promises. These obligations must be met, and with dollars that are fully adjusted for price increases.

Yet the federal budget must be balanced if we are to avoid default and national bankruptcy, which would destroy both funding for seniors and funding for the schools.

(While public schools should be locally controlled, federal funding must continue until otherwise replaced by state and local governments.) This is achievable if we simply reduce the bureaucrats, agencies, and special interests that are wasting the money designated for the children, seniors, and veterans – and follow this principle throughout our government.

Instead, entrenched politicians call for higher taxes "on the rich." The actual situation is the reverse. The high level of overall taxation that these politicians have already instituted is actually regressive, hurting the poor far more than it hurts the affluent. More taxes hurt more.

For example, politicians constantly call for higher taxes on oil companies. Since the profit of oil companies per gallon of gasoline is only a few cents, higher taxes must be passed on to customers in the form of higher prices. Who is hurt most by higher prices? The poor. It is the poor who have fewer dollars to spend that are hurt the most.

In addition, higher taxes destroy jobs, especially the jobs of poorer Americans. The upper middle class – the so-called "rich" – possess capital that funds American business and industry. When they are forced to sell their assets in order to pay taxes, these resources are lost from the economy, and the jobs that they supported are lost.

How Much Taxation Makes Common Sense?

The people with high incomes pay most of the taxes in the United States. They pay a higher percentage of income taxes, because the income tax system is graduated. In each of the tax brackets, there is a different tax rate. The more income you make, the higher bracket you're in and the higher tax percentage you pay. We are all familiar with this.

Test yourself on how much you know about the income tax system. Let's say that you define rich people as those people who are in the top 10% as far as income received. Ninety percent of Americans receive less money, on average, than people in this top bracket. What percentage of all the money collected by the federal government from the income tax do you think the top 10% of income-receiving Americans pay?

This is not a trick question. I want you to commit yourself mentally to a figure. I want you to say, if these people are in the top 10%, they ought to pay xx% of all income taxes. You want everybody to pay his fair share. So, what would you regard as a fair share percentage of all the money that the federal government collects from income tax. Write down a figure. Or, if you don't want to write it down, make a mental estimate. What percentage did you decide on? Nobody will know except you.

Would you say the top 10% should pay half or 50% of all the money collected by the federal government from the income tax? You think that would be fair? In other words, the top 10% should pay the same total amount of money as the other 90% pay to the federal government?

Would you be willing to teach your children that this is a fair way to collect taxes? Would you teach them that if 90% of the voters ganged up on 10% of the voters, it's legitimate for them to tell the 10% that they ought to reach into their bank accounts and come up with half the money? Do you think that would be fair?

What is the actual percentage? In the year 2009, the top 10% of all income earners in the United States paid not 50%, but 70% of all the money collected by the federal government from the income tax. This is a matter of public record.[32]

When someone tells you that the budget can be balanced, and expenditures can go up for lots of wonderful projects, if only the federal government would tax the rich, ask the person where the rich will get the money. What assets will they sell?

What is their incentive to work hard and take risks if they're going to be taxed so heavily that the top 10% winds up paying 90% of all money collected from the income tax. In any case, what is the evidence that the extra money collected from the rich will be sufficient to reduce significantly the budget deficit of more than $1 trillion. In fact, *tax rate increases* beyond a certain point *yield less revenue* for government.

> **"The moment the idea is admitted into society that property is not as sacred as the law of God, and there is not a force of law and public justice to protect it, anarchy and tyranny commence.**
>
> *John Adams*

There is no government revenue when the tax rate is 0%. As the tax rate rises, government revenue increases. When, however, the tax rate is 100%, government revenue is again 0%. There is no incentive to work. The laborer is not allowed to keep anything that he is paid.

So, revenue starts at 0%, rises to a maximum, and then falls back to 0% as the tax rate increases from 0% to 100%. When the tax rate is beyond the maximum of the curve, more taxes yield less revenue. The total of federal, state, and local taxes today is about 50%. This is beyond the maximum of the curve, so a higher tax rate will yield less revenue. Similarly, a lower tax rate will yield more revenue.

This paradoxical but true economic reality has been demonstrated several times in the American economy. When tax rates were lowered, overall tax revenue increased. Critics say otherwise, but they cite only inapplicable special cases. See *The End of Prosperity* by Arthur Laffer for a detailed explanation of this subject.[58]

Actually, the situation is even worse than this because of the regulatory tax. Workers and employers are required to spend a lot of their capital and time satisfying government regulations. This, too, is a tax. A very large one.

So, if tax rates are raised, a larger percentage of income will be transferred to government where it will be spent less wisely. And, total tax revenue – money received by the government – will drop because of the disincentive to earn.

My opponent is telling the voters he wants to "tax the rich." He should know very well that this will decrease federal revenue, destroy jobs, and hurt the voters.

"Tax the rich" is not an economic policy, it is an election gimmick to get votes. He is pandering to those voters who are envious of the rich. He poses as an enemy of the rich to get votes.[75] Remarkably, DeFazio himself is a millionaire. Do you really think that he plans to pay more taxes?

It is not common sense to raise taxes and thereby reduce government revenue. People dependent on government revenue for Social Security, Medicare, education, veterans benefits, and other programs will be hurt if revenue falls. Politicians know this. They think claiming to "tax the rich" will help them to remain in office.

If the government cannot balance the budget based

on taxation now, why do we think that it will balance the budget in the future? If Congress cannot balance its budget today, then one of these days lenders will look at the inability of the government to make its interest payments without more borrowing. They will recognize that the government is borrowing the money that it is using to repay earlier lenders. This is called a Ponzi scheme. Ponzi schemes eventually collapse. There are no exceptions.

Balancing the Budget

The federal budget can be balanced without decreasing essential expenditures. The 50 million seniors, the veterans, and 50 million school children that depend upon federal, state, and local funding need not be shortchanged.

To avoid government bankruptcy the budget must be balanced. Otherwise, those 50 million seniors, 50 million children, veterans, and all sorts of other people who are now depending upon government will be in real trouble.

The exact laws that must be passed to balance the budget when I get to Congress can take many forms.

Since I propose to cast votes on these issues, voters need to know how I think about this problem. Here is a list of specific actions that would greatly help to balance the budget.

1. Over-regulation and over-taxation of American individuals, businesses and industries should end. This will release private capital to fund increased economic activity, more jobs, and more money for everyone, including the government.

This involves reducing the number of unneeded bureaucrats the government employs and agency activities it carries out. Most regulatory agencies should be sharply reduced in size.

These agencies do many things that the Constitution leaves to the states and the people. These agencies did not exist during most of American history. Today, they empower and employ millions of bureaucrats whose regulatory actions make life miserable for those who wish to do business and create jobs in the United States.

The Department of Education and the Department of Energy should be closed. Both have entirely failed to solve the problems they were created to address and have, in fact, made those problems much worse.

Restoration of American liberty through reining in the agencies would be more effective than the largest tax cut in American history and would simultaneously cause a great increase in federal income. Not only would we save hundreds of billions of dollars of agency costs, the diminishing of their regulatory burden would revive our economy.

2. The government should get entirely out of the energy business, except for maintaining a small oversight group to make sure that safe practices in energy production are followed. Government subsidies of energy companies and federal impediments to energy companies should end. This will allow private industry to eliminate dependence on imported energy and close much of the trade deficit.

3. The capital gains tax should be eliminated. This tax causes extensive misallocation of American resources and wastes job-producing capital. This tax destroys jobs and capital by taxing illusory gains that are largely just inflationary price increases.

4. Budget-busting new programs, including socialized medicine, unnecessary military activity, stimulus pro-

grams, and other government-expanding schemes should be avoided.

5. The cost of medical care should be reduced and the quality increased. We must get the government out of the medical care industry. Our doctors must be free to deliver medical care without federal interference and without the very high costs imposed by the business and government special interests that Congress has improperly empowered.

Obamacare should be de-funded and the $500 billion transfer of funds out of Medicare (transferred by the Obamacare bill) should be put back into Medicare.

6. Government payments such as Social Security, Medicare, and veterans benefits should go as directly as possible to the people who depend upon them. Funding for the bureaucrats and special interests, in and out of government, who now unnecessarily deplete those payments should stop.

7. The funding of legitimate government activities, such as the Department of Defense, should be carried out without congressional micro-management, corrupt political deals, and unnecessary bureaucratic requirements.

Congressional meddling with the budget and activities of the Department of Defense, through which members of Congress waste defense dollars to please the clients of lobbyists and buy votes, wastes our defense dollars and decreases our defense preparedness. Our military professionals could give us more defense for less money if their expenditures were not politically manipulated.

8. The debasement of our national currency through money printing and other financial manipulations should end. This debasement raises prices, destroys savings, and creates economic uncertainties that destroy jobs and re-

duce prosperity.

9. Funding for Social Security and Medicare should be increased to make up for the price rises already caused by currency debasement.

10. Funding of the Veterans Administration should be increased, so promises made to our veterans can be kept.

Economic Liberty

The ideas listed above have a central objective – to increase American economic liberty. This is key to balancing the federal budget and getting our economy back on track. These ideas are also designed to keep our nation's promises, even though some of those promises were unwise.

Americans have lost much of their economic freedom. This has hurt employers and cost tens of millions of jobs.

With these burdens on their backs, Americans cannot compete effectively with workers in other countries, and many businesses have found it necessary to move abroad.

This is not merely a question of lower wages elsewhere. American products were once the highest quality and lowest priced in the world, even though American wages were the highest in the world.

The federal budget can be balanced if our economy returns to good health – a return that requires Congress to get the government out of the way of productive people and enterprises.

Unless this is done, the budget deficit will worsen and so will the economic affairs of our nation.

18

NATIONAL DEFENSE

The Congress shall have Power To lay and collect Taxes, Duties, Imposts and Excises, to pay the Debts and provide for the common Defence. . . . To declare War, grant Letters of Marque and Reprisal, and make Rules concerning Captures on Land and Water; . . . To provide for calling forth the Militia to execute the Laws of the Union, suppress Insurrections and repel Invasions;   Article 1, Section 8

The Congress, and only the Congress, has the constitutional authority to declare war. The Constitution is careful

> **We should compete with other nations by means of economic strength, a sound foreign policy, a vibrant space program, and common sense;**
>
> **We should have a military so strong that no one dare attack us and that assures victory if war comes;**
>
> **And, we should provide our citizens with an excellent civil defense system to protect them from natural, accidental, and man-made disasters.**
>
> **These measures lower chances of war and minimize the amount of suffering and death if war comes.**

to identify that branch of government which alone has the authority to involve the United States of America in military action.

During emergencies or perceived emergencies, however, people sometimes forget about the Constitution. Congress forgets about it most of the time, whether in war or peace. Precedents are established during periods of crisis, especially wartime, that undermine the Constitution, as well as the requirement to honor it.

There is no question that the Constitution authorizes the federal government to be the primary agency for the defense of the nation. The public has always understood that the government has an obligation to defend this nation from attack. The Congress has the authority and the duty to defend the territory and citizens of our country.

There was a time in the history of the United States when tranquility was virtually assured with respect to our relations with foreign nations. After 1783, there was no foreign nation, other than Great Britain, that was likely to invade the United States. The British had the power to interfere with our trade on the oceans, and so did the French. There was no practical threat of successful invasion by an army after the War of 1812.

The British did invade, briefly, in 1812, and burned the Capital. There was always the possibility that Britain would do it again, and both nations were wary of each other for a long time. But Canada was not about to invade the United States, and neither was Mexico.

Even the Japanese did not attempt a serious attack on the American mainland. They attacked Pearl Harbor. They wanted to destroy the American fleet, so that they could control the Pacific Ocean and Asian seas.

Not until the development of nuclear weapons was the United States at risk in modern times of a military attack on the American homeland.

An Armed Population

Americans have always been a well-armed people. Only Switzerland has a better-armed civilian population. The British learned during the American Revolution that an armed civilian force could be converted into an effectively armed military force in a very short period of time.

The technology of warfare until the 20th century favored a civilian population that could be rapidly mobilized into a defensive military force. The United States was unique in this respect.

Technological advance has changed this. Today, the machinery of national defense is far advanced, and people trained in its use must be constantly ready. Yet, Americans today have the least amount of military training in the history of the country. We are a well-armed people with respect to rifles, pistols, and sports weaponry. We are not well-trained in terms of organized military structure and military weapons.

We are fortunate to have the necessary resources to finance dedicated highly trained professional soldiers, sailors, and air and missile forces. There is very little possibility in the near future that any nation's military will attempt to attack our homeland. Our military is the best in the world, and we have a long heritage of skill and personal resolve among our millions of veterans. This minimizes the chance of war and assures our national sovereignty.

This does not mean that the United States military

should be used for invading, controlling, and directing foreign populations. Under these conditions, defensive foreign forces, not organized into conventional military units, have the ability to wear down an invading force.

The Soviet Union had the largest army on earth, but it could not conquer Afghanistan.

> "When you get into trouble 5,000 miles away from home, you've got to have been looking for it."   *Will Rogers*

The distinction between the defense of the homeland and the use of military forces in the invasion of distant countries should be carefully considered.

Only Congress is Permitted to Declare War

Some people – especially politicians who crave power – just naturally like to fight, especially when the fighting is done by others. These people tend to involve us in armed conflicts that are not necessary for the defense of our nation. They like to make use of our standing military.

Even when a conflict is necessary, they tend to find excuses to extend wars far longer than is prudent.

The Constitution is clear about one aspect. If the Congress of the United States does not declare war, this nation is not to be taken into a war. This constitutional principle has been ignored ever since the end of World War II, but that does not mean that it should not be followed.

If the Congress is unwilling to vote a formal declaration of war, our country should not go to war.

If it is not worth the political risk for congressmen to

> "The executive has no right, in any case, to decide the question, whether there is or is not cause for declaring war."
>
> *James Madison*

vote in favor of declaring war, then it is not worth the risk of a single American soldier, sailor, marine, or airman to fight in another country.

Preparation for War Preserves the Peace

We should conduct ourselves so that those in other countries admire us, our liberty, and the goods we offer in trade; so that they seek to emulate our liberty and prosperity; and so that they realize that an attack upon our country would be met with overwhelming force by the finest military that has ever existed. This would assure that we can live in peace and extend our way of life to other peoples – by example, not by force.

An effort should be made to assure that the money we spend on defense is allocated as effectively as possible. A large improvement could be made if the use of the defense budget by career politicians in Congress to aid in their re-elections were ended.

The purchase of weapon systems that the military does not want or need; the basing of troops in favor of certain congressional districts; and the congressional micromanaging of defense as a means to political power should all be ended.

Unrestricted budgets are generally far more effectively spent than restricted ones. Congress should simply appropriate a sum for the defense of our country and then turn the money over to our military professionals to spend as wisely as possible in providing for our defense. This should be done with congressional oversight that is carefully arranged so that it does not impair military activities.

Obviously, the Congress should occasionally review the effectiveness of our defenses, but it should not constantly micromanage military defense preparations for political purposes.

> **"To be prepared for war is one of the most effectual means of preserving peace."**
> *George Washington*

Being prepared for war – being so well prepared that potential enemies are deterred – is the best way to keep the peace. These preparations should be directed and guided by the best of our military professionals, not the most powerful of our politicians. And, war itself should be undertaken only when it is absolutely necessary for the defense of our country and after approval as specified in the Constitution.

We live in a dangerous world. So, we should not reduce our military defense. If, however, those resources are spent more wisely and are spent where possible within our borders, the effective economic burden will be reduced.

The United States should be an overwhelmingly well defended bastion and example of freedom to the entire world. It should not try to run the world. We must preserve our own liberty, continue in our own success, and provide to the world an example that many will decide to follow.

Defending Civilians

There is another important defense matter to consider that is rarely discussed in Congress these days. One time that it was discussed was in 1987 when Senators Pete Wilson and Steve Symms introduced in the Senate a "Sense of the Senate Resolution" that I wrote. This resolution was also introduced in the House of Representatives by Congressman Bilirakis. It is reproduced below.

This resolution had substantial support, but it was not put to a vote. The primary problem was that the building of blast and prompt radiation (radiation at the instant of the explosion) shelters – essential for survival of a generalized nuclear attack during the Cold War – was expensive.

However, in 1987, I also mentioned terrorism in the Resolution. A nuclear terrorist attack would be limited to one or a few locations and probably not give warning to people to enter the shelters. By entering the shelters after the attack, people could avoid deaths from fallout and fire, which comprise about two-thirds of the potential deaths. This could be achieved by fallout shelters alone, as were provided during the Kennedy Administration. This was a much less expensive program.

I think that the American people should have at least an inexpensive shelter-based civil defense to protect them from natural, accidental, and deliberate disasters.

It is very difficult to guard against a suicidal attack by someone who thinks he has little to lose and a great deal to gain by creating disruption in the lives of others.

We must protect ourselves without giving up our essential liberty - regardless of the threats. We must be able to survive any attack and yet preserve our freedom.

To implement an effective military defense you need to

understand the capabilities and incentives of your enemies. Today, our enemies are increasingly terrorist groups, but we must not forget about large nations that, if they wished, could hurt us far more.

The President of the United States cannot negotiate with terrorists; they can barely be identified. Even if he could negotiate with one group of them, he could not enforce the terms of the agreement on other groups.

> "Those who would give up essential liberty to purchase a little temporary safety deserve neither liberty nor safety."
> *Benjamin Franklin*

Basic to the defense of the United States today is a willingness of Americans to elect to Congress people who will vote to defend our homeland from our enemies. We also need to develop a foreign policy that is peaceful, so as to increase the profitability of trade and decrease the likelihood of attacks. Peace is a package deal. Peace means that the United States does not use its military forces to impose its will on other nations.

It is a responsibility of the United States government to implement a comprehensive civil defense program. I wrote about this 25 years ago in the book *Fighting Chance*.[59] To spend money on extended military action abroad and to avoid spending money on a civil defense system at home is the epitome of political hypocrisy.

Moreover, the cost of a sensible civil defense program today is much less than the system that was required to protect Americans during the Cold War.

If the citizens of the United States really are threatened

100TH CONGRESS
1ST SESSION **S. RES. 314**

Expressing the sense of the Senate regarding the American Civil Defense
Program.

IN THE SENATE OF THE UNITED STATES

NOVEMBER 4 (legislative day, OCTOBER 16), 1987

Mr. SYMMS (for himself and Mr. WILSON) submitted the following resolution;
which was referred to the Committee on Armed Services

RESOLUTION

Expressing the sense of the Senate regarding the American
Civil Defense Program.

Whereas in this age of nuclear energy, the people of the United
States are endangered by nuclear war, nuclear terrorist attacks, and nuclear accidents;

Whereas in the event of nuclear war the people are in the additional danger of starvation during the time before acquisition
and food transportation can be restored;

Whereas blast and radiation shelters and food storage methods
have been invented which can protect people from these nuclear dangers without evacuation;

Whereas blast and radiation shelters and food reserves have
been built to protect the peoples of Switzerland, the Union
of Soviet Socialist Republics and some other countries;

Whereas this United States Government has been established to
provide for the common defense of the people;

Whereas at present no defensive blast and radiation shelters or
distributed food reserves have been built for most of the
people of the United States;

Whereas the Department of Defense and the Department of Agriculture have the knowledge and resources to provide this
essential protection: Now, therefore, be it

1   *Resolved,* That it is the sense of the Senate that the

2 United States Department of Defense with the cooperation of

3 the Department of Agriculture should provide immediately to

4 this Congress a report on a program for the building of nucle-

5 ar blast and radiation shelters and for the storage of at least

6 one year's supply of food for every civilian and every military

7 person in the United States within walking distance of their

8 houses and places of work.

O

by terrorist attack (and they are), then it is the moral obligation of the government to do all it can to increase the
number of survivors of such an attack. It is the job of the
government to defend civilians.

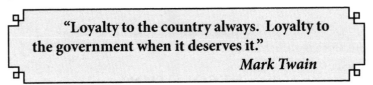

"Loyalty to the country always. Loyalty to
the government when it deserves it."
Mark Twain

Should terrorists succeed in detonating a nuclear
weapon in an American city, this could cause a million
deaths. Deaths from such an attack on a city are caused by
the nuclear blast and nuclear radiation produced during
the blast, by nuclear fallout, and by fire. Fallout and fire
extend over a much larger area and account for about two-
thirds of the deaths.

Simple, inexpensive fallout shelters as were marked and
provisioned in our cities during the Kennedy Administration would prevent most deaths from fallout and fire. So,
deaths from such an attack could be reduced by two-thirds
with such shelters, which could be provided at very low
cost. Great numbers of civilian deaths are not pleasant to
think about, but saving 700,000 lives is worthwhile, even
though 300,000 might still be lost.

It is difficult to take seriously the claim that the
United States government today is intent on protecting
the American people from terrorist attack by weapons
of mass destruction when it has installed no civil defense
protection whatever. We did have an emergency radiation
monitoring capability, but this was discontinued by the
Clinton Administration.

Obviously, our intelligence services should do their

best to discover and thwart terrorist attacks, but we should be prepared in case an attack does occur.

The defense of civilians is the primary purpose of the nation's military. The purpose of the military is not to protect multi-national corporate interests, even interests that contribute generously to congressional campaigns.

Our country has the finest military the world has ever known and an extraordinary force of men and women who constitute that military. The purpose of our military is to protect our country and citizens against external forces that truly threaten us. That is the way it should be used.

The world has changed. When George Washington urged that the United States refrain, when possible, from foreign entanglements and foreign wars, he was concerned about the negative economic and human costs of war, even wars that are "won."

The advance of technology has made George Washington's advice even more relevant. With modern technology, war has become far more dangerous.

Preventing War

The primary goal of the Department of Defense should be to prevent war – not to fight. Most military people understand this very well. They know war first hand.

When a central government becomes too big and the officials within it think of themselves as grandly superior to the citizenry, these people tend to strut around and think that they can impose their will on people in other countries, too. It is estimated that, during the 20th Century, more than 100 million people died in wars caused by governments that got out of control.

The Founding Fathers knew this. The restrictions that they placed upon government by means of the Constitution were intended to keep government restrained. In part, they were intended to reduce the tendency toward war.

> There is only one way in the world to prevent war, and this is, for every nation to tend to its own business. Trace any war that ever was and you will find some nation was trying to tell some other nation how to run their business.
>
> *Will Rogers*

Avoidance of war is another reason that we should reduce political power in Washington, even as we keep our military so powerful that no one will want war with us.

Veterans

No discussion of American defense can be complete without consideration of American veterans. Not only do veterans provide additional depth of experience and commitment to defend our country, but we must also see that they are properly honored and rewarded for their service.

Please see the chapter *Veterans* that follows for a discussion of this very important aspect of our national defense program.

Manned Exploration of Space

It is obvious that the interplanetary space around the earth is a potential battlefield. An aggressor with unrivaled control of outer space would have great advantages.

While it is all very well to negotiate treaties that de-militarize space, our country's security cannot rest entirely on such treaties. The defense of our nation in the space age requires that we have a vibrant – even if entirely peaceful – manned space program.

Like most government programs, America's manned space program has gradually become bureaucratized. As a result, far less has been accomplished for the dollars spent than during the first phase in the 1960s. Also, our engineering force has aged.

Apollo astronaut and the last man to pilot a space craft onto the surface of the Moon, former Senator Harrison Schmitt, has estimated that the average age of the engineers and scientists who designed and built the equipment that went to the Moon was 26 years. The average age in NASA is now over 50. Dr. Schmitt, a Caltech scientist, supports our campaign for Congress, as does Scott Carpenter, the second American to orbit the earth.

The Apollo Saturn V rockets that carried Americans to the Moon were the finest such equipment ever built. Not one of those rockets ever failed. Space scientist Lowell Wood estimated [33] that, for the cost of operating the space shuttle program during the 1980s, and 1990s, America could have sent another three-man Apollo mission to the Moon every six weeks.

We went to the Moon, and we should have long ago been on our way to Mars.

"Wait a minute!" You may say. "He wants the government limited to the duties specified in the Constitution. Does he think that each state should start its own space program – or that this should be entirely left to private enterprise?" Where is space exploration in the Constitution?

I think that we should have a manned space program for the same reason that we should have a sensible and, where possible, non-interventionist foreign policy. Both are essential parts of our national defense program because they lower the probability of war.

During the Cold War, competition in manned space flight took some of the risk out of the very dangerous nuclear confrontation. It was better to compete with the Soviets in building Moon rockets, Moon landers, and spacecraft, than in building ICBMs. The world came very close to war. It is quite possible that the manned Moon competition actually prevented a nuclear war.

Of war, it is often said that men just naturally like to fight – especially if other men are doing the fighting. I think it is better stated that men have an inborn desire to be a part of some great thing – to be, actually or vicariously, a part of something larger than themselves. We see this on a small scale in the enthusiasm that is shown in front of TV sets on weekends. Many viewers imagine themselves actually carrying the football.

I think this enthusiasm is caused by a desire to be a part of a great event, to transcend ourselves for a moment.

When I was in school, I did a lot of dramatic acting. One play we presented was *Dark of the Moon*. The character I played on the stage at Caltech, John Human, says at one point. "I look at them stars, all them planets a-twistin and changin' out thar in space. Then I know that this'n I'm standin' on, hit ain't so much, hit little, hit twistin' and changin' too. And I wanta be somethin' more'n jes' that!"

Americans are beginning to face a competition with China. There is a great danger that this will evolve into an eventual military competition, similar to the situation we faced during the Cold War. China has begun a space program. They have now docked two vehicles in space. They plan to go to the Moon and eventually to Mars.

Various technological arguments are advanced for returning to the Moon or going to Mars. I think we should go back to the Moon and to Mars as soon as possible for additional, more compelling reasons.

First, it is a far more benign way to compete with the Chinese than letting politicians and bureaucrats prance around threatening each other with nuclear weapons.

Second, it will provide an outlet for the emotional desire of all men to be a part of a great thing. When men travel to Mars, every person in the human race will be riding along with them.

Even though few of us will go, all of us will feel the excitement and wonder of the trip. All of us can wave our flags in support of our Mars Mission and work to see that our guys get there first. Each of us will, during that race be, as John Human dreamed, "somethin' more'n jes that."

Some people argue that much the same scientific goals can be accomplished with unmanned space probes, and at lower cost. This is true, but what will the people who pay for the programs get out of it? How is this justified?

A vibrant manned space program lowers the chance of war – just as a sensible foreign policy that stays out of the affairs of other countries lowers the chance of war. Exploration of space is a legitimate defense expenditure for our nation.

Our country should always be so well prepared for war that no aggressor ever dares to attack us.

And, we should reduce the chance of war by competing primarily in trade and technological achievement.

19

IMMIGRATION

It is the responsibility of Congress to keep the borders of our country secure, to facilitate legal immigration, and to make sure that the legal flow of citizens and noncitizens back and forth across our borders takes place with a minimum of impediments.

Why has Congress not fulfilled these responsibilities? First, some congressmen have made deals with lobbyists

> **A country without borders cannot remain a sovereign nation. Our borders must be secure.**
>
> **Failure of Congress to fulfill its responsibilities to secure our borders and conduct a common sense immigration policy has created a humanitarian crisis involving millions of illegals inside our country.**
>
> **Our borders must be secured; those without legal status must leave; and procedures for granting tourist, temporary worker, and path to citizenship status must be expeditious and fair.**
>
> **Illegals should be treated with compassion and charity; helped to leave the country; and provided with opportunities to return by legal means.**

whose clients benefit from cheap and vulnerable illegal labor. Second, some career congressmen hope to manipulate the political process by building political constituencies of illegals. Third, Congress has just shirked its responsibility.

So, we have a serious problem. Our borders are not secure. A country without borders is not a country. And, many millions of illegals are now in our country. If we let these people stay, then millions more will be induced to come. Yet, each illegal is not a statistic. He or she is a human being and must be treated as such.

To make matters worse, the proponents of the welfare state have made sure illegals are given access to our many welfare programs. This is bankrupting these programs.

Many illegals are hard-working, admirable people who are an asset to our country. Many others are poor people who lack skills and seek to live from American charity. Some illegals are criminals, yet others are people who came here decades ago and have become thoroughly Americanized "illegal citizens'" with extended families and deep roots in our communities.

As American liberty and justice have been gradually lost and American prosperity has therefore diminished and as the number of illegals has increased, many Americans have become more and more impatient with illegals. They want this problem solved.

Those states most affected by illegal migration are trying to cope with this problem, but congressionally empowered federal officials are impeding them.

There seems to be no entirely perfect, entirely charitable, and entirely sensible way to solve this problem that the negligence and corruption in Congress has created. Like our national financial obligations, reprehensible actions by career politicians have placed our country in a position where there is no really good way to correct this problem.

I often purchase groceries for the Robinson family at Food-4-Less in Medford, Oregon. Food-4-Less is open 24-hours per day, so I am sometimes there late at night when my other business in Medford is finished. The low prices attract many Hispanic families, especially during late hours. It is likely that many of these people are illegals.

I notice several things.

First, these people often shop as families. Two and even three generations are often seen shopping together. They are mostly Christian and very family oriented. So am I.

Second, a large majority of those shopping in Food-4-Less appear hard working and capable. If I were hiring men for serious work and reliability and could go only by looks alone, I would favor many of these men. For work requiring special technical skills, I would look more closely at each one. Latin America is not so technologically advanced as the United States, so fewer of these people have higher level technical experience.

Third, each is a human being and must be honorably treated as such. Most of them have come here to provide a better life for themselves and their families, both here and back home where many of them send their earnings. These people are not a faceless mass that should be objectified.

So, what do we do? Our borders must be secure and our immigration controlled. Otherwise, we will soon not be a sovereign country and all of our liberties will be imperiled. Yet, our career politicians have created a humanitarian dilemma.

To be sure, we should not elect or re-elect any more unprincipled politicians. But that does not, by itself, solve the problems they have already created.

Consider the following possibility.

1. Secure the borders immediately. Not with a ten-year plan, not with five-year plan, secure them now!

A country without borders is not a country, and there is little point in dealing with the illegals in our country when millions more are still pouring across our borders.

2. In order to help secure our borders, special advantages that draw some illegals to our country should end. Employment, welfare, and other advantages of legal residency should not be available to illegals, and laws regarding this should be enforced. Food and medical care should, however, be available to everyone. Also, the so-called "anchor baby" problem, wherein children born in the U.S. to illegals automatically become citizens, should be solved.

3. As the borders become secure – to be completed within one year – establish a one-year period during which every illegal in the United States must voluntarily leave our country and, if he or she wishes, apply – only from outside of the United States – for legal admission as a tourist, temporary worker, or new citizen.

Congress should pay charitable costs associated with this travel by the illegals. If an illegal cannot afford to leave our country, we should help pay his expenses.

I know! Why should we pay? We should pay for the same reason that we must pay vastly greater sums to correct other problems that our career politicians in Congress have created. If we want to stop paying, we had better throw these bums out in 2012.

4. Now, comes the hard part. Congress must establish common sense and charitable rules to govern the re-admission to the United States of some of these people and

see that these rules are applied fairly and expeditiously.

We need to fill our immigrant and guest worker needs with the best possible citizens, both from Latin America and from the rest of the world – in both labor-intensive occupations and in technologically advanced occupations.

The life that each illegal led while in our country should be a very significant factor in determining whether and under what status he or she can return, and that ruling must be made wisely and in a few days, not after months of bureaucratic diddling.

Illegals should not be given any special advantage over other applicants who do not have a history of illegal entry. All things being equal, a former illegal should have a modest disadvantage.

This is the "hard part" because there are so many different circumstances among the illegals.

The hard part is that decisions on re-entry will not be easily standardized. To expect bureaucrats to make decisions based on common sense is admittedly idealistic.

Nevertheless, guidelines must be established and followed as well as possible.

5. What about illegals who don't voluntarily leave? That's easy. When those who did not leave during the 12-month period are eventually found, one by one in the normal course of affairs, each should be taken to the border, deported, and not allowed to enter our country again.

If, for example, such an illegal seeks medical care for a serious illness at an American hospital, he or she should be admitted and provided with the best medical care of which the hospital is capable. After this has been done, he should be discharged from the hospital into the hands of the immigration authorities.

Most Americans are acquainted with illegals. They probably know an illegal who is an admirable person, and they do not want that individual treated uncharitably. Yet, most Americans are entirely fed up with the illegal immigration problem that Congress has created. They want it fixed. And they do not want the illegals to suffer unjustly.

Let me anticipate one objection. Some say, "There are millions of illegals. It is impossible for all of the illegals to leave the U. S., and any such effort will cost too much."

The cost of paying to resolve the illegal immigration problem is far less than going along as we are now and letting this problem damage and possibly bankrupt our medical, educational, and other institutions.

Moreover, the future cost to our country of trying to operate a country without borders is not acceptable. That cost is the loss of our liberty and our justice, privileges we have and rights that we protect by means of the rules of our sovereign Constitutional Republic.

If our borders are not secure, we will eventually lose our national sovereignty. The "invasion" of our country by many millions of illegals is actually a problem of national defense. We could alternatively call this a huge refugee problem – involving refugees from poverty and instability in other lands. It is a delicate matter. These "invaders" are not carrying guns (except for a few) and most of them seek only a better life, but the illegal problem still threatens our nation and our way of life.

States' Rights

The states most affected by the illegal problem have scrambled to deal with its injustices as best they can, especially in view of irresponsible congressional actions.

Arizona has been severely criticized and even been attacked in court by the federal government for passing legislation to protect itself from a vast influx of illegals, since the federal government failed to fulfil its responsibilities.

Other states are trying to enforce laws that penalize employers who violate citizenship employment laws by hiring illegals. Some other states are offering illegals special educational and other benefits.

We must understand that these states have a problem on their hands for which there is no good solution. They react, therefore, pragmatically to protect themselves.

Until this problem is solved, the states should be permitted – without federal interference – to handle their problems with illegals as best the people of those states determine. After this problem is solved, the question of state action in this matter will be moot.

Like many of our national difficulties, the "illegal" problem has been caused by very poor representation in Congress. We must elect citizen legislators with common sense to Congress in 2012, so that we will not have more such problems.

Fairness

Some will say that it isn't fair to make the illegals leave the U.S. in order to apply for legal status.

But, is it fair to say to the millions of people who have waited patiently to enter our country legally, "we are giving preference to those who have broken our laws, rather than to you, who have honored them?"

Some say fairness requires that Congress favor some corporations, so that more people will have jobs. But, is it fair that this favoritism will cause workers at competing corporations to lose their jobs?

Some say that fairness requires that Congress take the property of those who have more and give it to those who have less. But, is it fair to say to everyone, "no matter how hard you work, if you are rewarded for that work, Congress will take the reward that you have earned and give it to someone else. You will not be permitted to rise above others in our country, regardless of your talent and perseverance."

Actions have consequences – both seen and unseen. In his classic essay, *What is Seen and What is not Seen*, Frédéric Bastiat explains this in the case of *The Broken Window* and related circumstances. Every American should read this essay.

Henry Hazlitt, in his book *Economics in One Lesson*, provides another analysis of this.

It is a central fallacy found in much political demagoguery that the consequences of actions are evaluated solely on the basis of the apparent beneficial effects, while the unseen harmful effects are not considered.

20

WALL STREET

"I tell 'em this country is bigger than Wall Street, and if they don't believe me, I show 'em the map." *Will Rogers*

George Washington was inaugurated on Wall Street as our first President on April 30, 1789. The event was held at Federal Hall, 26 Wall Street, New York City.

George Washington was the embodiment of American Liberty; American Liberty was the enabler of American Exceptionalism; American Exceptionalism caused the American economy to become the most prosperous the

I support American corporations and the capital allocation industries that finance them – they provide Americans with products and jobs, but I oppose corporations that make deals with Congress to give them public money in subsidies and improper advantages over their competitors.

My opponent supports corporations, too – those that give him campaign cash at election time. Yet, he seeks re-election by demonizing the industry that provides corporate capital, which is "Wall Street."

Sea Drift As Originally Designed

Ted Robinson, Art's father, headed design and construction of the polyethylene plant at Sea Drift, Texas in the 1950s. Today, this petrochemical plant still enriches Americans by supplying essential materials and creating jobs. Congress has made it very difficult to build such industries in the United States today.

World has ever known; and Wall Street became the center of capital allocation for that prosperous economy.

American capital allocation has now spread throughout our country. Every brokerage office, every bank, and every individual investor watching and trading the markets on his computer screen plays a part in capital allocation. They are all a part of "Wall Street."

Most Americans are a part of this. If you have a pension, your pension fund manager is a part of Wall Street. If you own stocks, they are traded on Wall Street. If you work for a business, the capital allocation that allows that business to flourish is probably connected to Wall Street.

Today, "Wall Street" is spread all over the World, as electronically linked financial exchanges in many countries participate in capital allocation everywhere.

Sea Drift As Built

During Seadrift's design and construction, Ted Robinson and his coworkers labored to make the plant efficient, safe, easily expandable, and a credit to the people of Texas. Seadrift is environmentally sound. Government regulations in the 1950s were few, benign, and common sense.

The heart and soul of Wall Street is the productive use of profits and savings of people everywhere on Earth.

Capital is the summation of the accumulated profits and savings of individuals, businesses, and industries and the machines and other means of production that have been purchased with those profits and savings.

When an American is hired by a small business in Oregon, he is paid from the profits and savings of that business; profits and savings by others that the businessman may have borrowed; and the cash flow of the business.

If the allocation of capital to offer him a job was wise, his work produces more than he is paid; the business therefore has profits and savings; the business expands; and another worker can be hired.

If the decision was unwise or if some other factor like

government taxation and regulation prevents the business from prospering regardless of the worker's efforts, the capital allocated to his job is lost; the business contracts; and his job or that of another worker may be lost.

The wealth available to "create" a new job and career comes from profits, savings, and business cash flow.

Capital allocation for large businesses and industries is a special skill, requiring an industry itself. Stock prices that are quoted in the daily news are simply reports about the functioning of that industry – Wall Street.

The polyethylene plant at Sea Drift, Texas, for which my father directed the design and construction when I was a boy, was funded by the American capital allocation industry, just as were most of America's major industries.

Capital can also be allocated by Congress. Politicians seize the savings and profits of individuals, businesses, and industries through taxation and then allocate this capital themselves. Congress also seizes capital indirectly by passing laws enabling regulations that force private capital to be used in ways that Congress prefers.

Congress, being made up largely of career politicians, lawyers, and other people with little, if any, experience or skill with capital allocation, tends to waste capital, which costs the American people the loss of millions of jobs.

Congress also makes corrupt deals with dishonest people in the capital allocation industry.

These deals subvert the capital allocation process. Corrupt businessmen make deals with corrupt congressmen to give them capital that has not been earned by their businesses. This is done by direct payments of government subsidies; government loans and loan guarantees; indirect payments by laws that selectively damage the competitors of the businesses allied with Congress; and laws that selectively promote one company over another.

This corruption has become so widespread that almost all businesses and industries hire lobbyists who pander to Congress. Even honest, uncorrupted businessmen – most businessmen are honorable and honest – must lobby Congress to protect themselves from this corruption.

Also, very high wages are paid to some executives who have arranged for their companies to be subsidized and bailed out by taxpayers.

My opponent in District 4 is no stranger to this. A glance at the list of corporations and other special interests that pay for his re-election campaigns reveals the interests on Wall Street for which DeFazio has done special things.

Lobbyists broker and control the deals between congressional offices and special interests. Various perks are provided for congressional support, including campaign contributions. The book *Capitol Punishment* by Jack Abramoff describes this corrupt environment.

As the American economy has been sliding downward, the American public has been searching for the cause. The public is understandably very upset about this slide. Corrupt deals between Congress and dishonest people on Wall Street are a part of the cause.

As American businesses and industries have scrambled to save themselves from this decline, corrupt interests have had an advantage because they can call upon many congressmen to give them public money and preferences.

This has not gone undetected. The American people are furious about the huge payments made to corrupt elements of the capital allocation industry by Congress – payments to certain banks, businesses, and other special interests, including payments made to some (only a small group) of the special interests in Wall Street.

Demonizing Wall Street

Leftist politicians including my opponent are now conducting a frenzied condemnation of Wall Street as the cause of America's difficulties.

These politicians are trying to win votes by turning Americans against their own capital allocation industry – an industry essential for providing many American jobs and careers and an industry in which almost all Americans have a personal financial stake through their investments, pension funds, and employment.

These politicians are also using the politics of class warfare against this industry.

Yet, the political campaigns of Peter Defazio have been funded in large part by "Wall Street" itself. Without large campaign contributions from these elements, it is unlikely that my opponent would hold public office today.

DeFazio, who has become a millionaire while in Congress, campaigns in Oregon from an old Dodge Dart and likes to say that he is "independent as Oregon."

In fact, far from independent, he is entirely dependent upon the campaign cash of special interests, especially those in "Wall Street" for which he has done favors during his 25 years in Washington – including interests that do little business in Oregon.

DeFazio is now sending fund raising requests claiming that he has been targeted for defeat in 2012 by Wall Street. Yet, the only Wall Street targeting in view is the campaign cash he is getting from corporations for his campaign.

The Wall Street Campaign

Prominently in 2010 and already in 2012, my opponent is trying to convince voters that I, Art Robinson, am a tool of Wall Street. He said, in television ads, that he, DeFazio, will protect Oregon jobs from Wall Street and from Art Robinson's friends on Wall Street.

How does a research scientist and small businessman in Oregon become a tool of Wall Street? I really would like to know! Raising a family of six children and putting them through college and graduate school was a very difficult accomplishment for our family. Connections to Wall Street would surely have helped.

This is all politics. In campaign finance, incumbent career politicians usually have the advantage over challengers because they have had many years in Washington to give public money and power to the special interests that finance these campaigns. DeFazio has had 25 years to do this, and he has vigorously and successfully done so.

Yet, we are now being treated, in 2012, to the pathetic spectacle of our congressman running around whining that his opponent (a research scientist who has earned his way in life with his work in scientific research and education) is a tool of "Wall Street."

The truth is that I have essentially no connection to Wall Street – the capital allocation industry. And, DeFazio has extensive connections with Wall Street through his 25-years of dispensing favors in Congress.

His claim is an effort to smear Wall Street and to smear me by association, solely to dishonestly win votes.

Capital Trading

One part of the capital allocation industry that socialists attack is the capital trading industry. They like to demonize the "speculators." My opponent has been complaining a lot about speculators lately.

Let's say a farmer raises wheat, and a baking company needs that wheat. Their needs are filled by market middlemen, grain buyers and sellers.

This market is so large and so uncertain due to weather, business conditions, and other factors that the grain buyers and sellers "hedge" their activities in larger markets. In this case, they mostly hedge on the Chicago Board of Trade by buying and selling contracts for wheat.

A grain buyer "hedges" the wheat in his grain elevator by selling futures contracts allowing him to sell wheat later at fixed prices. This insulates him from future price changes.

Left to their own devices in a market between only producers, consumers, and ordinary middlemen and without the Board of Trade, these people would have difficulties.

Since the amount of grain produced and consumed varies greatly with time, business size, economic conditions, and many other unknowns, the difference between bid prices and ask prices would need to be very wide to allow for these risks. The farmer and the baker do not want unnecessary risks that could ruin their businesses. They need good stable prices.

If the speculative entrepreneurs were not in the market place, the price of bread and almost everything else we buy would be higher. A speculator whose trades, on average, smooth the market and move prices closer to a proper level tends to prosper. A speculator whose trades increase volatility and move markets away from good prices tends to lose money and is soon out of business.

So, we are helped by speculative traders, businessmen who assume these risks in order to make a profit. These businessmen constantly buy and sell. Therefore, the farmer and baker can always buy and sell just what they need.

Moreover, the farmer and the baker can always obtain more favorable prices because the traders smooth the market and eliminate the risk spread between the buy and sell prices. They create, through their activities, a fair price.

When the Russians invaded Afghanistan in 1979, President Jimmy Carter decided to use the incident for political advantage, so he banned American wheat sales to the Soviet Union and closed the Chicago Board of Trade.

This didn't hurt the Soviets much, since they just bought their grain elsewhere, but it destroyed the businesses of many Americans involved in grain distribution.

As one grain elevator operator pleaded in *The Wall Street Journal,* "We have got to have a price!"

It is this way with most markets for products, stocks, bonds, and items of capital required for markets. Traders provide the liquidity to make these markets work efficiently, reliably, and fairly for those who buy and sell – traders who are rewarded in profits for their work.

Desperate to win re-election, my opponent is advocating a tax on market trades that is so high that taxes and risk would combine to make short term trades unworkable and put many traders out of business. He claims that "speculators" have raised the prices of gasoline and other items.

In fact, it is money printing and interference with private enterprise by Mr. Defazio and other socialists in Congress that are most responsible for higher prices, but they are not going to admit this to voters.

Careful studies[70] have shown that even short term "fast" trading, as it is called, improves market liquidity and lowers the spreads between "bid" and "asked" prices. This benefits all market participants.

That his tax would do damage to the markets and would harm the residents of Oregon by lost jobs and careers, higher prices, and lowered prosperity is apparently of little interest to DeFazio. He has not been much interested in Wall Street during his past 25 years in Congress. Now, threatened with defeat, he seems to see this as an opportunity to use the politics of envy and bashing of the capital allocation markets to get votes for re-election.

American Anger

Many Americans are justifiably angry about the huge sums of money that corrupt career politicians in Congress have given to corporations, banks, and other very wealthy special interests on Wall Street and elsewhere.

In his book, Capitol Punishment,[56] former lobbyist and convicted felon (for actions that he took while becoming the most successful lobbyist in Washington) Jack Abramoff says that sometimes a congressman or his office did not specifically ask for campaign cash in return for a vote. This was so unusual that he made a practice of double checking in each case to make sure it had not been an oversight.

The situation might be summarized this way:

1. Congress hands out public funds to the voters. Some of these voters then vote for the incumbent congressmen.

2. Congress hands out public funds and other advantages to corporate interests. These corporations, in

return, give incumbents campaign cash to pay for lavish re-election campaigns.

3. With the purchased votes and the campaign cash, the incumbents are re-elected.

4. The re-elected career politicians then tax more away from the middle class, which is the primary source of savings and profits that create jobs. This loss of capital destroys jobs and puts more people on welfare, creating more votes for the politicians.

5. The results: the middle class is crushed by taxes; prosperity diminishes; corrupt businesses get public money; and corrupt politicians build even more power and money for themselves, managing to remain in congress sometimes longer than 25 years.

In this five-point cycle of corruption, only a small fraction of voters and corporations actually participate. Most Americans are honest, and are not this way. But, the few who do participate are often sufficient to tip elections and keep the politicians in power.

Most Americans are furious that this process is going on. Unfortunately, many of these people misplace their anger, failing to understand that it is corruption in Washington and especially in Congress that allows this process to continue.

And, those with just claims to public funds such as Social Security recipients and Veterans are not only deprived of proper funding but are also constantly threatened by the corrupt congressmen, who claim that their payments will stop if these congressmen are not reelected.

How long do these politicos stay in power?

The figure on page 5 in this book in the Chapter *Who is Art Robinson*, clearly tells the tale.

From an average of a little over 2 years that each House of Representatives member – each citizen volunteer – was in office during the first century of American Congresses, the average has risen to an average of more than 10 years that each House member – each career politician – now stays in office. The average tenure time is still rising.

The average for those who are most responsible for our country's problems is much longer than 10 years. The incumbent from Oregon District 4 has been there for 25 years. He is now stumping for higher taxes and more regulations and calling for the spending of even more money.

Occupy "Wall Street"

"Occupy" demonstrations have become common throughout our country. It is understandable that unrest is spreading as a result of the economic difficulties brought on by the misdeeds of Congress.

Socialists and other radicals (including my opponent who participated prominently in "Occupy Portland" activities) use these "occupy" demonstrations to manipulate these unfortunate people for political purposes. They seek to stimulate class warfare, for personal political gain.

The manipulators say that the issue is between the "99%" and the "1%." The "1%" are those in the top 1% of personal income, some of whom work in "Wall Street," the financial services industry.

This is wrong. We are all in the "100%." We are all Americans. Our danger comes from the "0.001%", especially some members the U.S. Congress, who seek money and power at the expense of us all.

21
FOREIGN TRADE

The Congress shall have Power To lay and collect Taxes, Duties, Imposts and Excises, to pay the Debts and provide for the common Defence and general Welfare of the United States; but all Duties, Imposts and Excises shall be uniform throughout the United States; Article I, Section 8: Part 1

The Constitution grants to Congress the power to tax imported goods. In 1788, this was a major form of taxation. The federal government was not allowed to tax personal incomes. There was no Internal Revenue Service.

Americans should trade freely with people throughout the world. We don't need trade agreements, especially not ones that favor special interests.

Import and export duties should be applied equally to all products and resources that cross our borders and be kept low, so that trade is not impeded.

Congress should restore our economic liberty, so that we can – as we once did – produce the highest quality, lowest cost products in the world, while paying our workers the highest wages in the world.

The government did tax imports that cross an American border from outside the nation. By restricting taxation primarily to tariffs, the Founding Fathers intended to keep the federal government income low, so that it could not significantly meddle in the lives of American citizens and would be less inclined toward war.

Taxes hurt. But at least this rule should surely be honored: Taxes should not be used to treat one business or industry preferentially at the expense of others.

One problem with current taxes on imported goods is that the taxes are not applied uniformly. There is no flat tax on all imports. Congress has written in loopholes for special interests.

There are too many taxes. We need fewer taxes.

The federal government taxes personal incomes. It taxes corporate incomes. It taxes almost everything that moves. As a percentage of federal revenue, tariffs in 2010 produced about $25 billion, or only about 1% of total federal tax revenue. [34]

A worse problem comes when the government passes import quotas. These produce no revenue for the government. These are favors to special-interest groups. The lobbyists make it worth a congressman's time – money for re-election campaigns – to write import quotas into laws. These are hidden from the public.

These quotas keep out goods. The public pays more for whatever they buy, but the money does not go directly to the federal government. It goes to the special interests who can sell their products at higher prices. It's a sweet deal.

Speaking of sweet deals, there are import restrictions on imported sugar. What is the result? Lost jobs and careers for Americans. Why? Because candy manufacturers set up plants abroad. There, they can buy sugar less expensively. Then they ship the candy into the U. S.[67,68]

> **"The political and commercial morals of the United States are not merely food for laughter, they are an entire banquet."**
>
> *Mark Twain*

It is like this in every industry that gets favors from the federal government by means of quotas. Some corporations are favored. Others lose.

Visible Winners, Invisible Losers

When Congress grants special favors to some to make them "winners," they almost always hurt others and make them "losers." The winners know when they win. They know why. The losers also know. But the voters rarely see who loses. They only see who wins.

The winners hire people. The losers fire people. Voters see the winners. The losers soon disappear.

The voters see that the winners are hiring. Some of the voters who know about the import quotas conclude: "The import quota was a good policy. Look at the extra jobs." But few of them ever notice the lost jobs.

What is seen is popular: "more jobs." That not seen is ignored: "lost jobs." Congress takes credit for the new jobs.

The people who favor the benefitted special interests say this: "We need more import quotas to protect American jobs." They do not say: "We need more import quotas to protect a relative handful of American jobs at the expense of three groups: (1) customers who pay more, (2) companies that can no longer export as many products, and (3) workers in other companies who lose jobs."

This is a racket. It ought to be stopped.

No More Hidden Subsidies

Congress has granted hidden subsidies to special interests for decades. Why? Because they are hidden. Citizens rarely figure out that special interests are getting fat and lazy because of federal subsidies.

Hidden losses also go on for decades. Citizens do not see what the subsidies to the special interests cost the interests that are not favored. So, there is little outrage. There is little sense of injustice.

But the special interests know that the voters would not be happy about these sweetheart deals. They might vote against a congressman who doles out tax money or favors to crony capitalists.

So, Congress hides the favors. A great way to hide them is with import quotas.

When Free Trade is Not Free Trade

NAFTA (the North American Free Trade Association) is not free trade. It is managed trade. It is trade regulated by international bureaucrats.

There is a sales strategy called bait-and-switch. It's illegal, but it's common. A company advertises a product for sale at a really low price. When the customer comes in – having spent time to get to the store – the salesman says: "Gee, I'm sorry. We have run out of that item. But take a look at this. It's much better." It's also more expensive. This takes people's time. It is sales based on deception.

The promoters of NAFTA used something similar to bait-and-switch. The bait: "free trade, lower priced goods, more exports." The switch: international control of trade and products by bureaucrats.

It isn't necessary to have treaties to reduce import taxes. Congress can simply vote to lower taxes. It isn't necessary for a treaty to eliminate import quotas. Congress can simply vote them away, one by one or in groups.

But what about situations where foreign interests sell goods to Americans at costs below their price of production in order to drive competing American companies out of business?

This is not new. American companies sometimes do the same thing to drive their competitors out of business. We have plenty of American laws concerning this. Common sense laws should be enforced for everyone doing business in our country.

Free trade does not require treaties. It requires only that government get out of the way.

It is said that Americans should "Buy American." Our family does this when we can. DeFazio says this to voters, but then he buys two houses in New Zealand.

My opponent says he opposes trade agreements. But he wrote a letter to President Bush asking him to negotiate a trade agreement with New Zealand. He is also a prominent member of the "Friends of New Zealand Congressional Caucus." [35]

When I was growing up and many of you were too, American products were the highest quality and lowest cost in the world - and American wages were highest in the world. No one needed to be encouraged to buy American.

> I have a suspicion about my opponent. Now, why would I be suspicious of him?
>
> I think that DeFazio and his wife may be planning to move to New Zealand when he leaves office. It is a beautiful country. They would live in one of their two houses there and use the other one for guests.
>
> Then, using his contacts in Washington, I think he hopes to be named U.S. Ambassador to New Zealand.
>
> If this is his dream, he should try to realize it soon. It would be better for the people of Oregon.

Over recent decades, American quality has diminished, costs have increased, and real wages have diminished. With half of everything Americans earn flowing into government coffers through over-taxation; over-regulation; and debt service from congressional over-borrowing, American liberty has diminished, and, in many industries, we cannot compete effectively.

The answer to this is to fire the career politicians who are destroying our country with self-serving taxation, regulation, and debt. Without big government on our backs, we will have no trouble again offering the world the best goods and services at the lowest prices, while we keep our wages high. We have done this before – before the era of big government.

22

MEDICAL CARE

*The powers not delegated to the United States by
the Constitution, nor prohibited by it to the States, are
reserved to the States respectively, or to the people.*
Amendment 10

I've got good news and bad news. The bad news is that
Obamacare will end access to quality medicine for most
Americans. The "good" news is that Obamacare threatens

> **Medical care is far too expensive. A government-
> industry-medical-legal monopoly controls medical
> care through a system of licensure, bureaucracy, and
> over-reaching regulation.**
>
> **This monopoly raises costs, controls physicians,
> and inhibits research and innovation. It is empow-
> ered by congressional laws and agencies.**
>
> **Obamacare increases the power of this monopoly,
> forces every American to participate, increases costs,
> and creates government rationing and control of life
> and death decisions.**
>
> **Congress should work to free physicians and
> patients from the medical care monopoly.**

to bankrupt the federal government if it is not stopped. When the voters realize that everything from Social Security to student loans may be lost to Obamacare, they will surely demand its end.

> **"If you think heath care is expensive now, wait until you see what it costs when it is free."**
> *P. J. O'Rourke*

But why must our country endure this roller coaster ride? Ask Peter DeFazio. He cast one of the deciding votes for Obamacare and socialized medicine. Some states have already begun to opt out of the program, and hundreds of corporations have already been given political waivers exempting them from participation. There are more than 30 court cases at the federal level that have challenged Obamacare. Perhaps the Supreme Court will rule against it, but regardless of this, it is bad for the American people.

In tax-financed fliers and other communications to voters, DeFazio now says that there are many things wrong with Obamacare. He knows that his vote for Obamacare is unpopular with voters.

Do we want a congressman who casts a deciding vote on legislation that will entirely remake more than 15% of the American economy and then, when voters complain, tries to cover for himself by saying that there are many things in the legislation that he doesn't like?

Even if the Supreme Court doesn't stop Obamacare, Congress still does not have to fund it. Congress funds everything that the federal government does. The federal government writes lots of laws and regulations, but, if the 2013-2014 session of the Congress refuses to fund a

H. R. 3590—146

"(B) QUALIFIED ENTITIES.—The Secretary shall determine what entities are qualified to receive enrollment HIT under subparagraph (A), taking into consideration the recommendations of the HIT Policy Committee and the HIT Standards Committee.".

SEC. 1562. CONFORMING AMENDMENTS.

(a) APPLICABILITY.—Section 2735 of the Public Health Service Act (42 U.S.C. 300gg–21), as so redesignated by section 1001(4), is amended—

(1) by striking subsection (a);

(2) in subsection (b)—

(A) in paragraph (1), by striking "1 through 3" and inserting "1 and 2"; and

(B) in paragraph (2)—

(i) in subparagraph (A), by striking "subparagraph (D)" and inserting "subparagraph (D) or (E)";

(ii) by striking "1 through 3" and inserting "1 and 2"; and

(iii) by adding at the end the following:

"(E) ELECTION NOT APPLICABLE.—The election described in subparagraph (A) shall not be available with respect to the provisions of subpart 1.";

(3) in subsection (c), by striking "1 through 3 shall not apply to any group" and inserting "1 and 2 shall not apply to any individual coverage or any group"; and

(4) in subsection (d)—

(A) in paragraph (1), by striking "1 through 3 shall not apply to any group" and inserting "1 and 2 shall not apply to any individual coverage or any group";

(B) in paragraph (2)—

(i) in the matter preceding subparagraph (A), by striking "1 through 3 shall not apply to any group" and inserting "1 and 2 shall not apply to any individual coverage or any group"; and

(ii) in subparagraph (C), by inserting "or, with respect to individual coverage, under any health insurance coverage maintained by the same health insurance issuer"; and

(C) in paragraph (3), by striking "any group" and inserting "any individual coverage or any group".

(b) DEFINITIONS.—Section 2791(d) of the Public Health Service Act (42 U.S.C. 300gg–91(d)) is amended by adding at the end the following:

"(20) QUALIFIED HEALTH PLAN.—The term 'qualified health plan' has the meaning given such term in section 1301(a) of the Patient Protection and Affordable Care Act.

"(21) EXCHANGE.—The term 'Exchange' means an American Health Benefit Exchange established under section 1311 of the Patient Protection and Affordable Care Act.".

(c) TECHNICAL AND CONFORMING AMENDMENTS.—Title XXVII of the Public Health Service Act (42 U.S.C. 300gg et seq.) is amended—

(1) in section 2704 (42 U.S.C. 300gg), as so redesignated by section 1201(2)—

(A) in subsection (c)—

Page 146 from the "Obamacare" Bill

Did DeFazio actually read and understand the 906 pages of this bill on his electronic reader as he claimed? He voted "yes," casting one of the deciding votes that passed the bill. Now he is trying to vote "no" by campaigning against major parts of the bill.

particular project, the project dies. Obamacare should be defunded.

There is political posturing to "repeal" Obamacare. This will not happen while President Obama is in office, and it will be much more difficult than de-funding even after he leaves office. Obviously, repeal would be desirable.

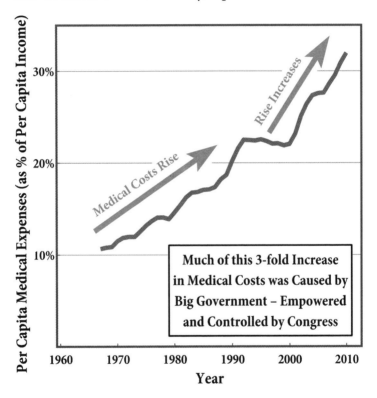

Cost of Medical Care in the U.S.

Medical Care costs as a percentage of personal income have increased 3-fold since 1970. This is largely due to the gradual conversion of medical care into a big government, Congress-empowered monopoly. Obamacare will raise medical costs even higher.

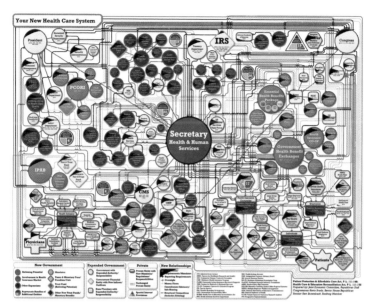

Organizational Chart of Obamacare[55]

This schematic contains only about 1/3 of the complete organizational structure. Under socialized medicine, a vast bureaucracy will waste a large part of the medical care money. This will be compensated for by gatekeepers and ruling boards that withhold medical care from seniors on the basis of age and facilitate other programs for medical care rationing.

Page 146 from the Obamacare Act is reproduced above. DeFazio claims to have read all 906 pages before voting. Do you think he did? Did he understand it?

Congress and Corporatism in Medicine

It is, of course, the very high cost of medical care today that causes many people to be interested in Obamacare. Medical care, as a percentage of average personal income, has already increased 3-fold since 1970. People do not realize that Obamacare will cost even more, but they do realize that the current system costs far too much.

Medical care is now 32% of average personal income as shown in the graph above. Health insurance, therefore, costs too much, and medical care without health insurance is even more expensive.

The reason for this high cost is that, based on congressionally delegated federal power and state laws, our medical system is already largely controlled by a self-serving governmental-corporate-medical-legal monopoly. Our doctors no longer control our medical care. They have become little more than slaves to this monopoly.

Licensure laws, governmental regulations, and a vast interlocking system of institutionalized restrictions have created an impenetrable monopoly that now stands between patients and physicians and medical facilities. This is the most powerful and expensive monopoly in human history – now demanding over 15% of the entire Gross Domestic Product of the United States for its services.

Not only the supply of medical goods and services, but also the evaluation of medical products and services is under monopolistic control – partly by physicians and institutions, but increasingly by insurers, lawyers, and governmental and quasi-governmental agencies.

If my son Matthew took his dog Rusty to the veterinarian, the veterinarian could measure, within a few minutes, a couple of dozen substances in a blood sample from Rusty – the same substances that will be measured if you go to a physician and his nurse takes an ordinary sample of your blood. The veterinarian does this with a personal computer and a simple peripheral. Some veterinarians send animal

Matthew & Rusty in 2003

Matthew's dog Rusty had more medical freedom than Matthew. The vast congressionally empowered medical monopoly controls medical care so tightly that costs have skyrocketed and medical freedom, access, and quality have shrunk.

blood samples to local hospitals, where they are analyzed by the same analytical devices used for human samples.

The veterinarian cannot, however, use his device to analyze a sample from Matthew. This is unlawful. It would also be unlawful for even a physician to measure Matthew's sample, without government approval of the device and certification of the doctor's lab under the Clinical Laboratory Improvement Act – a bureaucratic requirement that is beyond the means of most physicians.

The federal government – through bureaucrats paid and empowered by Congress – tightly controls the facilities and personnel allowed to make measurements on human specimens. Most measurements are done in corporate clinical laboratories, and most of those laboratories would refuse to measure a sample if Matthew asked them to do so. They would require a physician's order – an inconvenient and expensive requirement.

Yet, this example involves measurements that have been common for most of the past century. I am not talking about anything complicated or even the least bit dangerous. Matthew could have made these measurements himself when he was 12 years old, if he had access to the simple equipment. Trapped inside of a monopolistic wall of governmental corporatism, however, diagnostic measurements and access to them cost Americans huge amounts of money in unnecessary expenditures each year.

This is just a tiny part of the problem. Not only does this monopoly charge very high fees and prevent others from offering its services, it also strives to inhibit competition. Even Americans who buy vitamin supplements for preventive medicine are continually at risk of having their supplements withdrawn from the market by federal regulators that are paid by Congress.

Why is there no liberty here? Why is Matthew's freedom suppressed to less even than that of his dog Rusty? This monopoly sustains itself by the threat of governmental power that originates in unconstitutional laws passed by Congress.

Freedom in just the area of clinical testing as exemplified here would save the American people more than $100 billion medical dollars per year and lead to improvements in medical care.

The same people in Congress, who propose to subject us all to the huge costs and lower quality of Obamacare because the cost of medical care is too high for many Americans to afford, are the people who caused those costs to be too high in the first place.

It is not common sense to think that the congressmen who have caused this gaggle of freedom-suppressing laws can fix the problem with more freedom-suppressing laws.

Medical care in the U.S. is certainly too costly. We all realize this. Moreover, with medical care now absorbing more than 15% of our national income, it is having a large negative effect on the prosperity and careers of Americans and their families.

Yet, those who provide that care – physicians and those who work directly with them – are receiving a rapidly diminishing part of the money paid for medical care.

Instead, this vast government-empowered monopoly has grown so strong that it dictates every aspect of medical care, stifles innovation, and enslaves physicians, who must practice as they are told or lose their licenses to practice at all. All sorts of parasitic groups have attached themselves to this system, such as over-reaching tort lawyers who have driven the cost of medical malpractice insurance up so high that many doctors are forced out of medical practice because they cannot afford insurance.

American medical care, as a result of the momentum of the past, is still good, but we must get the government off the backs of our medical workers, or else this will cease to be the case. More government control is certainly not the answer.

The problems with government control are already evident. Our seniors have Medicare and certainly need it given the high cost of care due to government meddling, but they are finding that care increasingly rationed. Our veterans have medical care, but they, too, often find their care unacceptable in quality and quantity.

Increased government control of medical care under Obamacare – control of who will be sick and who will be well – who will live and who will die – gives power to government that is incompatible with American liberty.

Socialized Medicine

The main problem with all forms of socialized medicine is easy to explain. Medical care must be paid for by somebody. Without socialism, the person who needs medical care pays for it himself, or his insurance company pays for it. Then the physician or other medical care professional who provides the service has to meet the standards that are set by the person who is paying for the service.

If the federal government pays for medical care, Washington bureaucrats make personal medical decisions. To the extent that anyone surrenders the writing of the check to the federal government, he has surrendered authority over the person who is providing the service.

There is no escape from the connection between money and authority. Anyone who is unwilling to pay for a service, but who wants someone else to pay for the service, can be sure of this: *the standards of the service will be imposed and enforced by whomever pays for the service.*

If you want bureaucratic medicine, get the government to pay for it. But realize that as soon as the government pays for the services, the physician starts paying attention to what the bureaucrats in Washington want him to do, and he begins to ignore what his patients want him to do.

Washington bureaucrats can fine him or put him in

jail if he violates their rules. Patients can quit coming for treatment, but bureaucrats can end the physician's career, bankrupt him, and even imprison him.

Even before Obamacare most physicians have been increasingly building their practices around money from the government. Step-by-step, medical care has been bureaucratized and socialized.

> "The inherent vice of capitalism is the unequal sharing of the blessings. The inherent blessing of socialism is the equal sharing of the misery."
>
> *Winston Churchill*

Some say Obamacare isn't socialized medicine because there will still be privately owned insurance plans and medical facilities – at least in the beginning. Since these are under tight government control, they constitute corporate socialism. Consequently, costs will go up sharply and quality will go down. These are the hallmarks of socialism.

Older physicians will retire early, talented young people will not spend the money and time to become physicians, and the quality of medical care will decline.

Socialized medicine is bureaucratized medicine. Bureaucratized medicine leads to less efficient medicine and lower-quality medicine.

We can use this system for a while. Some people like it. Seemingly free services are popular. A high-value item delivered free of charge or at below-market prices seems attractive. But the problem is this: there is more demand than supply for something that is free. Who will decide who gets the care? Washington bureaucrats.

Medical Care in Decline

As medical care in the United States has gradually fallen more and more under the control of government and the special interests that Congress empowers, doctors are beginning to treat their patients according to bureaucratic rules and medical costs have skyrocketed.

The government is the customer—not the person who receives or increasingly does not receive service. The government sets the standards and the goals. The over-riding goal may be to save money for the government approved plan by restricting service. The health of "society" or of the budget, not the health or comfort of the patient, is the bottom line. Doctors who put their patients first may see their pay cut or may even find themselves out of a job altogether.

Payment depends on proper form-filling rather than productive work. Hospitals can spend as much on Medicare billing and compliance as they do on actual patient care. In the doctor's office, more staff may be shuffling paper about services than actually performing them.

Already, profound changes are occurring. Medicare beneficiaries are finding it increasingly difficult to find a physician willing to make an appointment for a new patient. Some physicians are restricting their practices to those who pay an up-front retainer fee for services.

The number of physicians in independent practice is declining rapidly, as more physicians become salaried employees of hospitals or large managed-care corporations. Even those who are still in independent practice often do not follow patients to the hospital, delegating that care to others. As is happening with much of American industry, medical services are also being out-sourced to Third World countries, where American-trained physicians offer services for a cash price to those able to travel.

No, there is nothing *called* a "death panel" in Obamacare. But there is the IPAB, the Independent Payment Advisory Board. This is made up of federally appointed bureaucrats who will dictate what can be paid for what medical services, starting with Medicare. They won't say that Mrs. Evans is going to be terminated, only that the treatment that would prolong her life will not be paid for.

Doctors who are paid for working more, do more work. They come in early, stay late, give up their lunch hours, work weekends, or improve efficiency so that they can help more patients.

But if you put a cap on the amount doctors can earn, many adopt a "work avoidance" strategy. Canadian surgeons, for example, sometimes go on vacation as soon as they have performed the allowed number of operations, no matter how many people are on the waiting list, disabled and in pain. Medical work is difficult and risky. Remove the potential reward, and doctors will work less, just as other people would – especially if you load on "disincentives" for working.

Do patients believe they are protected by doctors' ethics? The ancient Oath of Hippocrates forbids killing, even of the unborn. But modern ethics taught in medical schools dependent on government funding conforms to socialist ethics. The new physician is taught to comply with government directives and to strive for "the greatest good for the greatest number"– as determined by Washington.

The new physician is responsible for groups, not for individual patients. He isn't even called a physician, but rather a "provider" or "supplier" of services to "consumers," or "covered lives." Billing patterns are scrutinized, to catch and prosecute "outliers" – doctors who provide a lot more care than average. Once all medical records are computerized, it will be very convenient for bureaucrats to make sure all doctors follow the bureaucrats' dictates.

The "complete lives" system favored by "reformers" is based on age. Young children are a low priority because society has not yet "invested" much in them. Older people are a low priority because they don't have very many years of voting and paying taxes ahead of them. This is not considered to be age discrimination, because "every 65-year-old was once 25."

Every patient who is admitted to a hospital that takes government money has to be asked about "end-of-life choices." If your doctor doesn't go along with the program, he might be labeled a "disruptive physician," thrown off the hospital staff or insurance panel, and reported to the National Practitioner Data Bank.

Despite the increasing restrictions on treatments that can be offered to government-insured patients, Medicare and Medicaid are still very "popular" programs. As long as care seems to be "free" or nearly so, people like it.

Today, in the socialized "free" medical system in Greece there's the "envelope." That's for the bribe that you have to pay if you want good treatment. This might not come to the U.S. Americans might have to go to places like Greece to be allowed to buy care with their own hard-earned dollars, if the bureaucrats decide that American "national resources" should not be spent on patients like them.

In any system where goods and services are free or underpriced from the standpoint of the recipient, demand will always exceed supply. Thus the need for the "gatekeeper" who has the disagreeable job of deciding what care is to be authorized, and what is to be denied. This wasteful activity is very expensive to the taxpayer or organization that is paying for the "free" care, so medical dollars are lost.

When Medicare was rammed through Congress in 1965, soon after the assassination of President Kennedy, President Johnson feared that the program would fail. The American Medical Association was opposed to it, and so were many seniors. More than half of seniors had private insurance and were happy with it. They did not want to be pushed into socialized medicine.

So, to assure that his program would succeed, Johnson and Congress forced private insurers to cancel the policies of all Americans over age 65. Medicare was not a "public option competing on a level playing field." Medicare was the only source of primary medical coverage available to most Americans once they reached the age of 65.

Medical spending then accelerated much faster than economic growth. So, government is squeezing doctors harder and harder. Patients may not yet be able to see what they are not getting, but care is being cut in many ways.

Where are the high costs of medical care going? Some goes to pay for services that the government requires hospitals and doctors to provide to patients who simply don't pay their bills. Some is the result of cost-shifting from government programs like Medicare and Medicaid that underpay. Much is spent on claims filing and compliance with government rules.

There are additional costs affecting all American medical facilities: the huge costs of regulation of drugs and medical devices; litigation, which not only affects doctors' malpractice insurance but the cost of any item with a medical use; licensure and other regulatory costs that stifle innovation and restrict market entry; "certificates of need"; the "Clinical Laboratory Improvement Act"; requirements to keep records of medical garbage disposal; and more and more busywork requirements. Every time a politician wants credit for "improving" the medical system, the cost is another loss of medical care dollars.

Physician Liberty

Usually lost in all the discussion of how medical care *should* be paid for and delivered is the doctor's own human rights to liberty and justice.

Why should the fact that a doctor went to school and internship for $12+4+4+4 = 24$ years (and probably incurred enormous debts to pay for this education) authorize the government to take away his liberty?

Most patients prefer personal liberty. Most patients would not stand for their careers, lives, and finances to be regulated and micro-managed as closely as the doctors' are already controlled by government. They will be even more controlled under Obamacare.

Why, just because someone wants free medical care, does he have the right to insist that a doctor be enslaved and forced to give it to him?

Yes, doctors still have the right to leave the United States and practice abroad. How would most of their patients react if they were told that all of their affairs would be controlled as closely as a doctor's affairs are now controlled, and, if they don't like this, they are free to get out of their country or change professions?

Violation of the liberty and justice accorded to physicians can only have one ultimate outcome – fewer physicians and physicians with poorer skills. I have been told by several physician friends that, under the system now – much less Obamacare, they would never advise a young person to seek a career in medicine.

Our current doctors are trapped. They can submit to government control, retire, or leave the country. Many decide to submit, but not all, so we already have a shortage of doctors. How many really capable people will choose in the future to enter a profession that automatically ensures that they will lose their liberty?

In a sense, corrupt politicians are doing to the doctors the same thing they are trying to do to the "rich." They say to the voters, "I will take away the rich man's money and give it to you. Vote for me." They also say to the voters, "I will take away the physician's skills and give them to you. Vote for me." In effect, my opponent says both. He voted for Obamacare, and he is loudly calling for higher taxes on the rich.

When the great Russian writer Aleksandr Solzhenitsyn was asked, "How did the Communists enslave the Russian people? There were so many of you, and so few of them." He replied, "They came for us one at a time."

Our liberty and justice are no more secure than those of wealthy people and physicians. If we allow liberty and justice to be taken from them, eventually it will be our turn.

Medical Research

I have spent much of my life doing medical research. When I finished my education at Caltech and UCSD (University of California at San Diego) and was given a job on

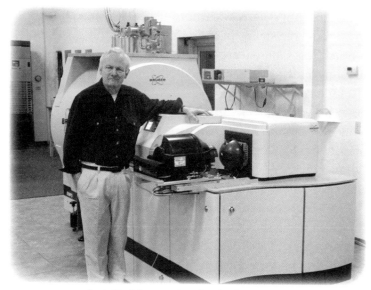

Art Robinson in the Laboratory

The Oregon Institute of Science and Medicine has one of the most outstanding and well equipped biochemistry research laboratories in the Northwest.

the faculty at UCSD, I decided to spend half of my time in basic research and half in medical research.

As a naive young scientist, I thought that all we needed to do was figure out better methods for preventive, diagnostic, and therapeutic medicine, and these would be used to increase the quality and length of human life.

During the next 45 years, the analytical and computational technology required for my work advanced at an unprecedented rate. The laboratory equipment that we have today at the Oregon Institute of Science and Medicine is miraculous as compared to that at UCSD in the 1960s. There have been great technological advances. My colleagues and I have played a small part in these events.

But, in applied diagnostic medicine, I have been very disappointed. Diagnostic medicine today is at least 50 years behind technological advance, and falls farther behind with each passing year.

For example, when you give a blood or urine sample to a doctor, a government-approved facility measures fewer than 25 substances in that sample. The substances measured and the interpretation of the measurements must

Noah Robinson in the Laboratory

Noah earned his BS in chemistry at SOU in 2 years and his PhD at Caltech in 3 years. His research on deamidation of peptides and proteins is respected throughout the world. Noah, his father, and his brother Matthew conduct research on Alzheimer's and Parkinson's diseases, the aging of human proteins, and improvements in medical diagnostics in the Oregon Institute of Science and Medicine laboratories.

be conducted just about the same way they were 50 years ago. To do otherwise risks governmental consequences. The bureaucrats define "medical care" as that of today or yesterday, or 50 years ago, and they don't like to change.

Yet, modern equipment can measure as many as 2,000 substances instead of just 25 in your samples, and modern computers can extract far more useful medical information from those measurements. This is not done. Why not?

Empowered by congressional laws, regulations, and bureaucrats whom Congress funds, a vast, entrenched governmental-corporate-legal-medical monopoly controls this field.

That monopoly is typified by the words of one corporate executive who explained it to me this way when I suggested improvements that his company could make in clinical laboratory procedures, "Why should we? We're making good money doing what we're doing." It is illegal for a doctor not to participate in the monopoly that has this attitude and not to follow its rules.

Consider one research area in which there have been remarkable improvements – medical imaging with Magnetic Resonance Imaging and Computerized Axial Tomography (MRI and CAT scan). Access to these machines has remained locked behind medical monopoly gatekeepers, and has cost hundreds, or sometimes thousands of dollars per scan and interpretation.

Yet, it could be offered directly to consumers, with no gatekeeper cost, for $100 or less in shopping centers and interpreted on the Internet. You would be given a CD containing your data, and then you send it to the best interpreters you can find on the Internet.

Consider overall diagnostic medicine. Most of us

know friends or relatives who have languished in sickness for months or years with illnesses that have not been diagnosed or successfully treated by their local physician. This is not necessarily the physician's fault. No one can know everything. But why not ask thousands of doctors instead of just one?

The Internet makes this possible, but it is not being done. Licensure and malpractice laws prevent American physicians from helping patients they do not physically examine or who reside in states where they are not licensed.

In addition to non-implementation of medical research discoveries, research itself is impeded by government. Nearly all medical research takes place in corporations linked to government or in government-funded universities and other government-funded centers. Scientists in these places must do the research that is dictated by the bureaucrats providing the funds and do it just as they say.

In the medical corporations, this means emphasis on treatments that government bureaucrats will allow the corporations to offer. It now costs an estimated $2 billion just to satisfy government requirements to develop and sell a new drug. Guess what that drug will have to cost in order to repay this money?

Only drugs that can be sold at very high cost are studied. Accountants make the research choices. Anything not patentable, such as nutrition in preventive medicine, is seldom studied. For inexpensive medical advances, there is no means to get back the enormous government-imposed costs.

In government-funded research centers, Washington bureaucrats have the final say on which research ideas will be studied. To be sure, they have "scientists" who advise them, but how skilled is a scientist likely to be who is willing to waste his time advising government bureaucrats?

Just processing government paperwork now occupies a large part of the time of our best medical scientists, so people of lesser ability who work for them must do most of the actual research.

As early as the 1970s, Linus Pauling and I realized that our work in nutrition, preventive medicine, and diagnostic medicine needed to be funded by non-governmental sources. Moreover, since most large foundations are guided and controlled by the medical monopoly, they were not much help to us either.

So, Linus and I co-founded the Institute for Orthomolecular Medicine, later called the Linus Pauling Institute of Science and Medicine. Our goal was to be funded entirely by private contributions, so that we could do the research

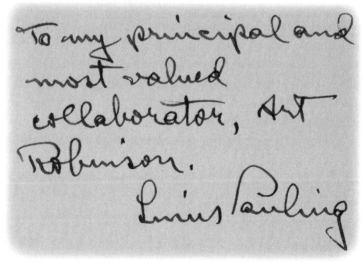

Book Inscription by Linus Pauling

"To my principal and most valued collaborator, Art Robinson."

we thought best. We succeeded in this, for a while.

Today, however, the Pauling Institute is at Oregon State University and receives politically controlled government money. Neither OSU nor LPI should be dependent upon politicians for their funds.

Laurelee and I moved to Oregon 30 years ago. With the help of our colleagues, we founded the Oregon Institute of Science and Medicine, which is entirely supported by private contributions. We do not use government money.

OISM does excellent work. We have a great advantage because we are free to do the research that we think best. Before World War II, when many scientists worked in endowed academic institutions and government meddling in research was minimal, those scientists had the freedom that we still enjoy.

In the movie *Fiddler on the Roof*, a rabbi is asked to offer a blessing for the Czar. The rabbi replies, "May God bless and keep the Czar – far away from us."

If this blessing were offered today and fulfilled so that the government was kept far away from our doctors and our medical researchers, medical care for all of the American people would markedly improve and become far less expensive.

23

VETERANS

The Congress shall have Power To . . . declare War, grant Letters of Marque and Reprisal, and make Rules concerning Captures on Land and Water;
Article I, Section 8, Part 11

Congress has the power to declare war. It therefore has the power to determine the terms of service offered to those who serve in the military. Part of those terms relate to the compensation of people in the military, including wages, retirement, and medical care.

Battlefield medical care today is very good. The percentage of wounded survivors has increased dramatically. An injured serviceman is treated effectively as soon as pos-

---

Congress does not provide sufficient funds to the Veterans Administration necessary keep the promises that it has made to veterans – especially in the case of medical care.

Funding for the Veterans Administration should be increased, so that it has sufficient resources to provide all veterans with everything our country has promised to them.

sible; then he is moved to a military hospital to be given the best possible medical care. This is an expense for the conduct of war.

The military also provides for injured soldiers who need rehabilitation. Our injured service men and women are being provided with first-rate medical care when they are in military service.

Yet, quality medical care is not always easily available at Veterans Administration hospitals. I have talked with many veterans, and a common complaint is that the quality and quantity of the care in VA hospitals is insufficient.

In the area of medical care for veterans, the congressman in their district should immediately intervene on behalf of veterans who are not receiving the medical care they deserve.

Congressmen should have staff members intervening on behalf of their constituents in cases where the government is short-changing a veteran. Most congressmen do have such staff members. It is an ordinary part of their job.

There is, however, no such thing as free medical care. Congress must appropriate sufficient funds to fulfill the promises that it has made to veterans, regardless of the fact that government run medical care is inherently inefficient.

Moreover, veterans should have the government-paid option to use non-VA medical facilities if they prefer.

Veterans in Oregon Congressional District 4

Congressional District 4 in Oregon has a lot of veterans and a lot of young men and women serving in the armed forces who will become veterans. The current incumbent congressman's staff handles veterans' complaints. This is entirely appropriate. A congressman is elected to represent the citizens of his district. He and his staff should spend a lot of time helping individual people in their district. That is their responsibility.

Calls for help from District 4 veterans happen over and over, and our congressman wins votes by helping.

But there is a problem. The calls keep coming. The congressman is living off the problem; he is gaining votes from the problem; but he is not fixing the problem. He really should be going over to the VA and asking: "Why am I getting all of these calls?"

Instead, he is getting care for those who call him, which is probably causing care to be withdrawn from those who don't call. The calls should be reduced to a very few. This should be his goal. He should be making sure that the VA is adequately funded, so he doesn't get the calls.

Congress promises medical care to veterans and then does not provide sufficient resources for that care. The Veterans' Administration is underfunded and over bureaucratized. So, it is short-changing the veterans. Congress must solve this problem.

Every veteran should have better federally supplied medical care and a better retirement program than any congressman.

Wildcards

Veterans are not just concerned about benefits. They are far more concerned about the nation they have defended. I have worked closely with veterans on two defense issues.

During the Cold War in the 1980s and 1990s, Laurelee and I organized about 8,000 Americans in a nationwide civil defense effort called "Fighting Chance." One of our activities was to build trailer-mounted civil defense shelter displays for the Federal Emergency Management Agency, FEMA, which they located at the national emergency training center and at state civil defense agencies. Many veterans worked with us in this effort.

We also published tens of thousands of copies of the book *Nuclear War Survival Skills* that FEMA distributed to emergency managers throughout the United States, and we developed an emergency food ration that FEMA adopted. We still distribute this information. Our civil defense work has always been an entirely non-profit project.

The American Legion borrowed the Pennsylvania display, covered the Pennsylvania State seal on the side with the American Legion seal, and toured fairs and other public events throughout the Northeast. They used it to teach millions of Americans about civil defense technology.

Later, during Operation Desert Storm, my colleagues and I, especially Cresson Kearny who initiated the project, worked to supply rifle protection bags to American soldiers. In the hasty run up to the war, the defense department forgot to manufacture rifle bags as specified in its equipment manuals. These were especially important to prevent rifle jamming in dusty desert conditions.

As our rifle bag program expanded, the Maine American Legion joined and increased our effort. Ultimately, we shipped 600,000 rifle bags and 4.5 million magazine protection bags to American troops. Another 170,000 rifle bags manufactured too late for the war were shipped, at Marine request, to Camp Lejune in the United States for future use. This project was entirely supported by voluntary work and contributions.

Delivering a Shelter Display to FEMA

This fully equipped civil defense shelter for use in public education was built by the Robinsons for the U.S. National Emergency Training Center in Maryland. When installed, it provides civilian protection from nuclear, biological, and chemical threats arising from accident, terrorism, or war – and safety in natural disasters.

Wars are often quickly organized affairs, so many soldiers fight with less than full equipment. Rifle bags, protecting rifles and easily torn off when necessary, were used by American assault troops in beach landings during World War II and by jungle soldiers in Vietnam. Often,

"Dr. Arthur Robinson, For Support of Desert Storm Troops - Oregon Institute of Science and Medicine - Department of Maine, The American Legion 1991"

however, these were not available. Sometimes, soldiers were found dead with jammed rifles in their hands.

We worked on many aspects of emergency preparedness. Unfortunately, Americans are still very poorly prepared for natural and man made disasters. For example, our nation once had portable emergency disaster hospitals. Open a semi-trailer, take out the contents, add doctors, and you had a fully equipped 200-bed tent-covered hospital. These hospitals were discontinued.

Our volunteer work in the 1980s and 1990s was a typical American activity. America has always benefited from hundreds of thousands of citizen "wild cards" – citizens who step forward voluntarily from private life to help in one way or another.

The FEMA annual report for 1988 included a wonderful memorial statement honoring Laurelee's contributions to civil defense, and the Maine American Legion presented us with an award in recognition of the rifle bag work.

An Errant Staple

One of our shelter displays, the one for Arizona, almost didn't make it. Manufactured by Oak Street Tank and Steel in Ashland, Oregon, we hauled the shelters to Cave Junction, where we installed the internal equipment.

We moved the shelters with an old mobile home delivery truck, modified with a room on the back for the six Robinson children. I used an ordinary driver's license because the DMV would not let me take the commercial driver's test with this truck and shelter rig, which they ruled did not require a commercial license. The children and I delivered shelters to FEMA locations all over the U.S.

When I picked up the shelter for the state of Arizona in Ashland, however, I was stopped by an officer at an Ashland truck weigh station.

"Let's see your wide load permit," he asked. I obediently complied, but then he asked, "Where is the map (showing roads allowed for the wide load)?

I gave it to him.

But then came the dreaded governmental regulatory question. "Why isn't the map attached to the permit?"

"I detached it from the permit, so that I could unfold it and read the map."

"The rule says the map must be attached to the permit. Where's your staple?"

Alas, I had no staple.

"Unload your truck right here. You can't proceed without the staple."

This was not going well, but he finally allowed me to keep the load, but ordered me to drive immediately to the Northbound Oregon-California DMV station on Highway 5 and get a staple.

On the way to the northbound DMV, however, I encountered another weigh station on Highway 5 southbound, with yet more bureaucratic requirements. "Where's your commercial driver's license," he demanded. My plea that the DMV had ruled I didn't need one fell on deaf ears.

And then came the revelation that I was already a known fugitive from red-tape, "We know all about you. We heard about you on the radio. You're the guy without the staple."

At length, I received another conditional probation to drive without a commercial drivers license only as far as the northbound DMV.

On the way, however, I accidentally missed the last turn before the Siskiyou mountains and found myself on the way to California. By now I was really worried. "They are going to make me drop this display at the station, and I have no way to get it back to Cave Junction. Plus, I am going to be late to Arizona."

So, I just naturally continued south and headed over the Siskiyou summit. Just over the border, I stopped and telephoned one of our volunteers. He brought the habitability equipment; we both worked through the night in the mountains installing it in the shelter; another friend brought the children to me; and we headed for Arizona.

The FEMA office in Arizona received its civil defense display on time, and the DMV is probably still looking for a guy driving a bomb shelter without the required staple.

Babies and Rest Stops

We had many adventures. Matthew was an infant when we were delivering the FEMA displays to state governments. These were fully functional and equipped nuclear blast shelters when buried underground.

I kept his diapers in the shelters. On occasion, we would stop in a fuel station, and I would change Matthew in the shelter. Matthew is, no doubt, the only PhD student in nuclear engineering in the U.S. who has had his diapers changed in mobile bomb shelters all over our country.

Once, in rural Wyoming, Noah, age 11, called from the back to request a bathroom stop. Since we had stopped not long before, his father was rather terse in explaining that he should have taken advantage of the earlier opportunity, but I did pull off the interstate.

While stopped, Noah discovered that the trailer was barely still attached. The hitch weld was almost broken in two, due to an error in manufacture. It would not have held much longer. This discovery and opportunity for repair saved us from a serious accident.

Noah received, on the spot from his much subdued father, a *Lifetime Bathroom Stop Award* – any time, anywhere, and without complaint. He now has a PhD from Caltech and is respected by scientists throughout the world for his research. He is our congressional campaign manager. And, that bathroom stop award still holds!

Medical Supplies

These displays were authentic. They lacked only actual medical supplies. For the one we built for the FEMA National Emergency Training Center at Emmitsburg, Maryland, Doctors for Disaster Preparedness even equipped the shelter with a full complement of medical supplies.

This turned out to cause a lot of trouble. The bureaucrats at the National Emergency Training Center were afraid to have antibiotics and other emergency medicines at their facility. They demanded that we remove them.

This, of course, makes perfect sense to bureaucrats, since rules are their stock in trade. Still, from the point of view of practical civil defense, what does it tell us about emergency preparedness, if the national center for emergency preparedness training not only doesn't have, but also doesn't want emergency medical supplies at its facility?

If we feel comfortable with sending hundreds of thousands of soldiers and hundreds of billions of dollars abroad for use in foreign wars, it would make sense to have at least a viable program for disasters arising from natural causes, terrorists, or wars that endanger our own citizens at home.

Veterans

While we have worked to improve things at home, however, American soldiers, sailors, and airmen have been fighting in serious wars abroad.

Our veterans are the men and women who did that fighting – they and their fellow warriors who died in those wars in order to preserve our freedom. They did not make the decisions as to the wars they would fight, but they risked and sacrificed themselves to preserve our liberty.

We owe each of our veterans a personal and national debt for the great service that they have given to our nation, and we must make sure that our own actions preserve the liberty for which they fought.

As to Veterans Affairs – provision for the health and needs of our veterans after military service, we must provide to every veteran the best that our nation has to offer.

Every veteran should have better medical care than any congressman. They should have better retirement programs, too. The sacrifices of those who serve our country in the military are far greater than those of any career politician or volunteer who serves in the U.S. Congress.

Service in Congress is a privilege. Many congressmen would say that Congress is their "career" – that they need "benefits" like any other employee. That is part of the problem in Washington. Our liberty should be safeguarded by citizen volunteers who serve short terms in Congress.

24

SOUND MONEY

The Congress shall have Power . . . To coin Money,
regulate the Value thereof, and of foreign Coin, and
fix the Standard of Weights and Measures;
Article I, Section 8, Part 5

No State shall . . . make any Thing but gold and
silver Coin a Tender in Payment of Debts;
Article 1, Section 10, Part 1

The Constitution is clear that Congress has the authority to coin money. The Constitution mentions only gold and silver coins. The section in which the authorization to

> While paper money is convenient, it has the disadvantage that, unless it is secured by gold, silver, or something else of intrinsic value, it can be printed in unlimited amounts. The Federal Reserve, authorized by Congress, has printed too much of ours. One dollar buys today what 5 cents bought in the 1940s.
>
> Inflation of money discourages saving and disrupts commercial activity, which reduces prosperity and jobs. Our country should have sound money.

coin money appears also mentions that Congress has the right to fix the standard of weights and measures.

The Founding Fathers did not call for paper money, because all of them had been through a disastrous period of American history with respect to paper money inflation during the War for Independence.

The war was partially financed by the printing press. The Continental government was unable to collect sufficient taxes from the states, so it printed money and, for a time, imposed price controls.

So, the army had difficulty buying supplies because the paper money had declined rapidly in value, and price controls made it difficult for farmers and other suppliers to deliver goods to the Army. At a low point during the war, George Washington could not buy food for his soldiers because farmers would not accept the printed money of the Continental Congress.

Our country is now repeating this experiment with paper money and getting the same result. Inflation has destroyed 95% of the value of the dollar since I was born.

Strictly interpreted, the Constitution does not permit paper money, only gold and silver. This was first violated by allowing government paper money backed by gold. Then the gold backing was removed. Capital gains taxes and special laws stopped the use of gold and silver.

With "capital gains" taxes on silver and gold, as the value of the dollar drops, the government takes gold and silver to pay taxes on artificial inflationary "gains."

Just repeal of these taxes and laws would permit gold and silver coins to circulate beside paper money. Americans could then choose, in each transaction, their preference. If this were done, either the coins would drive the paper out of circulation, or inflation of the paper money would stop. This is opposed by the Federal Reserve and Congress because they get a lot of political and economic power by printing money and inflating the money supply.

These people argue that they need to be able to print money in case the economy has a difficult problem. Why not just have Congress save money for a "rainy day?" This is what we ordinary people must do.

Coined Freedom

In the early years of the Republic, Spanish coins, known widely as *pieces of eight*, were often used. This coinage provided sound money. It was reliable, and it could not be debased by government inflationary actions. The price level stayed fairly constant during the whole period.

The Constitution also made it illegal for any state to pass a law requiring creditors to accept anything except gold and silver as a means of repaying debt. The constitutional convention considered the problems caused by paper money that was issued in Rhode Island. The other participants did not trust paper money, and the only reference to congressional authority in the Constitution regarding money is to establish coinage.

This sound money has been called "coined economic freedom." Every American citizen should be able under the Constitution and its original intent to use gold and silver as money – to guard his savings and conduct his business in money that cannot be debased by government. Congress does not now permit this.

The United States government provided sound money, either gold or silver, from 1788 until the Civil War. In 1862, the government began to issue paper money to pay for the war. The government decided it would not tax the people directly for all of its revenue, so the people were taxed indirectly with rising prices. The government stopped following the gold standard in 1861, and it was not restored until 1879. The result was price increases.

The United States was part of the international gold standard during the 19th century, except during the period of the Civil War and Reconstruction. From 1815 until 1914, most of the Western world was on a gold coin standard. During that hundred-year period, prices remained remarkably constant. People did not have to worry about prices going up.

Prices remained very stable. People could make plans for the future, knowing that the prices they would pay for goods and services later would be similar to the prices they were paying when they made their plans. This is one important reason that Western civilization in the 19th Century experienced the greatest period of economic growth in the history of mankind.

At the beginning of World War I in 1914, the countries embroiled in the war went off the gold standard. They relied on the invisible tax of inflation. The consequent rise of prices was visible, but the public didn't always understand that the government was behind this rise.

In 1933, the United States went off the gold standard by calling in the public's gold coins and making it unlawful for American citizens to own gold. It was claimed that this would help end the Great Depression. It didn't.

After World War II, the United States had most of the world's gold. So Congress, under congressional authority that it delegated to bankers and the President, convinced the world to use U.S. paper dollars as the world reserve currency. It was promised that these dollars would be gold backed. At any time, dollars could be exchanged for gold, except by American citizens.

This promise was honored by our politicians with the same forthright ethics that have gotten Congress its current 10% approval rating. They broke it. In 1971, they refused to honor the promise. President Nixon made the announcement.

Since then Congress, through the bankers and agencies Congress authorizes to do the job, has printed a blizzard of paper money and caused price increases all over the world. By getting to spend this printed money first, congressmen have purchased votes, power, and wealth for themselves at the expense of savers. As a consequence, prices have risen rapidly, and savings have been destroyed.

Savings is a very important source of capital. Capital is used to create jobs. Americans used to be savers. Each month, responsible citizens spent somewhat less than they earned and saved the rest, typically in a bank or savings and loan. The irresponsible printing of paper money under congressional authorization has greatly reduced this practice. Money saved in a bank, regardless of interest earned, just deteriorates in value.

The dollar is rapidly losing its value as a direct result of the congressionally authorized printing press – and from money "printing" with Federal Reserve computers.

So, still wanting to save for their futures, Americans have looked to other places to save their earnings. They have tried real estate, bonds, stocks, collectables – literally everything with intrinsic value. These markets, however, are volatile and uncertain. They are speculative.

So, America has become a nation of speculators rather than savers. Since savings are stolen by Congress and its allies the bankers through inflation, Americans have scrambled to find alternatives. Many people no longer follow frugal ways by saving their money in banks. As a result of money printing and the price increases that it causes, their savings are not safe in the banks.

Almost everyone with wealth is gambling – in the stock markets, in the bond markets, in real estate, and in other markets. If ordinary workers do not themselves do this, their pension funds are doing it for them.

It is widely realized that the U.S. Congress is corrupt, and that Congress cannot be trusted with the world reserve currency. China may try to replace the dollar - with gold backed Chinese money.

Consider the "rally" in the dollar value of U.S. stocks over the past two and one half years. The rally is there only because the government printed lots of paper money and caused stocks *priced in dollars* to rise. ***Priced in gold, silver, oil, gasoline, or a basket of world commodities, there has been no stock market rally.***

The two figures on pages 302 and 303 show the price of the Dow Stock Average in units of crude oil and in units of an average of world commodities. Commodity prices are a good comparison because their prices reflect the difficulty in producing them, a relatively stable measure of real value.

Notice that stock prices peaked near year 2000 and have decreased since. Can you see the stock "rally" of the past three years? No? That's because it isn't there!

The stock market has dropped 6-fold in terms of crude oil. Yet, in printed money, the "Dow price" is almost unchanged. The second graph uses a basket of commodities called the "Continuous Commodities Index." By this measure, the Dow has fallen 3-fold, and there is no rally.

Dividing the paper money price of gasoline by 3-fold, it is about $1.25 per gallon. Does that trigger a memory?

How could there be a stock market rally? The value of American businesses has been falling for 10 years, ever since it peaked in about the year 2000. Taxation, regulation, litigation, and debt are destroying American industry and business.

Congress doesn't want you to know this. The banks and stock brokers don't want you to know this. So, the government has printed a lot of money. Now, they are printing even more money to make things look as good as possible for the national elections in November 2012.

But, you know because you realize that economic life is becoming steadily more difficult and precarious even if you still have a job. By authorizing the printing of lots more dollars – trillions of more dollars – Congress makes dollar prices go up, but real wealth goes down. Unless you are a congressman or in a niche group that receives special favors from Congress, your chances for a prosperous life and fulfilling career are steadily diminishing.

When money is unsound, people turn to speculation – speculation in stocks, houses, land, and anything else of value that they hope will preserve their savings. Speculation drove the stock market up in the years before 2000. The unwinding of speculation plus the destruction of American business and industry by over-taxation, over-regulation, and over-indebtedness drove the stock market back down. As this occurred, the successive collapses of over-speculation in stocks and later in real estate added to

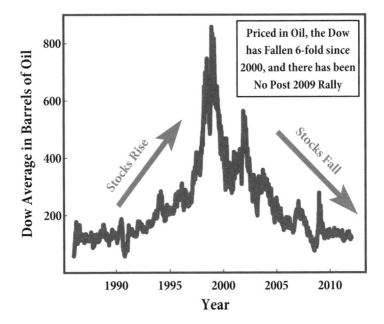

Dow Average Valued in Crude Oil

When the Dow stock average is graphed in crude oil, it is seen that the Dow has fallen 6-fold since 2000 and has not recovered. The same 6-fold drop is seen for gold, silver, and copper. This is twice the decline seen for a "basket" that includes agricultural items.

the downward trend.

The blizzard of paper money being printed by the government is increasing the *dollar* price of stocks. People are trying to use stocks as an inflation hedge to protect themselves from unsound money. Historically, however, it has been observed that stocks provide only about 30% protection from severe monetary inflation. They are likely, on average, to lose 70% of their wealth to the printing presses.

If one looks at real prices of goods and services over

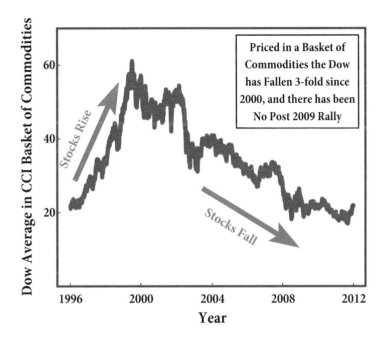

Priced in a Basket of
Commodities the Dow
has Fallen 3-fold since
2000, and there has been
No Post 2009 Rally

Dow Average Valued in a Basket of Commodities

When the Dow stock average is graphed in things of real value that cannot be inflated by congressionally authorized money printing, it is seen that the Dow has fallen dramatically since 2000 and has not recovered at all. Here the Continuous Commodity Index reveals a 3-fold collapse of the Dow.

long periods of time, he finds that prices have tended to be stable, with a downward trend. The downward trend results from improvements in methods of production. Yet, during my lifetime, prices in paper dollars of goods and services have increased about 20-fold.

Recent price increases have been masked in various ways, including the export of inflation to other countries because the dollar is used as the world reserve currency. The world has begun to break free of this restraint.

Americans have been badly hurt by the dishonest, un-backed fiat paper money that Congress has sponsored. As the world exits the dollar, they are going to be hurt a lot more. Can this still be stopped? Yes!

How? Elect honest citizens to Congress who will stop the inflationary money printing.

The Federal Reserve System

In the final days of 1913, when many in Congress had returned home for the Christmas vacation, the remaining House and Senate members passed the Federal Reserve Act, and President Wilson signed it into law within hours. That law delegated congressional control over American money to the Federal Reserve System, which is controlled by a committee of the Federal Reserve Bank.

As the American dollar has come to be used as currency throughout the world, the Federal Reserve Bank has become the most powerful bank in the world.

The Federal Reserve Bank became so powerful that Congress dared not even audit its activities. In principle, the "Fed" is supposed to supply Americans with honest and reliable money. Yet, there is not a single example in history where men were given the power to print money or debase coinage and did not abuse that power. The Fed has proved to be no exception.

The Fed should be completely audited – not just partially – and Congress should assert its constitutional authority to assure that Americans have a sound currency that is not inflated. If the Fed cannot do this – a goal that it has completely failed to meet so far and is unlikely ever to achieve – the Fed should be ended.

The Need for Sound Money

Money is a very important aspect of economic liberty. It serves several crucial purposes:

1. Money is a medium of exchange.

Suppose that the Rough and Ready lumber mill in Josephine County paid its workers in lumber – the product they manufacture. The workers would then need to trade this lumber for food, clothing, fuel and other things that their families need. Imagine these workers hauling their wages in trucks to Nelson's farm in Sauer's flat in order to trade wood for tomatoes and corn.

This inconvenience and many similar barter transactions would interfere with the division of labor throughout the economy. This would harm the economy and lead to less prosperity for the mill workers and the Nelsons.

Money solves this problem. The workers are paid in money and Nelson accepts money for his produce. Thus money serves as a medium of exchange.

2. Money serves as a store of capital.

Rough and Ready may decide to save some of its profits or the workers at Rough and Ready may decide to save part of their wages in the Evergreen Bank. Their savings then become available as capital for other businesses and provide jobs for other workers.

Here again, this use of money increases the efficiency of the economy and the prosperity of everyone.

Without using money, the mill workers could save part of their time and labor – and then use that time to work for the Taylor Sausage company. This would cause, however, an economic loss because most of the mill workers don't know much about making sausage.

If they instead save money and put it in the bank, Taylor can borrow it from the bank and hire more workers. If the new workers earn more for Taylor than they are paid in wages, everyone benefits. They have jobs, Taylor makes a profit, and Evergreen can pay interest to the mill workers. Taylor may decide to save his profits in the Evergreen Bank, too, or in the Sterling Bank or the South Valley Bank.

Capital, stored as money, makes possible the division of labor. The mill workers are specialists in producing boards. Nelson is a specialist in producing food. Everyone is more prosperous when people are able to work to produce the things that they are especially skilled in making.

Thus, savings and profits, made more convenient by money, serve as a source of capital – real capital, which can be used productively to create products and jobs. Capital cannot, however, be faked by printing money. Fake capital produces no net products or jobs.

Suppose the Fed, authorized by Congress, just prints up some new money and loans it to Evergreen. Can't Evergreen then loan this money to Taylor and thereby create more jobs? No. This doesn't work.

By printing more money, the Fed causes prices to rise, thereby taking real capital away from workers, businesses, and savers elsewhere in the economy. So, jobs elsewhere are lost. Money printing just moves capital from one group to another. It does not create new capital or additional jobs.

Moreover, since politicians and bureaucrats who did not work to produce the capital spend this money less wisely than would those who earned it, capital is actually lost when seized from the owners by inflation or taxes and cycled through government. So, there are fewer jobs.

The same holds true for borrowing or taxing by politicians. Net capital is not produced by these activities. It is

> If a mill worker is waylaid by a criminal and robbed, the mill worker becomes less prosperous. When government waylays the mill worker at every opportunity and seizes his capital through inflation, taxation, and borrowing, the mill worker becomes less prosperous, too.

just moved around to less productive uses.

3. Money serves as a measure of value.

When Robinson decides to harvest some trees on his land, he sends the logs over to Rough and Ready. How does the mill decide on a price for the logs? How does Rough and Ready decide how much to pay its workers, its fuel suppliers, its equipment suppliers, and the many other industries upon which it depends?

When the mill workers buy produce from Nelson, how does Nelson decide how much to charge, and how do the mill workers decide if Nelson's prices are reasonable?

These decisions are all made easier by money. A mill worker knows how long he must work to buy a dozen ears of sweet corn from Nelson. Everyone knows how much effort it takes for him to earn money, so he knows its value.

4. Money Facilitates Long Term Economic Decisions.

When Nelson buys additional farm equipment, he needs to be able to make a good estimate of the future price of his produce. If the money is sound, Nelson can assume that prices will be moderately stable – subject, of course, to weather and other factors that are the unavoidable risks of his business. If the money is not sound, Nelson will have trouble planning for the future, and his business will be less productive – providing fewer jobs and producing less.

Consider the hundreds of millions of transactions throughout the American economy similar to those of the mill workers and Nelson. With sound money, all of these transactions are facilitated and all Americans benefit.

In our current situation, where Congress causes economic confusion by creating money of unreliable value, jobs and prosperity are lost.

Congressional actions that have made our money unsound have cost the American people millions of jobs and tragic losses in prosperity and economic freedom.

Prices Should Decrease

My mother was very frugal. She carefully saved as much of my father's wages as she could. She played a little game. She tried to see how long she could pay the family expenses with a $20 bill. What will $20 buy today?

As prices rose as a result of inflationary money printing, however, her savings were taken from her.

Yet, prices should have decreased. Technological advance constantly makes things easier to make. With sound money, we could save part of our earnings, knowing that in the future they would buy more rather than less.

Money printing has stolen all of the productivity savings that should have made saved money more valuable. When government reports the "consumer price index," it under-reports the rise for political reasons. And, it also hides the fact that the index should have gone down.

Our nation needs sound money. It is a duty of Congress to see that sound money is assured.

25

NATURAL RESOURCES
AND THE ENVIRONMENT

Life is a wonderful privilege, but we are not able to live without using the resources of the earth. To even provide ourselves with food and shelter, we must use natural resources – and our modern civilization requires much more.

If you want reminders of why America is great, visit a hydroelectric dam, steel mill, nuclear power plant, coal mine, oil refinery, or petrochemical plant. On a recent trip to Houston, as I drove over the top of a highway overpass

> **Our economy and the survival of our civilization depends upon the use of natural resources.**
>
> **Congress has funded and empowered bureaucratic agencies that greatly restrict our access to natural resources – both private and public.**
>
> **From trees in Oregon and mines in Idaho, to oil deposits in Alaska and coal in West Virginia, Congress is restricting our access to natural resources.**
>
> **This destroys jobs and careers, reduces prosperity, and forces industries to move abroad. Congress should greatly reduce this intrusion on our freedom.**

at night, I found myself looking out over the glittering lights of a vast array of petrochemical plants that extended as far as my eyes could see.

My favorite airplane is the SR 71 Blackbird. There is a Blackbird at the Evergreen Aviation and Space Museum at McMinnville, Oregon. In service between 1964 and 1998, the Blackbird still holds the world speed record for an air-breathing airplane in level flight.

Flying faster than three times the speed of sound, the Blackbird had a simple solution for escape from enemy missiles. It simply accelerated and outran them. Fired at with more than 1,000 missiles, no Blackbird was ever shot down. The chief test pilot for the Blackbird was Robert Gilliland, who is our friend and a supporter of our campaign for Congress. Robert Gilliland has more hours above Mach 2 and Mach 3 than any other pilot.

Built at Lockheed by Kelly Johnson and his team, the Blackbirds are made of titanium. That titanium had to be mined from the earth and then traveled on a remarkable journey through marvelous men, machines, and additional natural resources before it flew its reconnaissance missions to the Soviet Union during the Cold War – missions that provided information that helped prevent nuclear war.

Everywhere one finds men and machines, there is reason to be in awe. Visit one of Oregon's remaining lumber mills or take a trip into the woods with a third-generation Oregon timber faller. Theirs, too, is a marvelous world.

Congress, however, apparently doesn't seem to think so. Living in their Washington cocoons, too many of these people do not engage in physical work.. They live in a world of limousines and airplanes that shuttle them around between their "very important" engagements – without any hands-on experience with the efforts that make the world work. Photo-ops with workers are as close as they ever get to real work.

The decisions to deprive southern Oregon timber companies of access to the natural resource of Oregon trees were made entirely on the basis of politics. Current federal efforts to deprive the people of District 4 of use of even more of their public lands and resources and to further encroach on private property are just more of the same.

My opponent encourages these intrusions. They are orchestrated by his political friends, while the economy is further depressed by rules that prevent use of natural resources.

The federal government broke its agreements with the counties of Oregon to lease the logging rights in their forests and share the revenues from this logging with the counties. These are called the O&C agreements and are very familiar to the people of District 4. My opponent accomplished nothing useful to stop this. His political self-interest lay with those who orchestrated it.

Instead, he helped obtain "welfare payments" to the county governments instead of justice. This conversion to welfare bought him votes. Voters became afraid to vote against him because the welfare payments might stop.

This was a textbook example of a politician living off the problem rather than solving it. Josephine County is 70% owned by the federal government, which pays no county taxes. The O&C logging agreements were supposed to make up for this. Now, the federal government has effectively closed these forests to logging.

Our congressman could have forced the federal government to honor the O&C agreements. This should have been his highest priority – beginning 20 years ago.

Deprived of access to their most valuable natural resource, District 4 counties face bankruptcy and sharp increases in property taxes.

Moreover, when the Biscuit Wildfire later burned vast stretches of forest in Oregon District 4, DeFazio stood idle while logging of the dead trees, replanting, and restoration of the forests was prohibited. Just the logging of those dead trees would have saved thousands of jobs in the lumber industry and kept District 4 counties solvent for many years.

Voters and taxpayers in Josephine County know very well that Peter DeFazio has worked in favor of his own interests and against their interests. This is the reason that I received 59% of the vote in Josephine County in 2010 and won majorities in Douglas, Curry, and Linn counties, too.

Now, my opponent is actually promoting a federal arrangement to take a million acres out of O&C forest lands. He also wants to designate 90,000 more acres as wilderness. "Wilderness" caused the horrific Biscuit Fire, which was allowed to burn while firefighters were refused access. These 90,000 acres are also rich in mineral resources.

Miners in southern Oregon, especially since gold prices now make the mining of this resource more practical, have also been having special difficulties with the government.

Are these miners getting any help from their congressman? Of course not. They and those who seek to develop other mineral resources get a cold shoulder from congressman DeFazio as they battle his anti-resource friends.

All across our country, similar scenarios are in progress where Congress and the bureaucracies it has funded stand between the American people and their natural resources.

The extraction, processing and use of oil, iron, coal,

natural gas, uranium, titanium, water, trees, farm land, and hundreds of other resources are constantly restricted by political opportunists. Congress favors those with the best publicity campaigns and the most campaign cash.

Steel is basic to our civilization. Yet, most remaining American steel mills are now re-users of scrap. The making of steel from iron ore has almost entirely moved abroad.

We are all too familiar with the usual claims. Essentially everyone who uses natural resources is advertised as a villain, "stripping our land of its beauty and wealth." They are said to be profligately destroying our children's future.

What future? A nation that does not permit its people to use their natural resources has no future.

The Constitution leaves to the states and the people all issues except those specifically delegated in the Constitution. The states and people are given complete control of their natural resources and environment except in rare instances, mostly where disputes cross state lines.

Congress should stop passing unconstitutional laws and should withhold funding from agencies that get between Americans and their natural resources. If we continue to be increasingly deprived of access to our resources, we cannot prosper.

The states are perfectly able to regulate resource use, so that it does not impair the environment. The states and the people are not going to ruin their own environments.

For most of our national history, we were not burdened with Washington over-regulation of our resources. Yet, our country remained a beautiful place to live and work – a place that some now claim will be ruined if it is left in the hands of the states and people who have preserved it.

Natural Resources from Abroad

It is, of course, possible for a country to use natural resources obtained from abroad. Our country grew prosperous using the natural resources within our borders and natural resources mined in other countries.

Energy is a special case. We have vast energy resources within our own country, but government has prevented us from using them. This has required that we send enormous amounts of capital abroad for oil and other energy resources and has badly damaged our economic health.

Strategically, it is best that a nation develop its own natural resources, so that it will not be deprived of needed materials in case of war. Congress did, in the past, stockpile natural resources for defense purposes, but this practice has largely and very imprudently been abandoned.

A nation must, however, export enough manufactured goods and natural resources to equal the goods and resources it obtains from other countries. Usually, the most wealthy countries excel in manufacturing activities. Less developed countries often serve as sources of natural resources. It is better to be in the former group.

As Congress has, by over-taxation, over-regulation, over-spending, and over-indebtedness destroyed much of our manufacturing and simultaneously restricted our access to our own natural resources, it has dealt our nation a double blow.

As our economy declines, those natural resources we are able to produce are increasingly being exported rather than being used by industries within our country. This is an ominous sign post on the unwise road that our nation, under congressional mismanagement, is traveling.

Preservation of Our Environment

Oregon District 4 has one of the most beautiful natural environments in the world. This was the most important factor that caused us to move our family here 32 years ago.

The environment in our district is a glowing testimony to the people who settled this region more than 150 years ago and those who have preserved its beauty for themselves and future generations.

The only real blight on the environment here is the vast region of burned forests from the Biscuit fire, the largest wildfire in Oregon history. This tragedy was caused by federal mismanagement of a "wilderness area" fire.

The fire was deliberately permitted to burn unchecked. Soon, it was too big to fight effectively and spread over a very wide region. Moreover, since further federal actions led to the burned area not being cleared and replanted, this environmental devastation will be with us for a long time.

Throughout the world, it is generally seen that the most wealthy nations have the best cared for environments. People and countries that are poor simply lack the financial and industrial resources to care for the environment. They cannot spare the time and money for environmental preservation. Poor people struggle just to stay alive.

During the past 32 years, I have noticed that the private property in Oregon District 4 is better cared for environmentally than public property. People who own land and resources generally take better care of them than do bureaucrats and politicians far away in Washington.

The greatest threat to the environment throughout our nation now is the economic instability that has been caused by irresponsible actions by Congress.

The U.S. Constitution clearly leaves environmental

concerns to the states and the people. The people who live in a particular environment are best suited to care for it.

When "environmentalists" call for more and more federal repression of the people in order to "save the environment," they actually hurt their own cause. Repression makes the people poorer, which hurts the environment.

Among the worst environments in our nation are poor ghettos in Eastern cities. The people in these places do not want this blight. They are just too poor to fix it.

All people, with very few exceptions, are environmentalists at heart. We just need sufficient regulation to assure that the exceptions are controlled. With sufficient freedom to maintain prosperity, Americans will do fine.

Liberty is the best protection for our nation's environment.

26

ENERGY FOR OREGON

*The powers not delegated to the United States by
the Constitution, nor prohibited by it to the States, are
reserved to the States respectively, or to the people*
Amendment 10

Inexpensive and abundant energy supplies are essential
to our industrial economy. Without these, our energy
intensive industries are not competitive, and those that
require large amounts of energy must move abroad, taking

> **Expensive imports of energy are a substantial
> part of our economic difficulties. High cost energy
> causes our industries to be less competitive and, in
> many cases, to move abroad. This destroys our jobs.**
>
> **The United States has vast natural resources with
> which to produce energy, but congressional restric-
> tions and regulations have inhibited their use.**
>
> **Other than very modest oversight, Congress
> should not meddle in our energy supply. Nuclear,
> coal, oil, gas, solar, wind, and other energy sources
> should be developed on a level competitive playing
> field without government subsidies or impediments.**

our careers, jobs, and national wealth with them.

Energy is also key to our personal lives, providing for fuel for our cars, electricity for our homes, and many other conveniences and necessities.

Energy should pose no problem at all for Americans. We have extensive technological knowledge for converting natural energy resources into usable energy, and we have such an abundance of those resources that we could not exhaust them in thousands of years.

America's ascendancy to become the economic miracle of the world was paralleled and made possible by our development of energy technology.

Some people think that the steam engine is a historical artifact, but much of our civilization still runs on steam today, utilizing steam turbines rather than pistons. Steam is produced from heat by burning wood, coal, natural gas, and oil, and by nuclear energy and then used in turbines to turn shafts that produce electrical and mechanical energy.

We also use internal combustion engines that burn natural gas, gasoline and diesel to turn those shafts.

Our cars, trucks, ships, factories, farms, and entire industrial civilization depend directly upon those spinning shafts, hundreds of millions of spinning shafts in marvelous machines throughout the world.

Those spinning shafts also produce more than 99% of our electricity, which makes possible our lights, computers, and a multitude of conveniences we now take for granted.

Electricity from those shafts keeps many of us warm in the winter and cool in the summer, and we directly burn fuels to keep us warm as well.

There are a multitude of ways to extract useful energy from our environment. Coal, oil, gas, nuclear, solar, wind, wave, and biochemical energies can be gathered in various ways and converted to our use.

As America developed from an agrarian economy to an industrial economy, the most important single industry was energy. Free enterprise, private capital, and energy engineers built a multitude of machines to provide us with low cost abundant energy. I still enjoy reading through my father's textbooks from college. At Iowa State University in the 1930s, he majored in steam power plant engineering.

Energy-producing technology did not need to cost the American taxpayer a single cent. Most of it arose spontaneously from the efforts of free people, working with private capital, and produced wonderful improvements in life for everyone, rich and poor, throughout our country.

Most Americans didn't need to understand this technology to reap its benefits. Engineers tried out every idea imaginable, and entrepreneurs provided private capital to fund most of these ideas. The resulting machines competed in the free market. Those that provided the greatest amount of useful energy at the lowest cost succeeded. Others failed.

On a level playing field of American industrial liberty, men with machines competed. We live wonderful lives today as a result of that competition. It is difficult to believe that those lives are now threatened by a shortage of energy.

What happened? Why, with this as our heritage, is our country so desperately short of energy that we have been borrowing and spending $300 billion per year – $3,000 for every American family, to import energy from other countries and are constantly being implored by our electric companies to "conserve" energy. Now under government control, these companies actually plead with us to use less of their own product!

What happened is that the Congress of the United States, acting entirely outside of its constitutional authority, decided to take charge of our energy industries, and Congress created a new bureaucracy to assist in this that it calls the "Department of Energy."

The reason given for creating the Department of Energy during the Carter Administration was to get America off dependence on foreign oil. Congress decided to dictate how we produce our energy. How has that worked out?

First, on the excuse of entirely bogus political lies about safety, Congress and the agencies it funds placed such onerous regulations on our nuclear industry that the building of safe, clean, and sustainable nuclear energy plants in the U.S. was completely stopped.

Second, Congress began to meddle in the coal, oil, and natural gas (hydrocarbon) industries. This gradually became more and more ridiculous. These self-important politicians now even claim that, by regulating our hydrocarbon industry, they can control the world's weather.

> **"Government's view of the economy could be summed up in a few short words: If it moves, tax it. If it keeps moving, regulate it. And if it stops moving, subsidize it."**
> *Ronald Reagan*

As a consequence of these congressional regulatory activities, our country is now critically short of energy; has lost many of its energy-intensive industries and jobs to other countries; and has run up an enormous national debt largely by buying energy abroad.

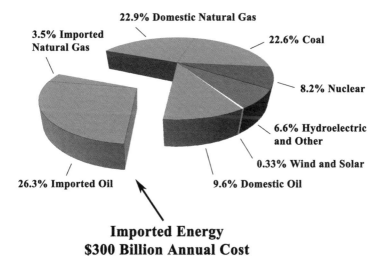

22.9% Domestic Natural Gas

3.5% Imported Natural Gas

22.6% Coal

8.2% Nuclear

6.6% Hydroelectric and Other

0.33% Wind and Solar

26.3% Imported Oil

9.6% Domestic Oil

Imported Energy
$300 Billion Annual Cost

Sources of United States Energy[17,36,37]

With oil at $60 per barrel, Americans *imported* about $300 billion in energy in 2007. Had Congress not interfered with energy production, Americans would have *exported* about $200 billion in energy. Now, with oil at $100 per barrel, but with the economy in recession and prices up, imports are about 20% of use and import costs are about the same as 2007. Congressional meddling has raised costs and reduced the supply of energy, making U.S. industries less competitive and causing many to move abroad.

If the Americans who invented and built our country's energy industries could zoom in on Washington today and see Peter DeFazio and his political cronies pretending to be able to decide out how America's energy should be produced, they would be astonished.

Surely even these people cannot possibly be so egotistical as to believe that they actually have the ability to direct America's energy engineers. Peter DeFazio has no education, no training, and no experience in any manufacturing enterprise whatever, much less energy engineering or science.

The figure above shows where we stand today as a result of congressional meddling in our energy industries.[17,36,37]

It shows values for 2007, before the current economic recession. Energy imports are currently about 20% of total use, primarily because our economy is now depressed.

Think about this chart. The United States is so dependent on imported energy that it has become increasingly indebted to foreigners in China, Japan, Russia, Saudi Arabia and other countries to pay for it. These debts are building up relentlessly.

Energy and Liberty

I am a physical scientist with degrees from Caltech and the University of California at San Diego.

For 18 years, I have written the 38-year-old publication *Access to Energy*, and have carefully researched many energy technologies.

The readers of *Access to Energy* include some of the nation's leading experts on energy. They send me information. I probably know more about energy than any current member of Congress.

And, as a congressman, I should not have anything at all to say about how America's energy is produced, except to make sure that my congressional colleagues and I stay out of the way.

The American industrial landscape should be a level competitive playing field when it comes to energy production, with no government subsidies and no government impediments to any efforts to produce energy, other than common sense safety rules.

If the U.S. Congress would get its nose out of the

energy industry, an abundant supply of energy would be made available at a low price by free enterprise, without the expenditure of a single taxpayer dollar.

If government stopped penalizing some energy industries and subsidizing others and got completely out of the way, within 10 years, or less Americans would be *exporting* $200 billion worth of energy each year, rather than *importing* $300 billion worth. We would cease to be a net importer. "Net" because we might still, for example, use oil from Canada and perhaps export electricity, which we would have in abundance, to Mexico.

The economic benefits would be even higher as our energy-intensive industries that have moved abroad returned, bringing their profits and jobs with them.

No one knows what mix of energy production we would have after those 10 years, although a reasonable guess can be made. We also don't know in which states that energy would be produced.

The Constitution gives the states and the people the authority to control their own destinies with respect to most things. It is likely that some states would decide to import energy from other states and to concentrate their own efforts on other industries that their citizens prefer.

Critics of this "hands off" policy may say that some federal regulation is justified. For example, what will be done if a group of drunken, incompetent engineers decide to build an unsafe nuclear power plant across the border from another state?

Obviously, a small amount of oversight is required. In the days when we were building nuclear power plants, this activity was overseen by the Atomic Energy Commission until 1974. Still operating today are 104 nuclear power plants, with an average age of 35 years, that were approved under their rules. Not a single human life has been lost as a result of power generation in those nuclear plants.

A small group of professionals, monitoring power plant construction and operation in cooperation with the states, would be more than sufficient. When the Department of Energy and its associated agencies are closed, a small part of their current budget should be used to pay expenses for a group like the former Atomic Energy Commission, closely watched by Congress to make sure it doesn't metastasize into yet another bloated example of over-regulation. This group could watch over safety in all forms of energy generation.

Two Deficits, Two Crises

Many Americans do not understand the relationship between the U.S. debt and their purchases of energy abroad. These are two sides of the same coin.

First, we are becoming ever-more indebted to foreign governments. Second, we are dependent on energy that we import from outside the United States. So, there are two huge deficits involved here: the financial deficit and the energy deficit. These two deficits are linked economically.

There may well come a day sometime soon when there is a crisis of financing for the United States government. Foreign central banks and private investors may no longer be willing to buy Treasury bills and Treasury bonds. These IOUs have been essential to the expansion of the American government, but this cannot go on much longer.

If that day comes, Americans are going to find out how dangerous it has been for the federal government to be dependent on foreign sources for the government's debt. They are also going to find out how dangerous it has been for Americans to be dependent on imported energy. They are likely to find out both of these things at the same time.

We may find ourselves so much in debt that foreign suppliers will not ship us energy. We will be in the same position as a nearly bankrupt business, when its suppliers will no longer fill its orders.

Congress, violating all dictates of common sense and even the U.S. Constitution itself, has set our country up for a disastrous financial and energy emergency – a danger comparable to that we faced during the Cold War.

On Edward Teller's office wall, as he and his colleagues raced against their Russian counterparts to keep America free during the Cold War, there hung an appeal that read:

"**Providence,**
"**Which looks after Drunkards and Children and Fools**
"**With silent miracles and other esoterica,**
"**Continue to suspend the customary rules**
"**And protect the United States of America."**

To prevent this dual crisis, which can only be avoided if we change our ways, American entrepreneurs must be free to develop new sources of abundant, low-cost energy.

Unfortunately, Congress has capitulated to the highly vocal, well-organized lobbyists who represent special interests. Congress has made it expensive or even illegal to develop viable alternatives to imported energy.

On the one hand, the government has wasted billions of dollars in subsidizing economically inefficient and unworkable energy alternatives, and on the other hand it has restricted the development of economically and technologically viable and proven sources of energy. It has spent the taxpayers' money on dead-end projects, and it has restricted the investment of private investors' money in projects that can actually deliver the energy we need.

It takes time to develop energy resources. Resource development is very expensive. And, it is now hampered by endless impediments imposed by Washington bureaucrats. So, if this dual crisis hits, Americans may find that they are suddenly without the energy that they need.

There is no more crucial resource than energy, other than the creativity and work of human beings. There is also no more restricted industry in the United States than the energy industry. This means that, if this crisis hits, the price of energy is going to go through the roof.

Of the 70% of needed energy we ordinarily produce, much is required for essentials, such as life-preserving heat in winter and food production. Loss of the imported 30% would actually reduce our discretionary supplies by 60% to 70%, including auto fuel and home electricity.

Look at your own monthly budget. What would happen if the price of gasoline tripled? What would happen if your heating and cooling bills also tripled? What would this do to your budget? You would probably not be able to find a lot of extra work to bring in extra money to pay for these expenses. You would not be in a position to cut back dramatically on your consumption of energy. So, what would you do? I mean this. What would you do?

Congress Seems Not to Care . . . Yet

The members of Congress who are in the pockets of special interests do not care. My opponent has an over 90% voting record approval rating with the radical environmentalist lobby.[13,14,15] He doesn't know anything about energy, but he knows where his campaign cash comes from.

These congressmen are implementing policies that are destroying the economic feasibility of developing large scale alternatives to imported energy. I don't mean "green" alternatives. I mean alternatives that will prevent the tripling or quadrupling of energy prices.

Congress has promised for almost 40 years that its policies would decrease our dependence on imported energy. The results, predictably, have been exactly the opposite. This dependence will backfire, overnight without warning, if foreign banks decide to cut off the flow of money. That will cut off the flow of energy.

When it becomes obvious that the endless bailouts by the American government have not worked, foreign governments may instruct their national central banks to stop buying U.S. debt. In the weeks and months following that decision, voters are going to have to sit down and rebalance their budgets, because the federal government did not have the political courage to balance its budget.

There is no plan in Congress to deal with this problem. There will be no relief from Congress because Congress cannot produce energy. Congress can pass laws. Congress can ask the Federal Reserve System to print up some new money. But Congress cannot generate abundant, low-cost energy or force people in other countries to give it to us.

Energy Specifics

The free market should provide our energy. No one is smart enough and no one has the right to direct the activities of 300 million free people. And, technology is always changing. Who can predict the future? We have numerous energy technologies. Some facts about energy are:

Nuclear Energy

The invention of nuclear electric power generation was the greatest technological advance in human history. For the first time, unlimited electricity could be available at a cost so low that it was irrelevant with respect to other costs. Electrical energy could become essentially free.

American engineers who made this advance began to build power plants. By the 1960s, these engineers were already producing a technological revolution.

A nuclear reactor analysis text written in 1976 that Joshua, Matthew, and Bethany Robinson used at Oregon State University says on page 3, "It is anticipated that some 500 nuclear power plants will be installed in the U.S. alone by the year 2000, with an electric generating capacity of about 500,000 megawatts electric at a capital investment of more than $600 billion, with this pattern being repeated throughout the world." An earlier printing of this book predicted 1,000 power plants, but this was revised because Congress had already begun to suppress nuclear energy.

Lobbyists for the power generation methods that nuclear would supplant were already at work in Congress. Also, the temptation to get its fingers into a $600 billion pie was just too much for politicians to resist.

These 500 power plants, which would have been

financed with private capital, were never built. Congress prevented it. About 100 plants were built and still operate today. These 500 plants would have been built as power stations with perhaps 10 power plants each, as planned for the Palo Verde nuclear power station near Phoenix. Congress prevented the completion of Palo Verde. Today it has only three plants instead of the originally planned ten.

Each plant at Palo Verde produces the electric power of two Hoover Dams. The three plants produce the power of six Hoover Dams. If Palo Verde had been completed, it would be producing the power of 20 Hoover Dams. The electricity cost from Palo Verde today is less than 2 cents per kwh - about one-fifth the cost of electricity in Oregon.

The 500 predicted power plants could have been built as just 50 power stations the size of Palo Verde, and each one of these stations could be built on a space the size of our modest farm in Southern Oregon.

These engineers wanted to build the equivalent of 20 Hoover Dams in every one of the 50 states of the United States, with a footprint so small that most people would never even realize they were there.

They would also have built fuel recycling facilities that could eliminate 97% of the volume of waste products from these power plants. Our government also prevented the building of these waste disposal facilities. The much vaunted "nuclear waste" problem is not a technological problem. It is a political problem.

To work properly, reactors require an optimum amount of fuel. Fuel assemblies are replaced while much of the fuel is still unused. When this fuel is re-purified, it can be re-used. During purification in recycling, the remaining radioactive waste is reduced to a very low volume. Many countries do this. Congress prevents it in the U.S.

These power stations would have been built with the technology of the 1960s and 1970s. Was it safe? Well, today we still have the remnants of this dream. There are 104 nuclear power plants operating in the United States. Their average age is 35 years, and there has never been a human life lost as a result of a nuclear accident in these plants.

Today, nuclear power is even less expensive, even safer, and even more desirable, and it could markedly improve the economy of Oregon. Founded on the vision of Professor José Reyes from Oregon State University, NuScale Power in Corvallis is developing small nuclear power units that can power small communities or industrial installations or can be installed in groups to produce large power units.

Still, NuScale faces huge regulatory impediments from the federal government in a very competitive environment. China, Japan, and Russia are working on similar projects for what promises to be a trillion dollar industry.

NuScale could develop into a large business and bring very great economic benefits to Oregon, creating thousands and eventually tens of thousands of high-wage jobs.

Will it do so? NuScale is not permitted to build even a working prototype of its product. NuScale must spend many more years producing expensive paper work for Washington bureaucrats before it is allowed to build its first unit. NuScale's foreign competitors do not have this impediment.

And, if NuScale succeeds, will the jobs it produces stay in Oregon or even in the United States? This is up to the Congress, which has a very poor record in such things.

We will never know the wonderful advances our civilization could have made had Congress not suppressed the development of nuclear energy. And, unless the meddling in our energy industries by Washington ends, our children and grandchildren may never see these things either.

Hydrocarbon Energy

Coal, oil, natural gas, and methane clathrates are all hydrocarbons. They vary in their sources and in the length of the chains of carbon atoms hooked together in their molecules. Natural gas is mostly methane and a lesser amount of ethane, while methane clathrates are primarily methane and water.

All four of these hydrocarbon types can be converted into one another. There are industrial plants operating today in South Africa that turn coal into oil as did the Germans during World War II – and plants operating in the Middle East that turn natural gas into oil.

Sasol Corporation is planning to build a plant in Louisiana that will convert natural gas into about 100,000 barrels per day of high-quality diesel fuel and other useful products. About 100 such plants would produce almost as much oil as Saudi Arabia, at a good profit. At $4 per million BTUs of natural gas (the current price is $2), plants of this type, already operating in Qatar, produce oil at $24 per barrel for gas plus the price of conversion to diesel fuel.

Currently, natural gas prices in the U. S. are decreasing as a result of new production methods. Moreover, when methane clathrates are included in future sources, the supply of hydrocarbons is essentially unlimited. We are not running out of hydrocarbons.

Portable hydrocarbon fuels produced in America from American natural resources at reasonable prices will be available to Americans indefinitely – unless voters continue to elect politicians who get in the way. Already, governmental interference over recent decades is causing prices to rise.

The earth contains enough hydrocarbons to provide for many thousands of years of human use, and there is some evidence that more hydrocarbons are possibly still being produced deep in the earth.

The price of hydrocarbons varies with the natural source. There are substantial differences in the cost of recovering them and great differences in the convenience of their use for various purposes. And, time is required to build the industries that process hydrocarbons, so sudden shortages can markedly drive up the price.

During the past 30 years, billions of people in China, India, Russia, and throughout Asia and Africa have gained much more economic freedom. These people are lifting themselves from poverty, struggling against tyranny, and beginning to use large amounts of hydrocarbon energy, too. So, there is a world-wide shortage of refined hydrocarbons, which has caused prices to rise.

Moreover, federal government meddling in the hydrocarbon industry has driven much of this industry out of the United States, so we have been importing hydrocarbons, especially oil, in large amounts.

To make matters worse, politicians are using fear to gain power over our hydrocarbon industries, just as they used fear of nuclear energy to take control of that resource.

In the 70s, they claimed that we were running out of hydrocarbons. That failing, they moved on to the claim that human use of hydrocarbons was catastrophically *cooling* the earth. When, however, world temperatures commenced a natural fluctuation upward, they quickly changed to the claim that human use of hydrocarbons is *warming* the earth. A world-wide propaganda campaign has fooled many people into fearing that hydrocarbon use can destroy the earth's climate.

The only proven environmental effect of human hydrocarbon use is that the amounts of plants and animals are increasing rapidly. Human industry is moving carbon from below ground and into the atmosphere where it fertilizes the growth of plants. Thus we have faster growth and more abundance of plants, which leads to more animals.

This effect is temporary. Atmospheric carbon dioxide not used by plants soon dissolves in the oceans. The oceans are so vast and already contain so much carbon dioxide that this human addition causes no significant increase.

When human technology moves on to nuclear energy and other energy sources, atmospheric carbon dioxide will quickly return to the levels of 200 years ago. Those of us living now should just enjoy this temporary increase in vegetation and animals, an unexpected gift from the industrial revolution.

The hypothesis that increased use of hydrocarbons causes the earth to warm substantially is quite old. This hypothesis was largely discredited by scientists who studied it carefully long ago. Recent research has shown even more definitively that this hypothesis is wrong. Human activities are not causing the earth to warm.[19]

The earth is in a prolonged warm period with very moderate natural cycles up and down. The most recent cooling cycle, called by scientists the "Little Ice Age", recently ended. The coldest period at the bottom of that cycle was a little over 200 years ago. George Washington was at Valley Forge during the coldest period in more than 1,000 years.

Temperatures have become more moderate. They are now at about the average of the past 3,000 years. They have risen about 2 °F since George Washington's time.

Exaggerating this slight rise, a gaggle of unprincipled people including tax-funded "climate" scientists, politicians, and businessmen, hope to make money and gain power by misinforming the public.

Do not be misled by this. See www.petitionproject. org for a list of more than 31,000 American physical scientists who reject the hypothesis of human-caused global warming and for a scientific review article based on the peer-reviewed scientific literature that explains why. Since my colleagues and I wrote this review in 2007, even more scientific data has shown that the hypothesis of human-caused global warming is wrong.

Technological change takes time. The vast infrastructure of energy production machinery upon which our civilization depends has required a long time to build. Many new energy technologies will become more useful in the future. Now, however, the technology of the entire human race depends on hydrocarbons. From ocean shipping to household heating, hundreds of millions of hydrocarbon-fueled machines make possible our way of life.

If those who advocate that we abandon those machines and that technology should by some terrible mistake succeed, this would cause the greatest holocaust of human death and suffering that the world has ever known.

There is, thankfully, little evidence that they will prevail. Yet, they have already caused much damage to the U.S. economy, by influencing their friends in the U.S. Congress.

Solar Energy

There is a lot of energy available in sunshine. We see this every day when the sun comes up and its warmth spreads over the land. Engineers have harnessed this energy for centuries, first in primitive ways and now with the solid-state technology of solar panels and other methods.

Using current technology, solar power lends itself to providing electricity in remote locations where no power grid – electric lines from power stations – is available. Solar power is also becoming increasingly popular as a way of assuring that electricity is available in small amounts at specific locations if the grid fails. The power grid has become increasingly fragile as a result of political meddling in the electricity industry.

Power independence through solar panels on one's roof requires, however, some caution. Most of these solar power systems are attached to the electric power grid in order to save money by avoiding batteries (required when there is little or no sunlight) and to please government apparatchiks who are providing tax subsidies. These depend upon the grid. They are not truly independent.

If the energy used by Americans today were supplied by current solar technology, about half of the state of California would need to be covered by solar panels at a cost of approximately $30 trillion. Obviously, this is impossible.

Two examples illustrate.

About two years ago in Florida, President Obama gave a speech opening the largest solar power plant ever built in the U.S. He praised this plant as an example of the future of American energy. This plant was built with tax money, and it works. It produces about $3 million worth of electricity per year, and it cost $150 million to build.

Even if it could be maintained at zero cost, this plant would require 50 years to return just its cost of construction, and the practical life of its equipment is estimated to be about 30 years.

This plant will never produce enough electricity to even pay for the cost of its construction and maintenance. It is just a giant tax-financed billboard for government power.

Closer to home, a smaller solar power plant is being installed along Interstate Highway 5 near Wilsonville, Oregon. This is part of a taxpayer financed project to begin a "solar highway." It is implied that solar power along the Interstate can someday power the automobiles. Advertising is to be installed at a nearby Highway 5 rest area telling travelers about this wonderful future.

According to numbers published in *The Oregonian*,[38,39] this project is expected to produce about $200,000 worth of electricity per year and to cost $10 million to build. So, just like Florida and with no maintenance cost at all, this project will require 50 years to generate enough electricity to pay its cost of construction. If we estimate that maintenance and advertising at the rest area will cost $100,000 per year, the payback period will be 100 years. Like the Florida plant, this project is just another tax financed advertisement for government "green" power.

Moreover, the Highway 5 project is being built by the Bank of America, under a contract to sell it to the state of Oregon after the bank has received all of the government subsidies, including those from Oregon. Hey, why not? It's only the public's money.

The Oregonian also reports[40] that the Trimet solar panel array at the Green Line Station in Portland will cost $370,000 and produce only about $3,700 in electricity each

year – a 100-year payback, without considering maintenance and the fact that the whole array will wear out long
before then.

The proponents of these solar projects, however, say
that the economics will change when electricity costs three
or four times more than it does today. If current Washington policies in Congress continue to suppress nuclear and
hydrocarbon energy, that may actually happen.

Some say "Cost, why worry? We 'prefer' solar power."
Yes, but if our competitors in other nations produce energy
at much lower cost, industries that require lots of power
will stay in those countries and more such U.S. industries
will move abroad. Do they "prefer" that our nation lose its
prosperity and offer our workers fewer and fewer jobs?

If so, they might wish to erect bleachers near the solar
projects. We can all sit in the sun and watch the electricity
being generated. We might as well because, if American
energy prices rise high enough to make these installations
practical, most of us will not have jobs to go to anyway.

Then, there are the solar power systems appearing on
the roofs of many homes and built largely with tax subsidies. Have you noticed that these are almost entirely on the
roofs of *expensive* homes? That is because they are financed
by tax breaks, which are valueless to those without large
tax bills. Somehow this regressive tax subsidy is of little
concern to congressmen, who constantly pretend to be
champions of the poor.

Projects like these and the billions of tax dollars that
have been wasted in subsidies to now-bankrupt solar
equipment companies have given solar power an unjusti-
fied bad reputation. This is actually very valuable technology. Left to the free market and without tax subsidies,

solar energy technology would advance more rapidly and without public expense.

Much political noise has been made, for example, about the bankruptcy of Solyndra Corporation, which received $535 million in tax subsidies from the U.S. Congress. The president spent the money. Congress appropriated it.

If Solyndra's lobbyists had not had their hands in the taxpayers' pockets, the company might still be in business. They were overwhelmed by changes in market prices for solar panels. With their business plan dependent upon government handouts rather than correct competitive decisions in the market place, Solyndra was ripe for failure.

Solar-electric panels have recently become far less expensive, but the panels are only part of these tax subsidized installations. The other required technology is also decreasing in cost, and the efficiency of the panels is gradually increasing.

Solar power, as technology improves over the next 20 years, will probably play an increasingly useful part in America's energy supplies, if that part is determined on the level playing field of a non-tax financed free market. Home electricity, for example, not including heating, might eventually be supplied at reasonable cost by solar-electric roof shingles. If solar energy remains under government control, however, its future is much more doubtful.

The huge amounts of electricity required to power industry and transportation will probably not be supplied by the energy of the sun any time soon.

There is, however, one very significant danger from solar-electric power. Politicians are pretending that it and its companion, tax-subsidized wind power, can now significantly substitute for hydrocarbon and nuclear power.

This is being used to convince the public that it is acceptable for politicians to destroy our nuclear and hydrocarbon power industries. This is dangerous. Nothing could be further from the truth.

Wind Energy

Wind power is much less promising than solar power because, not only is it intermittent and still very costly as is solar power, there is much less chance that it can significantly improve. Solar power technology can, in theory, improve perhaps at least 10-fold and possibly more. This is probably not true of wind power.

At present, wind power is just a tax-financed boondoggle. First, wind power is unpredictably intermittent. For every windmill installed, ordinary hydrocarbon power machinery must be installed, too, ready to operate immediately when the wind speed fluctuates. This assures that the cost of installation will always remain high.

Additionally, wind generators are maintenance intensive, with tens of thousands of small generators strung out across the country on tall towers. Have you noticed when driving through "wind farms" that older windmills are mostly not turning, and even some new ones are stopped?

Since most of these tax-financed windmills are new, this maintenance problem is largely being overlooked. In 20 years or so, most of the windmills we see today may not be turning at all. Many of them will probably be pulled down and scrapped.

Am I right? It should not matter, except to me, if I decide to invest my savings in wind or one of its competitors. Wind deserves and should receive the same economic chance as all other energy technologies, on a level playing field and without government subsidies or impediments.

Wind power does illustrate the hypocrisy of big-government politicians. If you were a wind turbine, you would already be in jail. Wind turbines kill tens of thousands of birds, including rare and protected species. If you were to kill protected species of birds day after day, week after week as do wind turbines, you would be imprisoned. Wind turbines do this, and it is entirely overlooked.

Energy Independence

Energy independence need not cost the American taxpayer a single cent. Indeed, it is the misuse of taxpayer dollars that is preventing American energy independence.

Congress just needs to get the government out of the way! The Department of Energy was established for the purpose of making the U.S. energy independent. Not only has it failed at this task, it has increased our dependence on foreign energy sources and has cost Americans millions of jobs by driving our energy-intensive industries abroad.

American energy independence can be restored in only one way: by the restoration of American liberty. Free, productive men and women built our country, including the energy industry. Freedom has been taxed and regulated away by politicians. We must remove these obstacles.

It is ridiculous and harmful for Congress to tax our energy industries and give the money to people in Washington who, in their entirely uninformed and inexperienced wisdom, decide how our energy should be provided.

27

THE SECOND AMENDMENT

A well regulated militia, being necessary to the security of a free state, the right of the people to keep and bear arms, shall not be infringed.
2nd Amendment

The Bill of Rights of the Constitution of the United States specifically prohibits government from enacting legislation infringing on the right of Americans to "keep and bear arms." The language is specific. In terms of American history, the intent was specific.

Every American knew this in 1776. Not all people were armed. They had the right to remain unarmed. Their neighbors had the right to remain armed. No one in the 13

> **Congress must prevent infringement of our Constitutional right to keep and bear arms.**
>
> **Firearms are an important part of our recreational culture, and they provide a means for personal self defense.**
>
> **Moreover, it has been definitively shown that, when some of the citizenry is armed, all citizens are very significantly protected from violent crime.**

colonies in 1776 had any doubt about this. It was basic to the American way of life. It is a fundamental right of the American people.

Will Criminals Obey Gun-Control Laws?

Some people seem to believe that if the United States government passes legislation against gun ownership, criminals will obey the law, turn in their guns to some local police department, and adopt knives and clubs as their weapons of choice.

Of course, few people really believe this. Yet voting to suppress gun ownership is illogical on any other presupposition about the nature of criminals. If gun-control laws are obeyed at all, they are obeyed by the prospective victims of criminals.

Gun-control laws are defended in the name of reducing violence, yet what they really do is transfer to criminals the ability to inflict violence, or the threat of violence, with far less risk of resistance. In states in which gun control laws have been made less restrictive, violent crime has decreased.

The graph shows the rapid decrease in violent crimes in a group of 20 states that adopted laws enhancing concealed carry of fire arms. In ten years, the incidence of violent crimes has been cut in half – and it is still decreasing. More than 200,000 violent crimes per year are now avoided in these states by increased firearms freedom.

Tragedies where unstable people kill unarmed Americans with guns are advertised widely by the press. Terrorist use of guns is also advertised. If some Americans are armed, these tragedies can often be cut short. Moreover,

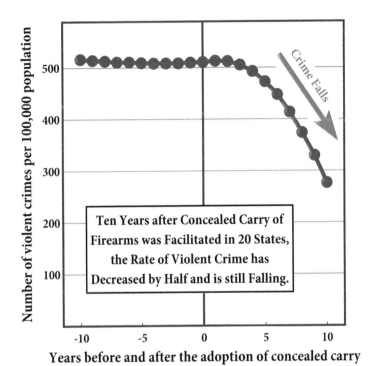

Concealed Carry Laws Reduce Violent Crime

The average incidence of violent crimes in 20 states that allowed or facilitated concealed firearms use by ordinary citizens has been cut in half in the first 10 years. Only a small percentage of citizens choose to carry firearms, but criminals don't know which ones. This figure is adapted with permission from *"More Guns, Less Crime"* by John Lott.

the scale of the tragedies is probably less than it would be if such people resorted to bombs instead of guns.

Gun-control laws are aimed directly at law-abiding citizens. These laws disarm citizens. This leaves them more defenseless against criminals who do not obey the law. Yet

> "The Constitution preserves the advantage of being armed which Americans possess over the people of almost every other nation where governments are afraid to trust the people with arms." *James Madison*

these laws are defended by the gun-control lobby in the name of "protecting" Americans.

The facts are obvious. Criminals do not obey the law. Criminals are armed. Criminals resort to violence. Criminals have no respect for the rights of law-abiding citizens. Gun-control legislation transfers power to the criminal class. It transfers power specifically to members of the criminal class who use or threaten violence.

Many Americans are not interested in guns, especially defensive handguns. Criminals, however, don't know who is armed. So, those citizens who carry guns protect everyone – usually not by use of their guns, but by their presence.

My children (now all young adults) and I all have Oregon concealed weapons permits. We were all fortunate to be trained by our friend, Jeff Cooper – I in the 1970s and the children in the 1990s.

Both the National Rifle Association and Gun Owners of America have given me an "A" rating.

Mr. DeFazio's ratings by these organizations are "B" and "D minus," respectively.

Politics and the Second Amendment

Many of the world's tyrannies have already disarmed their citizens, as have some relatively free countries.

The United States and Switzerland stand out as two

special countries that have not. The Swiss even keep the military rifles required for their nationwide compulsory military service in their homes.

Not so long ago, gun control laws were a mainstay of the Democrat Party, and they are still a major objective among some elements of that party.

This has turned out to be bad politics. American voters have defeated many candidates on this issue, so we don't hear quite so much gun control advocacy by politicians these days.

This will not always be the case. Gun tragedies are often exploited for propaganda against gun ownership. We must always be on guard to protect this constitutional right.

Recreational Firearms

The 2nd Amendment also protects the rights of citizens to bear arms for recreation. Recreational use of firearms is far more common in the United States than defensive use.

Jeff Cooper wrote many books. One book he wrote is entitled *To Ride, Shoot Straight, and Speak the Truth*. The book communicates an important message. In times past, it was considered every father's duty to give firearms training to his children.

Firearms are ubiquitous in our country, so one should be familiar with them. Unfamiliarity can lead to accidents.

Recreational use of firearms is the way in which most Americans today gain practical firearms knowledge.

Hunting and fishing are very popular in the rural areas of Oregon District 4. They are also important to the economies of these regions. Both, however, are being curtailed as more and more land is taken out of human use by federal actions and as impediments to hunting and fishing are increased by the federal government.

These misguided policies are not good for sportsmen and are also not good for prudent wildlife management policies.

The 10th Amendment applies here.

Oregon recreational activities and wildlife health should be entirely controlled by the people of Oregon and their state government, as constitutionally specified.

A common sense balance between hunting and fishing activities and Oregon wildlife health is far more likely to be achieved by people who live and work in Oregon than it is by politically motivated politicians and bureaucrats in Washington.

28

A SCIENTIST IN CONGRESS

The fear of the Lord is the instruction of wisdom;
and before honour is humility.

Proverbs 15:33

On the general principle that most disciplines have something to offer, it is a good idea for Congress to be made up of people from various walks of life.

At present, Congress is overloaded with lawyers and career politicians. This causes a lot of problems.

The most essential characteristic of a scientist is complete honesty in his work. Scientists study the truth about the natural world. That world will not change to conform to our preferences. It must be studied and described with utmost integrity.

Our country with its 300 million people is far more complicated than any ordinary scientific discipline. Yet, certain objective truths about America have been discovered. If we apply those truths with integrity to our national affairs, we can retain our liberty and live in a nation of prosperity, opportunity, and good will. Science can help with this.

I doubt that I have ever met a man or woman who didn't know many things that I don't know and didn't have many skills superior to my own. I probably also have not met anyone who is superior to me in all knowledge and all skills. We need citizen volunteers in Congress from all walks of life. I am a scientist. What are real scientists like? What sort of people do this kind of work?

The four scientists quoted below did remarkable things.

Isaac Newton was the greatest scientist who has ever lived. He single-handedly discovered not only many of the basic laws of physics, which underlies all other sciences, but he discovered ways of thinking about the natural world that have made the physical sciences possible.

J. Robert Oppenheimer led the Manhattan Project which developed the atomic bomb. His work, life, and travails encapsulate the era in which the greatest technological advance in history – the conversion of nuclear energy into electrical energy – occurred in parallel with the development of the most destructive technological advance – the development of the atomic bomb.

Robert Oppenheimer was also a politically liberal figure of his time, during a conservative era in science.

Albert Einstein made discoveries that led physics from the world of the seen and intuitive into the world of the unseen and non-intuitive, and enabled technological progress far beyond previous imagination.

Richard Feynman made contributions to the sciences of quantum electrodynamics and elementary particles. He is also especially well known for his ability to express both the simplicity and the unknowable complexity of scientific problems in terms that everyone can understand.

These men said:

"I do not know what I may appear to the world; but to myself I seem to have been only like a boy playing on the seashore, and diverting myself in now and then finding a smoother pebble or a prettier shell than ordinary, while the great ocean of truth lay all undiscovered before me."

Isaac Newton

"I think that today, if I know you and your friends through the country, you hold very close to the ancient imperatives – the imperatives of Christianity, of our traditions, of our country. I think you are not after novelty and improvisation in art or politics or philosophy, or manners. I think that, even if the end of our time should come, you are quite content that we live out these days faithful to the gospels, faithful to the ethic, faithful to the sense of responsibility which we have from times past.

J. Robert Oppenheimer
(Speaking to Caltech undergraduates)

"It is just 200 years ago that Newton closed his eyes. It behooves us at such a moment to remember this brilliant genius, who determined the course of western thought, research and practice to an extent that nobody before or since his time can touch."

Albert Einstein

"Let no one suppose, however, that the mighty work of Newton can really be superseded by this (Einstein's theory of relativity) or any other theory. His great and lucid ideas will retain their significance for all time as the foundation of our whole conceptual structure in the sphere of natural philosophy."

Albert Einstein

"In order to put his system into mathematical form at all, Newton had to devise the concept of differential quotients and propound the laws of motion in the form of total differential equations – perhaps the greatest advance in thought that a single individual was ever privileged to make."

Albert Einstein

In the section *What is Energy?* of the chapter, *Conservation of Energy* in *Lectures on Physics – Volume 1* by Richard Feynman, Robert Leighton, and Matthew Sands, which is based upon Richard Feynman's physics lectures to Caltech freshman students, Feynman gives his famous analogy about conservation of energy.

He describes the travails of a mother as she develops a mathematical formula governing the number of her son's blocks, which are found in a variety of places. Feynman then points out that:

"Energy has a large number of *different forms*, and there is a formula for each one. These are:

gravitational energy, kinetic energy, heat energy, elastic energy, electrical energy, chemical energy, radiant energy, nuclear energy, mass energy. . . . In order to verify the conservation of energy, we must be careful that we have not put any in or taken any out. . . If we total up the formulas for each of these contributions, it will not change except for energy going in and out.

"It is important to realize that in physics today, we have no knowledge of what energy *is*. We do not have a picture that energy comes in little blobs of a definite amount. It is not that way. . . . It is an abstract thing in that it does not tell us the mechanism or the *reasons* for the various formulas."

Richard Feynman

Humility

There is a fundamental similarity in the quotations of these four men. They all show extraordinary *humility.*

Newton compares himself to a child and his discoveries to a few pebbles and shells in the ocean.

Oppenheimer sees himself as a tiny player upon the historical stage of the gospels, ethics, and tradition.

Einstein speaks of his own contributions as far beneath Newton's, but also of Newton's as *privileges* that Newton was permitted.

And Feynman, in the modern era where supposed "scientists" speak "knowingly" of the origins of the universe and the origins of life, points out that neither he nor anyone else even knows what energy *is*, and uses the example of a mother, her boy, and his blocks to explain this.

Yet, the problems that these scientists spent their lives studying were very, very simple as compared to the civilization of the United States with its 300 million human inhabitants.

What then are we to think of a 25-year career politician who pretends to know how these 300 million people should conduct their lives and to be able to decide, much better than they, how their earnings should be spent?

And what are we to expect when we turn over our national affairs to him and other career politicians, many of whom have as little training, skills, accomplishments, and lack of humility as does he?

No one can correctly manage the affairs of 300 million people. Each of the 300 million people must guide his own affairs. That is why freedom works. Not only is freedom morally right, but it is the only effective way for large numbers of people to live together and individually prosper.

I am a scientist. During my education at Caltech and UCSD, I was privileged to be taught by or do research with several men whose work was recognized with Nobel Prizes and others whose work was of comparable quality and importance. This prepared me for a wonderful life in science.

My coworkers and I have conducted research in many interesting disciplines. We founded two fields of study. One comprises the biochemical processes and functions of amide molecular clocks in peptides and proteins. The second is called "metabolic profiling," which is today a growing part of the field of "metabolomics." We still work in these fields today at the Oregon Institute of Science and Medicine. We do excellent work.

When my son Noah and I submitted one research

paper, in which he had done most of the work, to a major journal for peer review, I was surprised when the editor accepted the paper after only one reviewer and himself had read it.

The one reviewer wrote only three words, "Brilliant, publish immediately."

Later, Noah and I wrote an entire book on the same subject. The book was initially sent to several hundred researchers working in our field for their suggested comments, with our request that they inform us as to any errors they noticed.

One of them wrote back to say, "I have read your research papers, so I would be very surprised to find even one error in this book."

We have also occasionally turned aside and used our training for work with a political component. During the Cold War, we built an effective nationwide effort to advance public knowledge and governmental interest in the science of civil defense – the protection of civilians from harm by natural disasters, terrorists, and war. We also worked on a project for American troops during the First Gulf War.

More recently, we conducted research into the scientific basis of the hypothesis of human-caused global warming.

Scientists work on virtually all aspects of the physical world. Some restrict their studies to relatively simple problems that they can expect to solve rigorously, and some undertake studies of problems so complex that they cannot expect to solve the problems – but instead only make useful progress toward eventual solutions. I have done both.

Two problems that hold a special fascination for many people are the origin of the universe and the origin of life.

These problems are so difficult that one wonders if the problems themselves can ever even be fully comprehended by the mind of man, much less solved. Still, it is perfectly legitimate to think about them. It is, however, bogus to advertise that one's ideas are proven truths, when, in fact, they are just unproven hypotheses.

As Richard Feynman, Robert Leighton, and Matthew Sands write:

> **"The principle of science, the definition, almost, is the following: The test of all knowledge is experiment. Experiment is the sole judge of scientific 'truth.'"**
> *Feynman, Leighton, and Sands*

As you might imagine, experiments that prove hypotheses about the origins of the universe and the origins of life are now well beyond human capabilities.

Yet, some people insist that current hypotheses about these two subjects – and about human-caused global warming – be taught to school children as rigorous scientific fact and that even slight deviations from this dogma not be considered at all.

This is advocated by "scientists" with so little humility they consider that their own ideas concerning problems that are the most difficult imaginable should be accepted as absolute truth.

It was amusing when DeFazio interjected this esoteric subject into the 2010 congressional campaign. He impugned my status as a scientist because, as DeFazio said, "he doesn't believe in evolution." DeFazio went on to make the ridiculous claim that the Oregon Institute of Science and Medicine where I work is "actually a survivalist compound." [41] See the chapter, *Corrections,* below for further information about this and my scientific credentials.

In so far as my thoughts are concerned, I know, from very extensive professional study, that the hypothesis of human-caused global warming has not been experimentally verified and that there is a large body of experimental evidence that actually invalidates it. The origins of the universe and life are very interesting scientifically unsolved problems, a view that I share with many of my colleagues, some of whom are prominent researchers of these subjects.

Scientists are problem solvers. They also must be rigorously honest. There is a wonderful essay on this by Richard Feynman entitled *Cargo Cult Science,* from a graduation talk that he presented at Caltech in 1974. After speaking about strict honesty in science and giving several examples, he closed with these remarks to the graduating young scientists:

> **"I have just one wish for you – the good luck to be somewhere where you are free to maintain the kind of integrity I have described, and where you do not feel forced by the need to maintain your position in the organization, or financial support, or so on, to lose your integrity. May you have that freedom."**
>
> *Richard Feynman*

Do members of Congress have this freedom? Most of them obviously don't think so. Will the voters give them this freedom? Will voters elect a scientist who thinks and acts with integrity? As Feynman would say, we can only find out by doing the experiment.

When human attributes come up against the physical world, the first characteristic that should exhibit itself in a good scientist is – *humility*. The quote I cited from Isaac Newton is an excellent illustration.

How does this relate to politics? Of what value will the methods of science be in Congress? Well, integrity in Congress would be a good thing to try – at least as a new experiment. Humility, too, might be useful.

You see, I think that liberty and justice are morally right, and that slavery is morally wrong, so I strongly advocate the protections for liberty and justice that our Founding Fathers put into our Constitution.

In addition, I think that the results of experimental and observational studies should guide our actions in situations that are too complicated for us to truly comprehend. So, look at the experimental results. Compare the lives of individual citizens in countries with oppressive big governments with those in our own country during its first 200 years.

It is self-evident that our Founding Fathers were right. Liberty and justice bring out the best in men – at least the best ever seen in human history.

It would obviously be foolish to abandon our experiment in liberty and instead adopt the methods of centralized governmental tyranny that have worked so much more poorly everywhere they have been tried. To do this would just not be common sense.

Moreover, as those who are motivated by the money and power they can get from centralized, all powerful Big Government have partially moved our country in their direction, we have seen the harmful results.

As our liberty has diminished, our lives have become more difficult. Our prosperity has decreased, our jobs and careers have been lost, and our happiness has diminished.

So, even though I am a scientist and certainly never expected to go into politics, I can no longer sit idly by as my country is taken in a wrong direction.

> "I have sworn upon the altar of God eternal hostility against every form of tyranny over the mind of man."
>
> *Thomas Jefferson*

The diminution of American liberty is definitely a form of tyranny over the mind of man.

When I was a young science student, an undergraduate at Caltech, I inadvertently became involved in an odd activity. Continuing my interests from high school, I played on the Caltech tennis team and participated as an actor in the annual campus play. This and my academic studies more than filled my time.

I decided not to accept the coach's offer to play football, which I have since regretted. In those years, the Rose Bowl stadium was also Caltech's home field. Had I accepted his offer, I would be able to tell you that I played in the Rose Bowl. I was 6' 1" and weighed about 170 pounds. The coach wanted me to start as a lineman, which shows you just how badly the team from our 600-student school was starved for players.

It turned out, however, that another young man from my high school in Houston, Texas was also in the freshman class. There were only 186 freshmen, so this was improbable, but it happened this way.

Well, my friend decided to run for freshman class president. "How," I thought, "am I going to let the people back home know that he holds a class office and I do not?" So, I ran for freshman class vice-president.

It turned out that he lost the election; I won; and then the man who beat him flunked out. This made me freshman class president.

In those days, one-third of the freshmen admitted each year did not graduate.

The next year I ran for sophomore class president, and won. Having now the bug, I ran for student body secretary and later for president of Dabney House and won both, but when I ran for student body president, I was beaten by Larry Rabinowitz, by 17 votes.

Thus chastened, I wisely retired from "politics" – until I saw the damage that the statists are doing to our country. So, like many other Americans, I volunteered.

There are tens of millions of us: farmers, doctors, plumbers, carpenters, machinists, housewives, scientists, entrepreneurs, firemen, soldiers, and many others – all now awakened to the necessity to bring common sense to Washington and all working in various ways to preserve American Liberty. This vast uprising of citizen volunteers will not be denied. There is no doubt as to the outcome.

And, as Thomas Paine would say, it is not common sense that a people will succumb to tyranny after 200 years of freedom, so we will win this current contest with those who wish to enslave us. It is also common sense for us to do so as soon as possible.

29

COUNTING THE VOTES

At election time, there always arises discussion about whether the votes are counted fairly. There are many examples of fraudulent registration and other irregularities.

The vote by mail system in Oregon is especially susceptible to fraud. Whether or not there has been fraud in Oregon vote counting is an ongoing controversy. Many voters contacted us in 2010 saying that they were concerned about this.

This is unfortunate. Voters should be able to have complete confidence in the voting system. **County clerks should not be burdened by a system that creates doubt.**

Vote by mail could become a very reliable system.

Honest vote counting is especially important to candidates. Why work hard in a campaign if the vote will be unfair? After the 2010 election, our campaign arranged a recount of a few precincts in each county, so that we could

> **The Oregon vote by mail system has unique advantages and disadvantages. The disadvantages involve the handling of the ballots.**
>
> **These problems should be solved, so that the voting public has more confidence in the system.**

learn more about the vote counting system.

Even if every vote in Oregon is being counted entirely correctly, there is a serious problem with our system.

It would be so easy to commit fraud in this system that many voters lack confidence in it.

In 1961, a group of Caltech students picked the locks guarding the Rose Bowl card stunts and changed the cards. Viewers at the game and on national television were then treated to the Caltech mascot and the word "Caltech" spelled out in the stands. This is a famous college prank.

Caltech Card Stunt

Rose Bowl halftime 1961. Used with permission by *Engineering and Science*, published by the California Institute of Technology.

With a couple of the Caltech students who accomplished this to help, anyone could change the outcome of a congressional election in Oregon. It would be easy to simply pick the locks on clerks' doors or perhaps gain access otherwise to the ballots. Then real ballots could be replaced by newly-marked fraudulent ballots in the way done for the stunts at the Rose Bowl game.

(I was a student at Caltech in 1961, so I had best point out that I was not one of the students who did this. It may otherwise be in my opponent's next campaign flier.)

Voters in Oregon receive their ballots in the mail long before the election. The filled out ballots are placed in an inner, unmarked envelope. This is sealed and placed in an outer envelope that must be signed by the voter. The outer envelopes are used to verify the voter's identity and then discarded. This protects voter privacy.

Mailed or placed in vote collection boxes, the ballots eventually make their way to the county clerk's facilities and are opened and counted. Herein lie the problems.

1. Counting by computerized ballot scanners begins before election day, so any computer professional with access to the counting machines can gain valuable information for the last days of the campaign. We must trust that no one does this.

The Secretary of State may say that the computers are secure, but "secure" computer systems are broken into frequently, including those of large businesses and federal agencies with far more resources to provide security. Credit card, bank account, and even classified secret U.S. government information has been stolen.

2. Many of the ballots are re-filled out at the clerk's office because they are judged unfit to go through the counting machines. For example, in the November 2010 general election in Lane County, an estimated 10% of the ballots were replaced by re-marked ballots. We must trust that this is done correctly.

3. A large supply of blank ballots is present in the

clerks' facilities, to be used for the ballot correction work.

4. The ballots are kept in the facility for many days and nights before and during the counting.

5. The counting itself, even during a ballot recount, cannot be monitored by members of the public, representatives of the candidates, or anyone else.

This last is in violation of the spirit of Oregon law, which specifies that vote counting may be observed by representatives of political parties, candidates, and the public.

The Democrat Secretary of State in Oregon has interpreted the law to mean that people can "observe" ballots being counted – but *they must do so from so far away that the observers cannot see the marks on the ballots.* The clerks specifically state that observers are not to be permitted to see the marks on the ballots. When counted, the ballots no longer have the voter's name, so this is not for privacy.

When we conducted our test recount, Noah and Matthew decided to take binoculars with them to overcome this. They were told to cease use of the binoculars or leave the building. They were permitted only to, in the clerks' words, "observe the process." They were not allowed to see the marks on the ballots.

Since it is of little use for the public to observe the vote counting if they are not able to see the marks on the ballots, this interpretation defeats the intent of public monitoring.

Various remedies would help. For example, the ballots could be guarded 24-hours per day by selected people from opposing campaigns. This would not avoid the risks of ballot changes before the ballots arrive at the clerk's office, but it would prevent the Rose Bowl method.

The intent of the observer law should be followed so

that the public can actually monitor the vote counting. The current policy prevents any oversight by the public.

All sorts of improvements could be made.

Still, vote-by-mail has an inherent flaw. There is a lot of time between the voting and the counting. This creates an opportunity to commit fraud, but it can be remedied.

A simple and very effective improvement would be to put random code numbers on the ballots and on a tear off ballot tab that is kept by the voter. These numbers would be read by the counting machines. Later, the numbers and the votes cast on each ballot would be made available, especially on the Internet.

Privacy would be maintained because only the voter has his tab. He could check on the Internet to see that his vote was counted properly. There would be little risk from voters making false claims later because any challenge could be checked with the actual ballot. If the vote turned out to be correctly counted, the challenging voter could be billed to pay for the checking.

To be sure, checking enough votes to validate an election would still be laborious. With, however, a definitive way of doing so, the risks to those committing fraud would be much increased and public confidence enhanced.

Part IV

SETTING THE RECORD STRAIGHT

30

CORRECTION OF DEFAZIO MISREPRESENTATIONS

*"One of the most striking differences between
a cat and a lie is that a cat only has nine lives."*

Mark Twain

In the 2010 campaign, Peter DeFazio refused to debate me in person. He did submit to four "forums" where he

> In 2010, Mr. DeFazio refused to debate me, although he did participate in four forums arranged by his friends.
>
> Instead, he conducted a campaign of smears and character assassination made up of misleading and false claims. He has begun the same in 2012. His 2010 claims are corrected in the pages that follow.
>
> In 2012, we should debate the issues. He and I represent quite different views of the role of Congress and of common sense government policies. Voters deserve a forthright discussion of those issues.

Harvesting Hay on the Robinson Farm

One family lives on this farm – the Robinsons. Our family has lived and worked here for more than 30 years. On MSNBC national network television, Peter DeFazio falsely stated that this is a "survivalist compound." What would he be willing to say about any other family in Oregon District 4 that he decides to attack?

chose the forum organizers, but the candidates were not permitted to debate or question each other.

Mr. DeFazio, for the most part, avoided discussion of real public issues and policies. His 2010 campaign consisted primarily of a million dollar media blitz during the last weeks before the election that was devoted to smearing his opponent with false statements rather than promoting his own policies. Given the effects that 25 years of those policies have had on the voters of Oregon District 4, his refusal to debate is not surprising.

As the DeFazio 2012 campaign begins, we are hearing from him and his friends much the same campaign of defamation that he ran in 2010. Therefore, it is useful to set the record straight concerning his 2010 claims.

1. DeFazio: On MSNBC network television said: "this is a guy [Robinson] who lives on Social Security in a survivalist compound in a corner of my district." [42]

Truth: I live with my family on a farm that we purchased when we moved to Oregon in 1980. This is an ordinary family farm, with farmhouse and barns. It is not a "compound" for survival or anything else.

I derive most of my income from my work as research professor at the Oregon Institute of Science and Medicine and from the newsletter *Access to Energy*. I do receive Social Security payments that are approximately equal, after taxes, to my annual payments into Social Security, with, therefore, essentially no net income from that source.

DeFazio owns four homes, two in Oregon and two located in New Zealand. Presumably he lives at these locations.

2. DeFazio: On MSNBC network television: "My opponent has a long history of being a, you know, corporate shill." DeFazio then goes on to suggest that I received money from Exxon Mobil. [42]

Truth: I have never received money from Exxon Mobil or any other oil company for any purpose. I have no "history" of working for or receiving money from any organization, other than for my work at the non-profit organizations the University of California at San Diego, Stanford, the Linus Pauling Institute, and the Oregon Institute of Science and Medicine.

3. DeFazio: "Well He . . . he . . . he offers himself as a research scientist, but he doesn't believe in evolution. What he's researching at his institute, which is actually a survivalist compound, is the beneficial effects of radioactivity on us."[41] (Air America, October 12, 2010)

Truth: I have degrees in chemistry from the California Institute of Technology and the University of California at San Diego. I have served on the faculty of UCSD; as a research associate at Stanford University; as research professor (and co-founder and president) of the Linus Pauling Institute of Science and Medicine; and as research professor and president of the Oregon Institute of Science and Medicine.

I have published numerous original, peer-reviewed research articles in highly respected scientific publications including:
1. *Proceedings of the National Academy of Sciences, U.S.*
2. *Journal of the American Chemical Society*
3. *Science*
4. *Nature*
5. *Clinical Chemistry*
6. *Clinical Biochemistry*
7. *Journal of Solid State Chemistry*
8. *Journal of Organic Chemistry*
9. *Mechanisms of Aging and Development*
10. *Proceedings of National Society of Autistic Children*
11. *Experimental Gerontology*

12. *Life Sciences*
13. *Current Topics in Cellular Regulation*
14. *Molecular Vision*
15. *Journal of Peptide and Protein Research*
16. *Journal of Chromatography*
17. *Peptide Science*
18. *Journal of International Research Communications*
19. *Helvetica Chimica Acta* (Swiss Chemical Society)
20. *Annals of the New York Academy of Sciences*
21. *Canadian Journal of Physics*
22. *Proceedings American Soc. of Mass Spectrometry*
23. *Analytical Chemistry*
24. *Inorganic Chemistry*
25. *Analytical Biochemistry*
26. *Journal of American Physicians and Surgeons*
27. *Journal of Peptide Research*
28. *Journal of Orthomolecular Psychiatry*
29. *Rapid Communications in Mass Spectrometry*
30. Many research books and reviews
31. I am co-author with my son Noah of the book, *Molecular Clocks: Deamidation of Asparaginyl and Glutaminyl Residues in Peptides and Proteins.*

My favorite research publication is "Structure-dependent Nonenzymatic Deamidation of Glutaminyl and Asparaginyl Pentapeptides" by N. E. Robinson, Z. W. Robinson, B. R. Robinson, A. L. Robinson, J. A. Robinson, M. L. Robinson, and A. B. Robinson, *Journal of Peptide Research* (2004), Volume 63, pp 426-436. All six of my children and I carried out this work.

My research articles have ranged in subject from nuclear physics to nutrition. I am especially well known for work on protein amide molecular clocks, which serve as timers of biological processes, and for my work on the diagnosis of disease and quantitative measurement of human health by means of metabolic profiling.

I have also co-authored two influential and very widely read scientific research review articles on the subject of human-caused global warming, and I write and publish the newsletter *Access to Energy*, which is devoted to science and public affairs, especially on the subject of energy. The readers of *Access to Energy* are about one-third scientists and two-thirds from other professions.

My wife Laurelee was also a scientist, and all six of our children are educated as scientists and engineers.

The Oregon Institute of Science and Medicine is an excellent research institution, with a research laboratory in biochemistry rivaling and in some ways superior to those at Oregon State University and the University of Oregon. To call this a "survivalist compound" is an outright lie.

I have not done any original research on the subject of radiation hormesis, the science of the effects – positive and negative – of radiation on human health, but I have reported on the work of others in my newsletter *Access to Energy*.

4. DeFazio said that Robinson wants to put nuclear waste in Oregon drinking water. [44]

Truth: I have never advocated that anything, much less nuclear waste, be put into the public water supply.

I have always been opposed to the addition of anything (other than minimal and unavoidable residual amounts of bactericides left over from water purification) to the public water supplies.

DeFazio's claim is an out-of-context distortion of the articles I have written on radiation and health. I have pointed out that, in some cases, radiation dangers were being exaggerated, since the radiation levels in question did not exceed the Environmental Protection Agency's very strict standards for drinking water.

So far as I know, Peter DeFazio has never written anything authoritative about nuclear science. He has written materials in which he opposes the development of nuclear energy in the U.S.[46]

5.   DeFazio has painted me on TV ads as a tool of Wall Street.[42] His 2012 contribution requests to donors say that he needs money to protect him from Wall Street, which he says has targeted him.

Truth: I have essentially no connection to Wall Street.

As a result of my writings on science and public policy and my work in Washington, DC on emergency preparedness, medical research, and environmental science, I am moderately well-known.

Early in the 2010 campaign, three readers of my newsletter, a scientist and investor and his daughters living near New York City, contributed the maximum amounts of $2,400 each to the Robinson campaign. There were about 100 contributions of this amount to our campaign in 2010.

Learning of this contributor from the published FEC reports, DeFazio ridiculed this donor in public during a public forum because, as DeFazio claimed, the contributor is rich. DeFazio's objective appeared to be to use the politics of envy against the contributor and me and deter other potential contributors to the Robinson campaign.

After the same forum, in a huff after being bested in the forum, DeFazio also insulted a lady in the audience who tried to speak with him. Because of this, a few days later, she contributed $2,100 to the Robinson campaign.

It is unknown how much DeFazio's behavior cost his campaign, but the New York donor later made substantial contributions to an independent expenditure group that ran TV ads against DeFazio.

Having spent my life in science and in the western United States, I have had almost no contact with "Wall Street" – the financial services industry, and we did not have significant corporate support for our campaign. See the earlier chapter *Campaign Finance* for details.

DeFazio, by comparison, receives more than half of his campaign contributions from "Wall Street" corporations and other special interests.[5,6] His campaign received campaign contributions - totaling more than $1,350,000 from special interest organizations between 2008 and 2012, mostly from corporations, unions, and other special interests having little connection with Oregon.

"Wall Street" is not just a street in New York City. It serves now as a designator for the entire American financial services industry. The majority of Americans do business with this industry, either directly through their investments or indirectly through their pension funds, insurance policies, and other assets. The financial services industry is an important capital allocation tool in our economy.

6.   DeFazio has said in many forums and publications that I want to close the public schools.[44]

Truth: I definitely do not want to close the schools. DeFazio quotes out of context from many hundreds of pages of text that I have written and numerous speeches that I have given about education – especially education in academic subjects – during my lifetime as an educator in public educational institutions and in the home school community. See the chapter *Academic Excellence in Public Schools* for a more detailed explanation of my statements and views.

Peter DeFazio has voted against numerous efforts to improve the schools. He voted "no" on state and local merit pay for teachers, teacher testing, tenure reform, vouchers, charter schools, education savings accounts, and state waivers from federal rules.

Peter DeFazio even voted against vouchers for Washington, D.C.s mostly minority students who sought to escape the very poor schools to which they were assigned.

7. DeFazio's campaign painted me as a racist by reference to articles that appeared on the Internet immediately after I became a candidate against DeFazio and by reference to an article I wrote in *Access to Energy* supporting the student admission standards of Caltech.

As soon as I started to run against DeFazio in 2010, articles from his supporters appeared, claiming that books I publish for children by the author G. A. Henty are racist.

DeFazio's approved moderator during the Coos Bay 2010 forum mentioned Henty and implied that I publish books by a racist.[47]

DeFazio himself demurred, apparently trying to distance himself personally, but let the claim stand by his reference to the Internet. Simultaneously, DeFazio's own campaign Internet site was advertising my "racism" in the Caltech instance.

Truth: The book in question was *By Sheer Pluck* by G. A. Henty, first published over a century ago and now published by my family. We publish all 99 of Henty's excellent historical novels, which have been widely used in American schools. The adventure stories in the novels help students remember the historical events.

In this book a fictional older man in 1850 comments both positively and negatively on different tribes that he meets in Africa. Some are even cannibals.

This older man is representative of his time, as are many of the characters portrayed in Mark Twain's famous novels *Tom Sawyer* and *Huckleberry Finn* – among the most anti-racist novels in all of American literature.

The centerpiece of the Henty novel, *By Sheer Pluck,* is a 30-page soliloquy by a black African native who grew up in a period of constant tribal warfare in which he and his tribe engaged in the capture and selling into slavery of black Africans from other tribes.

The native describes how he himself is eventually captured and sold into slavery; endures the vicissitudes of slavery in the New World; eventually escapes to Canada; and "by sheer pluck" works hard, becomes a wealthy man, and finally returns to Africa, bringing Western Civilization to his own tribe.

This eloquent 30-page indictment of racism and slavery and celebration of the accomplishments of a black African man under great adversity was apparently of little interest to DeFazio's friends, who focused on the few prejudicial lines spoken by a fictitious character elsewhere in the book.

Also, of apparently little interest was our publication of the autobiography of Booker T. Washington, the works of Mark Twain, and books by many other anti-racist authors.

Do DeFazio's retainers suggest that our publication of Henty's novels about the French Revolution shows that we think that all upper-class Frenchmen should be beheaded?

Perhaps they think that our publication of Henty's novel about ancient Egypt shows that we favor the worship of cats and crocodiles.

And, DeFazio would probably not care to meet the many African American home schooling Americans who enthusiastically use the Robinson curriculum and books, including those of G.A. Henty, for their children.

In the instance of my support of Caltech, Caltech admits about 200 of the most brilliant and well-educated high school graduates to its freshman class each year. Caltech has not lowered its admission standards to accommodate "affirmative action."

With American public schools providing especially poor educations to many minority students (see the earlier chapter *Academic Excellence in Public Schools*), fewer minority students qualify for admission to Caltech.

More minority students might qualify for Caltech if DeFazio stopped voting "no," on school improvements.

8. DeFazio: "Robinson has said he would end entitlement programs like Social Security, Medicare, student financial aid, and some Veterans Administration programs".[49]

Truth: DeFazio's statement is false. I have consistently called for *increases* in Social Security payments and improvements in Medicare for senior citizens. I have also called for *increased* funding for the Veteran's Administration.

I have pointed out that Social Security payments have lagged badly behind price increases. They must be increased to catch up. The federal budget must be balanced, but not by short-changing seniors for benefits they have paid for and counted on.

DeFazio, however, voted for Obamacare, which takes $500 billion out of Medicare. He also voted during the past 25 years for the use of Social Security funds on all sorts of other programs – expenditures that depleted Social Security funds and used them for other purposes.

9. DeFazio: "Art Robinson has bragged publicly he intends to 'buy' this congressional seat."[49]

Truth: I never made any such statement. Moreover, DeFazio's claim is odd, since DeFazio receives so much corporate and special interest campaign funding that his campaign has always had more funds than the Robinson campaign. See Chapter 6 on *Campaign Finances* for the exact numbers.

In addition, DeFazio uses his congressional perks for hundreds of thousands of dollars in effectively additional campaign advertising at taxpayer expense.

The Robinson campaign has received greater total amounts of contributions from individuals than has the DeFazio campaign, but this has been overbalanced by the large amounts of special interest money that DeFazio also receives.

10. DeFazio: Robinson is "pathological," a "nutjob," and other similar epithets.[42,50]

Truth: Do voters really want a congressman who habitually substitutes silly comments like this for debate of the issues with his opponent?

11. DeFazio: Robinson advocates that "Energy company CEO's shouldn't pay taxes."[54]
This appeared on a large, expensive billboard on Interstate 5 south of Roseburg. The sign deceptively displayed a picture of me, and was designed to look like a Robinson campaign ad. On the billboard, Robinson was saying,
"Energy company CEO's shouldn't pay taxes."
The required disclaimer crediting the billboard to DeFazio was too small to read from a passing car.

Truth: This billboard is entirely fraudulent.
DeFazio could, with equivalent honesty, have claimed that a proposal that, "national civil defense supplies of emergency food should be freely available to all Americans in case of nuclear attack" could be characterized as, "millionaires should be given free food."
I have written many articles about national emergency preparedness and about the best response to such emergencies. The best possible industrial response to an energy emergency (or to many other similar emergencies that are now likely because essential American industries have been driven abroad by the actions of Congress) could save many lives. That response would be improved if the government temporarily removed impediments to industrial production. Since taxation is one of those impediments, it

could be suspended for a while.

This would provide more capital for the fast expansion of industrial production and increased motivation to solve the crisis quickly. Thus, the needed production facilities could be built more rapidly.

This is not unlike actions that government already often takes to lower taxes on essential industries that are lagging behind, even if there is no emergency. In the period before World War II, President Roosevelt took many of the constraints off industries, so that they could prepare for the war effort – even though Roosevelt himself had designed and implemented some of those restraints.

Even when thinking and writing about these unusual circumstances, however, I have never singled out the CEOs (chief executive officers) of any industry, much less energy, for special tax advantages. This would be ridiculous.

Similar entirely false statements by DeFazio include:

"He [Robinson] thinks big energy companies should be exempt from all federal regulation and should not have to pay taxes."[49]

[Robinson's] vision for America is that "big oil and its executives run everything and the special interests pay no taxes at all." See radio ad on page 48.

12. DeFazio: The Robinson campaign is supported by funds from secret possibly criminal sources.[42]

DeFazio appeared on national television, claiming that I had secret donors, and he enthusiastically participated in and endorsed a Rachel Maddow MSNBC show in which I was accused of accepting help from "money launderers."[42]

Truth: There is no truth whatever in DeFazio's claim.

DeFazio holds the public in very low regard. In this case, he depended upon public lack of knowledge that the election laws required reporting of quarterly campaign contributions on October 15, 2010.

So, a couple of weeks before that date, DeFazio began claiming that an independent expenditure supporting Robinson had not reported the identity of its donors – thereby, as DeFazio claimed, it and Art Robinson were supported by secret donors.

The truth was that no campaign, including DeFazio's, had yet reported because this was before the reporting date. DeFazio, himself, could just as fairly have been accused of the same so-called "money laundering."

The independent expenditure organization later reported its donors by October 15 as required by law just as did the Robinson and DeFazio campaigns, and the DeFazio-Maddow "secret donor" parade quietly faded away.

13. DeFazio: "[Robinson] signed a pledge that protects tax breaks for corporations that ship American jobs overseas."[62]

Truth: What I signed was a simple pledge not to raise taxes. The American people are already suffering from over-taxation. I said nothing about and do not support special tax breaks for corporations who ship jobs overseas.

14. DeFazio, through his surrogates Dean Byers, a Democrat party official and John Sowell, a *News Review* writer, has spread a claim that the Robinson family has

actually not provided more than $600,000 in Robinson curriculum fellowships to home school families over the past 17 years as we have stated – and actually done.

This DeFazio claim was contained in a complaint by Byers to the Oregon Secretary of State, which DeFazio told the press he "thinks has merit." Sowell made sure DeFazio's claim was published widely in the national press.

DeFazio makes a prominent political advertisement of almost $350,000 in scholarships that he says he has provided to students. When the Robinson family scholarships appeared beside DeFazio's in the Oregon voters' pamphlet, DeFazio apparently could not stand the competition.

No one has questioned the DeFazio scholarships. He advertises them widely at election time. Yet, when it turned out that his opponent and his family also give scholarships to students, DeFazio and his retainers quickly spread a political smear that the Robinson scholarships were bogus.

Truth: The Robinson Self-teaching Homeschool Curriculum has been marketed to families and students for 17 years. During that 17 years, its curriculum magazine and card deck advertisements have carried a notice of the scholarship program to which those who cannot afford the $195 price (for 12 years of education for all children in one family) can apply.

By this scholarship program, the Robinson family makes sure that families are able to use their curriculum regardless of their ability to pay. Scholarships are financed from the profits of this Robinson family business. Over the 17 years, the Robinson family has given more than $600,000 in these scholarships to students.

An estimated 60,000 home school students now use

the Robinson curriculum. It has won many awards and is highly respected in the home school community.

15. DeFazio, in 2012 campaign ads, is claiming that the problems that arose at OSU affecting the three Robinson students and Professor Jack Higginbotham did not occur. He incorrectly uses my public statement at the time – that I do not have definitive proof of the motivations of those involved – to claim that nothing took place at all.

Truth: The students and professor were attacked in unprincipled ways that, to the best of my knowledge, were unprecedented in American academia. These events at OSU have been an ongoing tragedy for the students, their professor, and OSU. The misbehavior of only a few OSU staff members, coupled with an unwise and failed cover-up effort by OSU officials, caused much harm.

The separate personal visits of Congressman Peter De-Fazio and his disgraced friend former Congressman David Wu to the OSU nuclear engineering department during the time of these events – visits with the people who attacked the students and their professor – do not prove that DeFazio was involved.

Mr. DeFazio had not shown any interest in the nuclear engineering department before this time. Perhaps he was just curious about the three Robinson students, whose outstanding academic performance was inconvenient for his campaign against me on education issues. The people who visited with him may have just been angling for some of the earmark money that these congressmen dispense.

Much has been written about the OSU events. Some people believe that, in taking public action to stop these misdeeds, I lowered the chance of being elected to Congress. Yet, this was the only way to save the career of Professor Higginbotham (the President of the OSU Faculty Senate) and the educations of these three students. I would have taken exactly the same actions even if the student's names had not been Robinson.

16. As DeFazio's 2012 campaign unfolds, we are seeing indications of an even more strident level of negative campaigning, involving more false statements, out of context quotations, and other dishonesty.

He uses a sort of "straw man" strategy. First, stringing together several false statements, he creates a non-existent "Art Robinson" of his own fictional invention. Then he campaigns against the fiction.

He spends a lot of money advertising his fictional "straw man" opponent on mailed fliers, radio, television, and the Internet. While doing this, he runs lots of polls to see which of his false claims are most effective. He then modifies the "straw man" accordingly.

There must be some occupation where DeFazio's skills in this would be useful. That would not, however, include the Congress of the United States.

CONCLUSION

The United States shall guarantee to every State
in this Union a Republican Form of Government,
Article IV, Section 4

Congress Counts

I don't know when you are reading this book. At the time that I am writing it, we do not yet know who the candidates for President in 2012 will be. Hopefully, the

---

The most important decision made by voters is selection of our representatives in Congress. Congress is the most powerful branch of government.

It was intended that the Congress be filled by citizen volunteers who served short terms and made sure our government followed the Constitution.

Now, Congress is filled by career politicians who serve far too long. A conflict arises between their career interests and our national interests. The Congress now is not even acting with common sense.

This has jeopardized our prosperity, our jobs, our safety, the futures of our children and grandchildren, and our liberty itself .

choices will be good. Oregonians have only a small voice in the presidential candidate selection and election.

Oregonians have a much larger voice in the composition of the U.S. House of Representatives. While the media constantly glorifies the presidency, it is the U.S. Congress that has the primary ability to lead or mislead our country. Congress has far more power under the Constitution than either the President or the Supreme Court.

The Founding Fathers gave us a Constitutional Republic to protect our lives and liberty – to assure that we had a small government and were protected from big government. They created a Congress with responsibility to preserve our Constitutional Republic. And, they gave us the power to replace Congress frequently. Thus, it is in our own power to preserve our freedom.

Congress controls the national purse. Congress decides whether there will be peace or war. And, most importantly, Congress decides whether or not we live in Liberty and Justice under our Constitutional Republic or drift astray into tyranny.

Our country has stumbled, but it has not fallen. It is in danger, but it is not lost. It is our job in 2012 to preserve our nation by replacing the Congress that has gone astray and getting our government back on track.

We must have a Congress made up of citizen volunteers who act with integrity.

We cannot expect those in Congress who have gone off track, to correct the problems that they have created. We need to elect a new Congress with Common Sense.

Goals

We will know that we are succeeding when:

1. **Our economy is thriving, and there are abundant employment opportunities.**
2. **The federal budget is balanced.**
3. **The national debt is being repaid.**
4. **Our senior citizens and veterans are not frightened that they will be abandoned.**
5. **All of us are able to go about our lives without being constantly interfered with by regulations.**
6. **Our public schools are academically excellent.**
7. **Our money is sound.**
8. **The hourly news is not constantly filled by reports of intrigues in Washington.**
9. **Congress acts entirely in accordance with the U.S. Constitution, the rules of our Republic.**

The people of District 4 in Oregon have suffered especially severely from the errors of Congress. We need new congressional representation.

Please cast your vote for Art Robinson!

P.O. Box 1250, Cave Junction, OR 97523
www.ArtForCongress.com
Ph. 1-541-255-2785

Web Site, Facebook and Campaign Materials

Our website address is: www.ArtForCongress.com. To sign up as a volunteer, request yard signs, car door magnets, buttons, other campaign literature, or to make a contribution, visit our website, or use the contact information below:

Art Robinson for Congress
P.O. Box 1250, Cave Junction, OR 97523.
Ph.1-541-255-2785
art@rfc2012.com

Our campaign presence on Facebook is rapidly growing, and our campaign web site is becoming increasingly useful. As of this writing, we have more than 118,000 Facebook friends. A link to Facebook is available on our website. Please monitor and contribute to these Internet activities as the campaign goes forward.

Attend political meetings and work as much as you are able on behalf of the many worthy candidates who are seeking office. This election counts. Our congressional campaign in District 4 is only one part of it.

Please vote for Art Robinson for Congress!

I will make sure that my work in Congress fully justifies the confidence that you place in me though your vote.

APPENDIX
History and Economics

And the Lord said unto Samuel . . . shew them the manner of the king that shall reign over them.

And Samuel [said to the people], This will be the manner of the king that shall reign over you:

He will take your sons and appoint them for himself . .

And he will appoint him captains over thousands . . .to make his instruments of war. . .

And he will take your daughters. . .

And he will take your fields. . .and your oliveyards. . .

And he will take . . . your seed. . . and your vineyards

And he will take your menservants, and your maidservants, and your goodliest young men. . .

And he will take. . . your sheep: and ye shall be his servants.

And ye shall cry out in that day because of your king, which ye shall have chosen you. . .

Nevertheless the people refused to obey. . . and they said . . . we will have a king over us.

That we also may be like all the nations. . .

First Samuel 8:7-20

The Tide of History

Since that time 3,000 years ago when Samuel futilely tried to warn his people, the nations of the world have been ruled by big governments. They have been ruled by all sorts of "kings." These have been called kings, conquerors, tyrants, chancellors, presidents, assemblies, premiers, rulers, leaders, parliaments, and all sorts of other names.

They have not always been single individuals. Sometimes they have been groups of individuals. Their power has been justified by force, theocracy, expediency, socialism, fascism, communism, and in all sorts of other ways.

All of these systems, with occasional brief departures, can be summarized in two words – **Big Government**.

Moreover, big government – overly centralized power – has almost always ultimately led to slavery, poverty, and war. Eventually, those who rule over others become so full of themselves that they lose all semblance of common sense.

Swimming Against the Tide

Our Founding Fathers decided to swim against this tide of history. They formed a **Small Government** with very limited powers. They placed individual life, liberty, and property above the status of government and wrote a Constitution specifically designed to protect the people from big government.

That Constitution worked well for about 200 years. There were ups and downs for our country, but through that time we remained guided by it. It is still partially working today, but our Constitution has been losing the battle between individual freedom and those who seek power

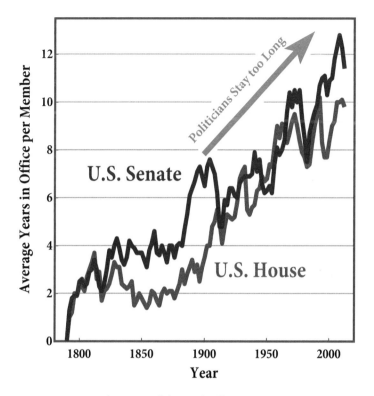

Average Years in Congress

During the first century, the average tenure of members of the House and Senate was 2 and 4 years, respectively. These averages include those in their first years, so average tenure was a little longer. Those members were citizen volunteers. Today, the averages are 10 and 12. These members are career politicians. Their careers create a conflict of interest between their self-interests and the best interests of our nation.

and money from big government – because Congress has not been doing its job, and members of Congress have not been fulfilling their oath of office.

The rise of big government has been accompanied

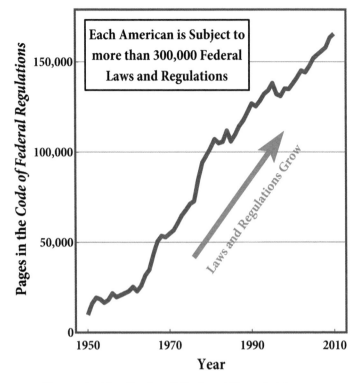

Pages in the Code of Federal Regulations

This measures the Congressionally funded growth of Big Government intrusion into our lives. There are now more than 300,000 laws and regulations on the backs of all Americans. Thus, by this measure, we are 8-fold less free than in the 1950s. This has diminished liberty, damaged our economy, and destroyed jobs.

by an increased tendency for people to seek "careers" as politicians. Lengths of time stayed in Congress were stable for the first hundred years, but have been rising ever since. They have risen 5-fold between 1850 and today.

As America floated through the 1950s, she was the greatest achievement that mankind had ever seen. A full

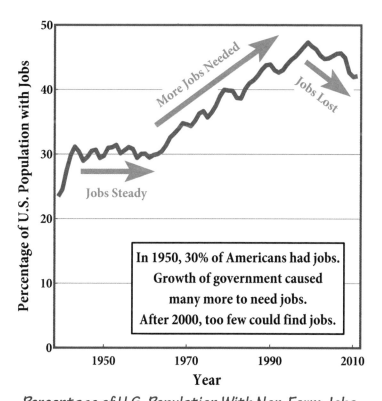

Percentage of U.S. Population With Non-Farm Jobs

Initially at 30%, employment rose from the 1970s to 2000. By then 50 million more people needed work. As Congress weakened the economy, living standards were more difficult to maintain. After 2000, needing even more work, fewer people could find it.

century of liberty, justice, and sound money had facilitated extraordinary human achievements.

She was beginning to be dragged down by big government, but America was like a giant flywheel. She was just too successful to stop suddenly.

The tide of history – the tendency for people to choose "kings" – was, however, beginning to tug at her. America's

Percentage of Population Employed in Manufacturing, Mining, & Logging

The percentage of Americans working in manufacturing, mining, and logging fell steadily until 2000, when the drop worsened. These job losses were caused by Congress. Between 2000 and 2010, an average of 10 factories and 2,000 manufacturing jobs were lost every day.

golden age of liberty, prosperity, and exceptionalism began to succumb to big government.

Through the 1970s, 1980s, and 1990s, more and more Americans had to take employment because the governmental drag on our economy made it increasingly difficult

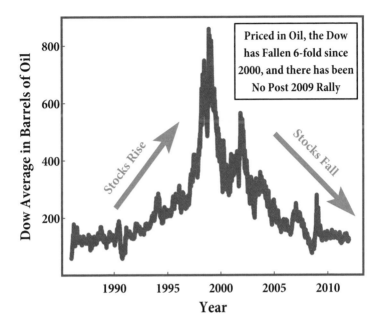

Dow stock average priced in barrels of oil.

Measured vs. real value rather than dollars, the Dow peaked in 2000, and has declined dramatically since. There has been no real stock rally from the lows of 2009.

for families to maintain their prosperity.

Between 2000 and 2010, the United States lost the equivalent of 10 factories and 2,000 manufacturing jobs – *every day*. Employment in manufacturing dropped gradually to 6% by the year 2000, and then more rapidly to 4% by 2010.

The U.S. stockmarket would have reflected this decline, but was resuscitated in dollar terms by Federal Reserve money printing and loose credit practices. This money printing has destroyed the real return on savings, which is very harmful to seniors and others who depend on savings.

The speculative blow off in about the year 2000 was followed by a disastrous decline of between 3-fold and 6-fold, depending upon how the real value is computed.

Under the stimulus of more money printing, the dollar value of the stockmarket has recovered during the past 3 years, but no rebound in real value has taken place.

This period of decline is chronicled in American employment. It was steady at 30% of the population in the 1950s, but as more and more Americans sought work in efforts to sustain their prosperity and overcome the effects of congressional expansion of the government, employment rose to 47%.

Then, however, the accumulating toll of government accelerated. In about 2000, employment began to drop and is today 42%. This destroyed 15 million jobs.

Moreover, extrapolating the rise from 30% to 47%, an estimated 52% of Americans needed employment in 2010. So, we now actually lack an estimated 30 million jobs.

Flywheel

The great flywheel of American industry after World War II had unprecedented momentum. It seemed that nothing on earth could stop it. But, it depended upon American liberty and justice. It depended upon the American system that placed the freedom of the individual above the power of the state.

Not all Americans realized this. Most Americans just lived within the custom and culture that they inherited and enjoyed it. But, some wanted America changed.

These were people to whom personal money and power were more important than liberty and justice for all. They were selfish people – a type of person always present in the human race – who seek power over other people.

Some such people find satisfaction in controlling small groups of people. Others seek more. Some seek power over whole nations. These people have created the big governments that have dominated human affairs for thousands of years. And, those big governments have caused vast amounts of war, human suffering, slavery, and death.

Big government has grown slowly in the United States. It has inched forward in thousands of increments. The 300,000 laws and regulations in the *Code of Federal Regulations* did not appear overnight.

Congressional Responsibility

As I have detailed in this book, the Founding Fathers left most of the responsibility for adhering to the Constitutional assurances of small government in the hands of the U.S. Congress – and the American people, who have the power to replace members of the House of Representatives every two years. Senators were designated as representatives of state governments, but this was changed by the 17th Amendment.

The American people are not happy with the antics of the Congress. Congress now has a poll-reported approval rating of only about 10%. Yet, these career politicians keep getting re-elected. The reason for this is that they have voted themselves great financial and other election advantages over challengers.

The economic travails of our country and most of our country's other problems as discussed in this book are directly traceable to wrong actions by the U.S. Congress.

District 4 in Oregon is especially disadvantaged because, not only has its 25-year congressman voted to grow big government, but he has also done very little to shield the citizens of District 4 from the harmful actions of that governmental growth.

Weakened by poor representation in Congress, Oregon District 4 is especially economically depressed. This, however, can be changed by simply getting federal government over-taxation, over-regulation, over-indebtedness, over-involvement in our personal lives, and other impediments out of the way.

We should remove from Congress the career politicians who have held us hostage to their own careers, and return to a Congress of citizen legislators who govern honestly with common sense.

BIBLIOGRAPHY

1. *U.S. Declaration of Independence*
2. *U.S. Constitution*
3. *John Adams* – David McCullough
4. *The American Crisis* – Thomas Paine
5. *Autobiography of Benjamin Franklin*
6. *The Big Short* – Michael Lewis
7. *Capitol Punishment* – Jack Abramoff
8. *Cargo Cult Science* – Richard Feynman
9. *A Child's History of England* – Charles Dickens
10. *Clathrate Hydrates of Natural Gases* – E. Dendy Sloan and Carolyn Koh
11. *Common Sense* – Thomas Paine
12. *Crash Proof* – Peter Schiff
13. *The Diaries of George Washington*
14. *Early Warning Report* – Richard Maybury
15. *Economics in One Lesson* – Henry Hazlitt
16. *The End of Prosperity* – Arthur Laffer
17. *Engines of Commerce* – Vaclav Smil
18. *Essays in Science* – Albert Einstein
19. *The Federalist Papers*
20. *The Feynman Lectures on Physics* – Richard Feynman,

Robert Leighton, and Matthew Sands
21. *Fighting Chance* – Arthur Robinson and Gary North
22. *For Spacious Skies* – Scott Carpenter
23. *The Gods of the Copy Book Headings* – Rudyard Kipling
24. *Greeks and Romans Bearing Gifts* – Carl J. Richard
25. *Health Hazards of not going Nuclear* – Petr Beckman
26. *Holy Bible* – King James Version
27. *By Sheer Pluck, In the Reign of Terror, St. Bartholomew's Eve,* and *No Surrender* – G. A. Henty
28. *The Law* – Frédéric Bastiat
29. *Liberty Defined* – Ron Paul
30. *Not Yours to Give* – David Crockett
31. *Nuclear War Survival Skills* – Cresson Kearny
32. *Radiant Science, Dark Politics* – Martin Kamen
33. *Return to the Moon: Exploration, Enterprise, and Energy in the Human Settlement of Space* – Harrison Schmitt
34. *To Ride, Shoot Straight, and Speak the Truth* – Jeff Cooper
35. *The Road to Serfdom* – Friedrich Hayek
36. *Skunk Works* – Ben Rich
37. *South* – Ernest Shackleton
38. *The Ultimate Resource II* – Julian Simon
39. *Up From Slavery* – Booker T. Washington
40. *Wealth of Nations* – Adam Smith
41. *What is Seen and What is Not Seen* – Frédéric Bastiat

REFERENCES

1. Princeton University Press, *The Ultimate Resource 2*, Julian L. Simon

2. Bernie Sanders's America, "A Socialist Senator's Monstrous Fantasies," James Taranto, *The Wall Street Journal*, December 13, 2011, http://online.wsj.com/article/SB10001424052970203430404577096631574167496.html

3. "The War on Political Free Speech," Bradley A. Smith, *The Wall Street Journal*, January 23, 2012

4. "How Donor Disclosure Hurts Democracy", James L. Huffman, *The Wall Street Journal*, April 11, 2011, http://online.wsj.com/article/SB10001424052748704415104576250503491062220.html

5. www.opensecrets.org

6. www.fec.gov

7. See the liberal online rating site: http://www.thepoliticalguide.com/Profiles/House/Oregon/Peter_DeFazio/Views/Debt,_Deficit,_Spending,_and_the_Size_of_Government/

8. U.S. Census Bureau, www.census.gov

9. American Recovery and Reinvestment Act of 2009, January 28, 2009, H.R. 1

10. American Recovery and Reinvestment Act of 2009, January 28, 2009, H.R. 1

11. www.npr.org, February 17, 2009

12. National Taxpayers Union http://www.ntu.org/on-capitol-hill/ntu-rates-congress/members/house/peter-defazio.html

13. http://www.ontheissues.org/House/Peter_Defazio_Environment.htm

14. http://www.lcv.org/scorecard/past-scorecards/pdf/scorec-are-2010.pdf

15. http://www.progressivepunch.org/members.htm?issue=N0&sea rch=selectName&member=OR4&chamber=House&zip=&x=37 &y=8

16. *Greeks & Romans Bearing Gifts*, Carl J. Richard, Rowman & Littlefield Publishers, Inc., Lanham, MD.

17. www.petitionproject.org

18. Access to Energy, April 2009, Vol. 36, No. 9.

19. *Journal of the American Medical Association*, Jun 18, 2008, Ezekial Emanuel

20. Bureau of Economic Analysis, www.bea.gov

21. http://www.downsizinggovernment.org/content/federal-worker-pay-blasts-off

22. *The Federal Register*, www.federalregister.gov

23. *Three Felonies a Day*, Harvey A. Silverglate, Encounter Books, 2009

24. "You Commit Three Felonies a Day," *The Wall Street Journal*, L. Gordon Crovitz, September 27, 2009.

25. "Harvey Silverglate on Three Felonies A Day," *Forbes*, July 16, 2010.

26. http://www.washingtonpost.com/solyndra-politics-infused-obama-energy-programs/2011/12/14/gIQA4HllHP_story.html

27. http://articles.chicagotribune.com/2011-11-17/news/ct-edit-solyndra-20111117_1_solyndra-loan-guarantee-renewable-energy

28. http://www.issues2000.org/House/Peter_Defazio_Education.htm

29. Lyndon Johnson, Remarks in Pittsburgh at the Steelworkers Union Hall, April 24, 1964.

30. http://www.treasury.gov/resource-center/data-chart-center/tic/Documents/mfh.txt

31. *Peter DeFazio Reports*, – January 2012, (Mailed at taxpayer expense to voters of Oregon District 4).

32. http://www.kiplinger.com/features/archives/how-your-income-stacks-up.html

33. Lowell Wood, Talk to Doctors for Disaster Preparedness, Las Vegas, NV, September 1991.

34. http://en.wikipedia.org/wiki/Tariffs_in_United_States_history

35. Friends of New Zealand Congressional Caucus, http://usnzcouncil.org/node/329
36. Annual Energy Review, U.S. Energy Information Administration.
37. *Journal of American Physicians and Surgeons* (2007) 12, 79-90.
38. http://www.oregonlive.com/wilsonville/index.ssf/2011/05/oregon_department_of_transport.html
39. http://www.solarfeeds.com/the-baldock-solar-highway-breaksground/
40. http://blog.oregonlive.com/commuting/2011/11/trimets_plan_for_solar_panels.html
41. David Bender, "Ring of Fire," *Air America*, October 12, 2010. http://www.youtube.com/watch?v=ZGiIFDPTGhs
42. MSNBC, *Rachel Maddow Show,* Peter DeFazio, guest, – October 1, 2010 – http://www.youtube.com/watch?v=OShFOIYri8o
43. MSNBC, *Rachel Maddow Show*, Art Robinson, guest, – October 7, 2010.
44. DeFazio for Congress, radio commercials and other campaign literature.
45. Nuclear Power Risk from Radiation, Bernard Cohen, www.physics.isu.edu/radinf/np-risk.htm
46. *The Register Guard*, February 20, 1998, Section 6C.
47. Coos Bay Forum Sponsored by "The League of Women Voters," Moderated by Tim Novotny, October 18, 2010, Egyptian Theater.
48. DeFazio Campaign Mailing June 2010 and other DeFazio advertisements.
49. Email from Peter DeFazio, sent to MoveOn.org e-mail list. Sunday, September 26, 2010.
50. *The Eugene Register Guard*, September 19th, 2011.
51. *The Oregonian*, October 28th, 2011.
52. http://thatsmycongress.com/house/repDeFazioOR4112.html
53. http://www.irregulartimes.com/house/DeFazioOR4.html
54. "Energy company CEO's shouldn't pay taxes" was displayed on a large billboard on highway 5 near Roseburg. The sign was made to look like an Art Robinson advertisement, with a "Paid for by Peter DeFazio for Congress" disclaimer which was too small to read as you drove by.
55. "America's New Health Care System Revealed," by Congressman Kevin Brady. www.house.gov/apps/list/press/tx08_brady/

pr_100728_hc_chart.html
56. *Capitol Punishment* - Jack Abramoff, WND Books.
57. Solid Evidence to Support Home Schooling" by Michael P. Farris in *The Wall Street Journal*, March 5, 1997, p A18
58. *The End of Prosperity* by Arthur Laffer
59. *Fighting Chance,* Robinson, A.B., North G., Oregon Institute of Science and Medicine.
60. www.progressivepunch.org
61. heritageactionscorecard.com
62. DeFazio for Congress campaign advertising mailed to Oregon voters in 2010. Titled "Peter DeFazio versus Art Robinson, Get the Facts."
63. DeFazio letter in response to debate invitation. May 27, 2010.
64. 1988 Yellowstone National Park Fires, www.yellowstoneparknet.com/history_museums/fires.php
65. *Greeks and Romans Bearing Gifts* – Carl J. Richard
66. Albany Democrat Herald, "OSU nets $183.7M in Federal Grants," Thursday, August 4, 2011.
67. "U.S. Bakers, Candy Makers Seek More Sugar Imports," by Leslie Josephs, *The Wall Street Journal*, March 17, 2011
68. www.cato.org/pubs/tbb/tbb_0607_46.pdf
69. Congressional CBO summary. The Budget and Economic Outlook: Fiscal Years 2011 to 2021.
70. "High-Frequency Traders, It Seems, Help Forex Market," by Eva Szalay and Jacob Bunge, *The Wall Street Journal*, September 28, 2011.
71. "Evaluation of the DC Opportunity Scholarship Program," June 2010, U.S. Department of Education.
72. "Obama's War on School Vouchers," *The Wall Street Journal*, Jason L. Riley, February 14, 2012.
73. "Sticking it to the Littlest Guys: Obama Chooses Teacher Unions Over Inner-City Kids," Troy Senik, Center for Individual Freedom, February 16, 2012.
74. Congressional Research Service, www.crs.gov.
75. http://photos.oregonlive.com/oregonian/2011/10/pink_martini_plays_pioneer_cou_7.html
76. H.R. 1683, 111th Congress - March 24, 2009.
77. H.R. 2003, 112th Congress - May 26, 2011.

INDEX

ABOUT THE AUTHOR

Dr. Art Robinson is a scientist, educated at Caltech and the University of California at San Diego. He then served on the faculty of UCSD; as Associate of the Department of Chemistry at Stanford; and as President and Research Professor of the Linus Pauling Institute.

Since 1981, he has been President and Research Professor of the Oregon Institute of Science and Medicine, founded by him, his scientist wife Laurelee and several colleagues, including Drs. Martin Kamen and R. Bruce Merrifield.

Dr. Robinson has four sons and two daughters, who all have university degrees in science. So far, three of them have received doctorate degrees.

The Robinsons have lived on their family farm in Josephine County for 32 years. After Laurelee's death in 1988 when their children were 12, 10, 8, 6, 6 years and 18 months old, the seven of them (including their dad) grew up together on their farm and worked to earn the six children' college and graduate educations.

The Robinsons publish the Robinson Self-teaching Home School Curriculum, used by about 60,000 home school students; more than 100 books; the newsletter *Access to Energy*; and educational materials for emergency preparedness.

Their Oregon Institute carries out research on biochemical molecular clocks, Alzheimer's and Parkinson's diseases, various aspects of human aging, and advanced analytical methods for use in diagnostic and preventive medicine. Its research facilities are among the best equipped in the Northwest.

ACKNOWLEDGMENTS

I have written this book with the help, advice, and encouragement of my family and many friends and colleagues. To protect them from becoming targets of my opponent during the 2012 congressional campaign, I have decided to refrain from naming them here until a later edition is published.